The

Vol I
141-143
& 140-141

I BELIEVE
IN THE HOLY SPIRIT

I

The Holy Spirit in the 'Economy'
Revelation and Experience
of the Spirit

Principal works by Yves Congar

Chrétiens désunis (1937): *Divided Christendom* (1939)
Esquisses du Mystère de l'Eglise (1941; 2nd ed. 1953): in *The Mystery of the Church* (1960)
Vraie et fausse réforme dans l'Eglise (1950)
Le Christ, Marie et l'Eglise (1952): *Christ, Our Lady and the Church* (1957)
Jalons pour une théologie du laïcat (1953): *Lay People in the Church* (1957)
Le Mystère du Temple (*Lectio divina* series; 1958): *The Mystery of the Temple* (1962)
Vaste monde, ma paroisse (1959): *The Wide World my Parish* (1961)
La Tradition et les traditions (2 vols, 1960, 1963): *Tradition and Traditions* (1966)
Les Voies du Dieu vivant (1962): *The Revelation of God* (1968) and *Faith and Spiritual Life* (1969)
La Foi et la Théologie (*Le mystère chrétien*, 1; 1962)
Sacerdoce et laïcat (1963): *Priest and Layman* (1967)/*A Gospel Priesthood* (1967) and *Christians Active in the World* (1968)
Sainte Eglise (1963)
La Tradition et la vie de l'Eglise (1963): *Tradition and the Life of the Church/The Meaning of Tradition* (1964)
Pour une Eglise servante et pauvre (1963): *Power and Poverty in the Church* (1964)
Chrétiens en dialogue (1964): *Dialogue between Christians* (1966)
Jésus-Christ, notre Médiateur, notre Seigneur (1965): *Jesus Christ* (1966)
Situation et tâches présentes de la théologie (1967)
L'Ecclésiologie du haut Moyen Age (1968)
L'Eglise de S. Augustin à l'époque moderne (*Histoire des Dogmes* series; 1970)
L'Eglise une, sainte, catholique, apostolique (*Mysterium Salutis*, 15; 1970)
Ministères et communion ecclésiale (1971)
Un peuple messianique. Salut et libération (1975)
Eglise catholique et France moderne (1978)
Je crois en l'Esprit Saint (3 vols, 1979, 1980): *I Believe in the Holy Spirit* (3 vols, 1983)

YVES M. J. CONGAR

I BELIEVE IN
THE HOLY SPIRIT

VOLUME I

The Holy Spirit in the 'Economy'

Revelation and Experience
of the Spirit

TRANSLATED BY
DAVID SMITH

THE SEABURY PRESS
NEW YORK

•

GEOFFREY CHAPMAN
LONDON

84/1054

A Geoffrey Chapman book published by
Cassell Ltd.
1 Vincent Square, London SW1P 2PN

The Seabury Press
815 Second Avenue, New York, NY 10017

First published in French as *Je crois en l'Esprit Saint*, I: *L'expérience de l'Esprit*
© Les Editions du Cerf, 1979

English translation first published 1983

Typeset in VIP Times by
D. P. Media Limited, Hitchin, Hertfordshire

Printed and bound in Hungary

Library of Congress Cataloging in Publication Data

Congar, Yves, 1904–
  I believe in the Holy Spirit.

  Translation of: Je crois en l'Esprit Saint.
  Contents: v. 1. The Holy Spirit in the 'economy'—v. 2. 'He is Lord and giver of life'—v. 3.
The river of the water of life (Rev 22:1) flows in the East and in the West.
  1. Holy Spirit.   I. Title.
BT121.2.C59713 1983   231'.3   82–19420

          Geoffrey Chapman:
          ISBN 0 225 66353 8 (this volume)
               0 225 66352 X (three-volume set)

          The Seabury Press:
          ISBN 0-8164-0518-2 (this volume)
               0-8164-0540-9 (three-volume set)

To
Nicole Legrain and Nicolas Walty
without whom this work
would never have been published
with gratitude and in friendship

GENERAL INTRODUCTION

This work, which I have been wanting to write for years, is dedicated to the Holy Spirit. The present 'Renewal' movement, all too frequently known as 'charismatic renewal', will have a place in it, but it is not the source of my wish to embark on the work, which in fact preceded it. It simply gives to our undertaking a contemporary interest and even an urgency with which I am favourably disposed to comply.

What are our standpoint and our point of departure to be? What will be the conditions governing our approach? They will follow the classical rules of faith seeking understanding. Faith, after all, seeks to understand what it holds and experiences, and it owes what it holds to what it has received from inspired or canonical Scriptures. It is through these Scriptures that God speaks to us and communicates to us what we have to know if we are to respond to his loving plan for us. The Christian, however, is a man who has been preceded by others. Generations of believers have reflected about faith before us and they have also experienced the Spirit. We seek an understanding of faith not alone, but with them, and also with contemporary witnesses to Christian experience, since the Spirit blows today as he did yesterday.

This questioning of Christian experience is very necessary because revelation and knowledge of the Spirit are affected by a certain lack of conceptual mediation. The ideas available to us when we speak of the Father and the Son are fairly well defined and easy enough to understand. They refer to fatherhood and begetting on the one hand and the bond between parent and offspring on the other. These two terms point in fact to the first and second Persons; being relative terms, they characterize those two Persons as mutually related.

The term 'Spirit', however, has none of these associations. The whole terminology used to speak of the third Person is common and absolute. The word 'Spirit' is equally suitable for the Father and the Son, as is 'Holy', but they are not terms signifying a person. 'Procession' can also be used of the Word, the Son. There is no revelation in the objective sense of the Person of the Holy Spirit as there is of the Person of the Word, the Son, in Jesus and, through that Person, of the Person of the Father. In this context, it has been suggested that the Holy Spirit empties himself, in a kind of kenosis, of his own personality in order to be in a relationship, on the one hand, with 'God' and Christ and, on the other, with men, who are called to realize the image of God and his Son. 'In order to reveal himself, he did not, like Yahweh in the

Old Testament and Jesus in the New, use the personal pronoun "I".[1] The Holy Spirit is revealed to us and known to us not in himself, or at least not directly in himself, but through what he brings about in us.[2] On the other hand, whereas the activities of understanding can be perceived in him in a very translucent way and therefore defined, those of affection and love have not yet been similarly analysed.[3] These difficulties will be considered when we turn our attention to a theology of the third Person.

My intention in this work is to divide the whole study into three parts, each part occupying one volume. I have no carefully preconceived and detailed plan, but rather a project and an intention. This can be outlined as follows:

I. THE 'ECONOMY' AND THE EXPERIENCE OF THE SPIRIT
    (A) According to the canonical Scriptures
    (B) In the life of the Church through the ages

II. 'HE IS LORD AND GIVER OF LIFE'
    (A) The Spirit animates the Church:
        The Church is made by the Spirit. He is the co-instituting principle of the Church
        The Holy Spirit makes the Church one. He is the principle of communion
        The Holy Spirit is the principle of catholicity
        The Spirit keeps the Church 'apostolic'
        The Spirit is the principle of holiness in the Church
    (B) The breath of God in our personal lives:
        The Spirit and man in God's plan
        The gift of the Spirit in the messianic era
        'God has sent the Spirit of his Son into our hearts'
        Life in the Spirit and according to the Spirit
        The Holy Spirit and our prayer
        The Spirit and the struggle against the flesh. The spirit and freedom
        The gifts and the fruits of the Spirit
    (C) The Renewal in the Spirit. Promises and questions
        The positive aspect of the charismatic renewal
        Questions:
        What title should be used?
        Spectacular charisms
        Baptism in the Spirit
        The Renewal and ecumenism
    (D) 'In the unity of the Holy Spirit, all honour and glory'

III. THE 'THEOLOGY OF THE SPIRIT'
    (A) The third Person. Circumincession

(B) The Spirit and the incarnate Word
(C) Appropriation?
(D) East and West:
       The *Filioque*
       The Epiclesis. The Eucharist and the Holy Spirit

I shall, then, begin my study in the classical manner by an investigation of the canonical Scriptures. For whatever the extent and the variety of the activity, and therefore the manifestations of the Spirit, the meaning of that activity and those manifestations is vouchsafed to us in an 'inspired' and therefore for us normative way in canonical Scripture. In this investigation, however, there will be no need to discuss the relationship between the history of salvation, which is coterminous with the history of mankind as such, and the history of revelation, or between what has been called 'transcendental revelation' and 'categorial revelation'.[4] All Catholic theologians agree that the canonical Scriptures bear witness to that revelation and that they act as our criteria in our evaluation of our experience of God.

But this is not all. The Scriptures comprise 46 documents in the Old Testament and 27 in the New, compiled over a period lasting more than a millennium by various authors or groups of authors, many of whom are unknown to us. They cannot simply be treated as a whole, without distinction. On the other hand, I cannot, in this context, undertake a complete study, which would call for a series of detailed monographs. I shall therefore follow the chronological order of the written documents of the Bible. This will enable us to distinguish not only a development and even a progress in the revelation of the Spirit, but also a certain diversity in the way in which the subject of the Spirit is presented by the different authors.

There is, of course, a problem here, raised by modern exegesis. Greatly improved methods are used today, but this has frequently meant the classical groups of proof-texts have been broken up. It has been shown, for example, that Luke's presentation of the activity of the Holy Spirit is different from Paul's, but very often what one exegete claims to have established is contradicted by another, and the original ideas contained in one monograph make the arguments in another seem outdated. It is obvious, then, that the Church cannot wait to live and confess its faith until the exegetes have reached complete agreement or until Luke and Paul or Mark and John are made to dovetail neatly into each other. The Church has never in fact yielded to the temptation to melt the four gospels down into a single one, but has always regarded the four evangelists as the animals of Ezekiel, each one walking straight ahead. It has spoken of the gospel as 'tetramorphic' and has included these four forms as they are in a 'canon', the unity of which corresponds to the unity of God himself.

It is in the image of God himself that the Church honours diversity in unity. It experiences and preserves that unity in its Tradition, which is the vital handing on of 'all that she herself is and all that she believes'.[5] There is always the risk that, because of this unity, the most prominent shades of meaning, which form the wealth of the documents from which the Church lives, will be blurred by Tradition. For this reason, we are encouraged to look for and affirm these subtle differences within the Church itself. In every family, each child has its own character and its own individual tastes. The Church is similarly the family and the home in which we live. The unity of the Church is fully Catholic.

With these comments in mind, I shall provide the reader with what is inevitably an elementary and incomplete series of experiences and manifestations of the Spirit. I shall do this firstly at the level of the revelation to which the Scriptures bear witness and then at the level of the life of the Church throughout its two millennia of history.

I have no illusions about what I am doing. The task that I am undertaking will strike some readers as too difficult and others, who are specialists, as too elementary. Each of the sub-sections of this work could be the subject of a full scholarly monograph. In many cases, such monographs already exist. I have read, used and cited many of them, but have only retained what is necessary for my own purpose.

My purpose is above all to know and to teach. I know that it is not enough to stop there. For the Christian, knowledge is there for the sake of communion and love. I believe intensely in the essential union of theological study and a life of praise—the doxology and practice of the liturgy in which, by celebrating them, we are in communion with the mysteries. It is arguable that I ought to have quoted the texts themselves more often, instead of simply giving the references. It is, of course, essential to go to them, read them and enjoy them. The Scriptures are the forecourt of the kingdom of God. It is also the Holy Spirit who takes us into this forecourt. May he help us to speak of him in the chapters that follow!

Each one of us has his own gifts, his own means and his own vocation. Mine are as a Christian who prays and as a theologian who reads a great number of books and takes many notes. May I therefore be allowed to sing my own song! The Spirit is breath. The wind sings in the trees. I would like, then, to be an Aeolian harp and let the breath of God make the strings vibrate and sing. Let me stretch and tune the strings—that will be the austere task of research. And then let the Spirit make them sing a clear and tuneful song of prayer and life!

NOTES

1. H. Mühlen, *Mysterium Salutis*, XIII (Paris, 1972), p. 182.
2. This was the opinion of St Bernard, *Sermo 88 de diversis*, 1 (*PL* 183, 706); *De Pentecoste sermo*, 1 (*ibid.*, 323).
3. See Thomas Aquinas, *ST* Ia, q. 37, a. 1; *Comp.*, c. 59.
4. See C. Geffré, 'Esquisse d'une théologie de la révélation', P. Ricœur *et al.*, *La Révélation* (Brussels, 1977), pp. 171–205.
5. Dogmatic Constitution on Revelation, *Dei Verbum*, 8, 1.

CONTENTS

ABBREVIATIONS USED IN THIS BOOK

AAS   Acta Apostolicae Sedis
Anal. Greg.   Analecta Gregoriana
Anal. Praemonstr.   Analecta Praemonstratensia
Arch. Fr. Praedic.   Archivum Fratrum Praedicatorum
Bib   Biblica
Bibl. August.   Bibliothèque augustinienne
Bibl. Œcum.   Bibliothèque œcuménique
Bibl. théol.   Bibliothèque théologique
Bibl. Thom.   Bibliothèque thomiste
BWANT   Beiträge zur Wissenschaft vom Alten und Neuen Testament
BZ   Biblische Zeitschrift
CBQ   Catholii Biblical Quarterly
CC   Corpus christianorum
COD   J. Alberigo et al. (eds), *Conciliorum Œcumenicorum Decreta*
Denz.   1st ed. of *DS* (below)
Doc. cath.   La documentation catholique
DS   H. Denzinger, rev. A. Schönmetzer, *Enchiridion Symbolorum*
DTC   Dictionnaire de théologie catholique
ETL   Ephemerides Theologicae Lovanienses
Et. Théol. et Rel.   Etudes théologiques et religieuses
Fliche and Martin   A. Fliche and V. Martin, *Histoire de l'Eglise*
GCS   Griechische christliche Schriftsteller
Greg   Gregorianum
Jaffé (Loewenfeld)   P. Jaffé *et al.* (eds), *Regesta Pontificum Romanorum* (2nd ed.
   rev. S. Loewenfeld *et al.*)
JTS   Journal of Theological Studies
LTK   Lexikon für Theologie und Kirche
Mansi   J. D. Mansi (ed.), *Sacrorum Conciliorum nova et amplissima Collectio*
M-D   La Maison-Dieu
MOPH   Monumenta Ordinis Fratrum Praedicatorum Historica
NRT   Nouvelle Revue théologique
NTS   New Testament Studies
OED   Oxford English Dictionary
Or. Chr. Anal.   Orientalia christiana analecta
Or. Chr. Period.   Orientalia christiana periodica
PG   Migne, *Patrologia Graeca*
PL   Migne, *Patrologia Latina*
RAM   Revue d'ascétique et de mystique
RB   Revue biblique

ABBREVIATIONS

RHE   Revue d'histoire ecclésiastique
RSPT   Revue des sciences philosophiques et théologiques
RSR   Recherches de science religieuse
RTAM   Recherches de théologie ancienne et médiévale
RThom   Revue thomiste
RTP   Revue de théologie et de philosophie
SC   Sources chrétiennes
SE   Sciences ecclésiastiques
ST   Summa Theologica
Strack and Billerbeck   H. L. Strack and P. Billerbeck, *Kommentar zum Neuen Testament aus Talmud und Midrasch*
TDNT   G. Kittel and G. Friedrich (eds), *Theological Dictionary of the New Testament* (Eng. tr.)
ThSt   Theological Studies
TZ   Theologische Zeitschrift
VS   La Vie spirituelle
WA   Weimar edition of Luther's *Werke*
ZKT   Zeitschrift für katholische Theologie
ZNW   Zeitschrift für neutestamentliche Wissenschaft

VOLUME I

THE HOLY SPIRIT
IN THE 'ECONOMY'

REVELATION AND EXPERIENCE
OF THE SPIRIT

A NOTE ON 'EXPERIENCE'

I have given this volume the sub-title 'Revelation and Experience of the Spirit'. This refers to the ways that are offered to our objective knowledge of the Spirit, not to our subjective personal experience.

Revelation consists of what God himself has communicated to us through the history of his people as interpreted by the inspired prophets and wise men of Israel and later, in regard to the decisive event of Jesus Christ, the evangelists, the apostles and their spokesmen. My first task will therefore be to examine the Scriptures. If, however, it is true that God continues to act in history and in men's lives after the period that is usually called 'constitutive' and that he does so through the Spirit, then we surely have something to learn from the period that has followed the constitutive era, since it is rooted in that era. We should not interpret simplistically the idea that revelation closed with the death of the last apostle. God has certainly enabled us to know something since that time. Our experience of the Spirit has continued since then. It is as intense and urgent as it ever was in the past, even though what we can learn from the constitutive period continues to be normative. This is what constitutes the interplay between Scripture and living tradition. That is also why I shall retrace the history, not of the activity of the Spirit, which would be impossible, but of certain particularly meaningful aspects of the knowledge that has been gained and expressed of the Spirit. I shall not, strictly speaking, be retracing the history of dogma. I shall rather be following history in order to explore the idea that Christians have expressed about the activity of the Holy Spirit and in this I shall try to go beyond the dogma of the third Person.

By 'experience', I mean our perception of the reality of God as he comes to us, is active in us and operates through us, drawing us to him in communion and friendship, as one being exists for the other. This experience falls short of vision and does not do away with the distance that we are aware of in our knowledge of God himself, but overcomes it at the level of a presence of God in us as the beloved end of our life, a presence that makes itself felt in signs and in the effects of peace, joy, certainty, consolation, enlightenment and all that goes with love. The experience that the great mystics have described is a special and indeed exceptional degree of this perception of a presence of God who is given to us so that we can 'enjoy' his presence as a living object of knowledge and love. On this side of what is exceptional, there is what is ordinary—our experience of God's presence and activity in the appeals and signs that occur in our prayer, our practice of the sacraments of faith, the life of the Church and the love of God and our neighbour.

We can, of course, only become conscious of this experience and express it in terms or concepts that are our own. 'It is the Spirit himself bearing witness with our spirit that we are children of God' (Rom 8:16). We find ourselves in finding God. This is the religious experience *par excellence*,[1] an experience which, it cannot be doubted, brings its own certainty. This certainty is confirmed by the fact that our experience and the way that we express it is in accordance with that of the 'cloud of witnesses' mentioned by the author of the letter to the Hebrews (12:1) and that of all other believers. Although we have a practical assurance, we can never say with total certainty—unless we have a private revelation—that we are in a 'state of grace'. Short of a direct vision of God that is without any created concept, there is no way of perceiving God and his activity that does not make use of our own mental resources and is not involved with those resources.

The whole context of Christian life, our effective service of others in response to charity and to the appeals and demands that are contrary to our 'carnal' selves are evidence that all this does not come from ourselves, but from God. The theme of the gospels and St Paul of the struggle between the flesh and the Spirit corresponds to a reality that forms part of the Christian experience.

I shall not trace the course of that experience in the ways in which it is expressed as a living reality in spiritual writings and the lives of the saints. I shall try to interpret that reality theologically, not by studying or analysing the spiritual life, but rather by attempting to evolve a theology of the Holy Spirit and his rôle in the Church. In this context, I shall be concerned with theoretical aspects or objective dimensions of our knowledge of the Spirit.

NOTE

1. This is the definition given by J. Mouroux, *L'expérience chrétienne. Introduction à une théologie* (Paris, 1952), pp. 21, 25, 48, 369. This definition is also accepted by D. Mollat, *L'expérience de l'Esprit-Saint selon le Nouveau Testament*, 2nd ed. (Paris, 1973), p. 7, and M. J. le Guillou, *Les témoins sont parmi nous. L'expérience de Dieu dans l'Esprit-Saint* (Paris, 1976). For an idea of Christian experience other than that of Mouroux, see H. U. von Balthasar, *La Gloire et la Croix. Les aspects esthétiques de la Révélation* (Paris, 1965; Fr. tr. of *Herrlichkeit*), I, pp. 185–360. For experience of faith: P. Jacquemont, J.-P. Jossua and B. Quelquejeu, *Une foi exposée* (Paris, 1972), pp. 171–174. For a note on the use of the word 'experience', see *Revue Internationale Catholique Communio*, I, 8 (November 1976). The number of *Concilium* on 'Revelation and Experience' (113; March 1978) contains little that is strictly relevant to our subject.

PART ONE
THE CANONICAL SCRIPTURES

NOTE

1

THE OLD TESTAMENT

THE WORD[1]

The Hebrew word *rûaḥ*, which is almost always translated by the Greek *pneuma*, means breath, air, wind or soul. In the Old Testament especially, but also quite often in the New, to translate it as 'breath' gives a realism and an emphasis to the data reported and to the biblical texts that our word 'spirit' does not suggest so well. The translation 'breath' has been used by D. Lys (see note 1 below), M.-A. Chevallier and, in books that do not claim to be scholarly, but are nonetheless very solid, by Jean Isaac, A.-M. Henry, T. Maertens, G. A. Maloney and others.[2]

The word *rûaḥ* occurs 378 times in the Old Testament and these occurrences can be divided into three roughly equal groups. It is used in the first place to denote wind or a breath of air. Secondly, it is used for the force that vivifies man—the principle of life or breath and the seat of knowledge and feeling. Finally, it indicates the life of God himself, the force by which he acts and causes action, both at the physical and at the 'spiritual' level.

Rûaḥ-breath is not in any sense opposed to 'body' or 'corporeal'. Even in profane Greek and the language of philosophy, *pneuma* expresses the living and generating substance that is diffused in animals, plants and all things. It is a subtle corporeality rather than an incorporeal substance. The *rûaḥ*-breath of the Old Testament is not disincarnate. It is rather what animates the body. It is opposed to 'flesh', but then 'flesh' is not the same as 'body'. 'Flesh' is the purely earthly reality of man and is characterized by the fact that it is weak and corruptible: 'The Egyptians are men and not God; their horses are flesh and not spirit' Isaiah declared (31:3) in order to dissuade the Jews from looking to them for support. It was a question of knowing the source of real strength and life. In Gen 6:3, the way is prepared for the flood by God's declaration: 'My breath shall not abide in man for ever, for he is flesh'. Men were, in other words, living only according to their own earthly principle.

The Greeks thought in categories of substance, but the Jews were concerned with force, energy and the principle of action. The spirit-breath was for them what acts and causes to act and, in the case of the Breath of God, what animates and causes to act in order to realize God's plan. It always refers to a life-energy. Cardinal Daniélou expressed this idea perhaps a little

3

too insistently in stressing the opposition between Greek and Hebrew thought, but certainly in a very striking and pedagogically successful way:

> What do we mean when we speak of 'spirit' and say that 'God is spirit'? Are we speaking Greek or Hebrew? If we are speaking Greek, we are saying that God is immaterial. If we are speaking Hebrew, we are saying that God is a storm and an irresistible force. This is why, when we speak of spirituality, a great deal is ambiguous. Does spirituality mean becoming immaterial or does it mean being animated by the Holy Spirit?[3]

It is clear, then, that the real meaning of the word cannot be understood simply by consulting a dictionary. As James Barr pointed out in his criticism of Kittel's *Wörterbuch*, it is its use in a particular context, in which it refers to a given subject or intention, that determines the value of the word. *Rûaḥ-pneuma* can, for example, simply mean the wind (as in Jn 3:8; Acts 2:1–4, 6). Elsewhere, it can mean the breath of God that communicates life (Ex 15:8–10; Ps 33:6) and consequently man's breath, the principle and sign of life (Gen 7:22; Ps 104:29–30; also very frequently in Job). We also speak about man's 'last breath' and 'expiring'. It is also breath or animation that enables a task to be accomplished, especially if it is in some way the work of God. This was so in the case of Bezalel's task of furnishing the sanctuary (Ex 31:3ff.). It is, as we shall see later, even more true in the matter of leading the people of God, conducting their wars and prophesying.

The breath-spirit (the Spirit) is qualified in various ways according to the effects that it, as a principle, produces. The Old Testament speaks, for example, of the spirit of intelligence (Ex 31:3) and of the spirit of wisdom (Deut 31:3; 34:9) and of jealousy (Num 5:14; all these texts are in P[4]). It even speaks of 'an evil spirit from the Lord' (1 Sam 16:14; 18:10 = D; cf. Judg 9:23).[5] The most interesting way in which it is qualified, however, is when the spirit or breath is said to be *of God*, in other words, when it expresses the subject by whose power various effects are produced in the world or in man, and especially in those who receive the gifts of leadership or prophecy or who become religious men and so on.[6] Sometimes the 'spirit of the Lord' or the 'spirit of God' simply refers to God himself, as for example in Is 40:13; 63:10: 'But they rebelled and grieved his Holy Spirit'.

This quotation brings us to the term that is so important for us here, an expression that is also used in the penitential psalm, 51:11, the 'holy spirit'. The spirit is holy because it comes from God and its reality belongs to the sphere of God's existence. There is no need to find any other reason for the holiness of the spirit. God is holy because he is God, but in the case of this spirit (or Spirit), the Old Testament does not emphasize the value of sanctification very much, at least not in the sense of an inner principle of perfection in life; such holiness is rather the result of observing the Torah. The Spirit-Breath is first and foremost what causes man to act so that God's plan in history may be fulfilled.

4

THE ACTION OF THE BREATH OF YAHWEH

Certain external effects, for which there are parallels and similarities in other religions, such as shamanism, were attributed to the breath-spirit (the Spirit) at a given period and in the earliest documents. What is ascribed to the forces of nature in shamanism, however, is always attributed to God (Yahweh) in the Old Testament. New data were contributed by the authors of the prophetic books, penetrating more deeply into man's innermost self.

The Spirit has effects on man and brings about an experience of seeing and wisdom. The Yahwistic and Elohistic accounts of Balaam show him manipulated by Yahweh and, despite himself, pronouncing a divine oracle: 'Balaam lifted up his eyes and saw Israel encamping tribe by tribe. And the spirit of God came upon him and he took up his discourse and said: "The oracle of Balaam, the son of Beor, the oracle of the man . . . who sees the vision of the Almighty, falling down, but having his eyes uncovered . . ." ' (Num 24:2ff. = J).

Samuel was the first of the prophets, whose greatness cannot be disputed, but the editor who was working at the time of King Josiah and was responsible for 1 Sam 9:9 said: 'He who is now called a "prophet" was formerly called a "seer" '. The 'seer' Samuel is really a 'prophet'; he has an inspired way of speaking about what has to be done. He tells Saul, for example: 'You will meet a band of prophets . . . they will be in the grip of a prophetic trance. And the spirit (breath) of the Lord will come mightily upon you and you will enter into a trance with them and be turned into another man' (10:5–6). This is precisely what happened (see 10:10ff.). A similar occurrence is recorded later in the same book (19:20–24) in the case of the messenger sent by Saul to Samuel, who was at the head of a group of prophets in a prophetic trance: 'The Spirit (the breath) of God came upon the messengers of Saul and they also entered into a trance'. The same happened to Saul himself when he followed his messengers to the same place. Even in the fairly rudimentary conditions of this event, we become aware of what is always true even in the most exalted activities caused by the Spirit, that is, the effects on man and his psyche in cases of guidance and inspiration that are attributed to the Breath of God himself. God, in other words, never seizes hold of man without involving him completely, including his psychosomatic being.

At the same time, in texts of the same period as the one quoted and even earlier, the spirit (or Spirit) that comes from God gives a discernment and wisdom that are in accordance with what is normal. What these experiences have in common with the preceding ones, however, is that they guarantee that God's plan for his people will be carried out.[7] Pharaoh, for example, says of Joseph: 'Can we find such a man as this in whom is the Spirit of God?' (Gen 41:38 = E). There is also the case of the seventy elders to whom God distributed some of the spirit that was in Moses (Num 11:16ff., 25). They began to prophesy and, as Joshua was scandalized by such an unselective extension of this privilege, Moses told him: 'Would that all the Lord's people were prophets, that the Lord would put his spirit (his breath) upon them!' (11:29). When Moses was in sight of the promised land and was about to die, however, God inspired him to act in order to secure his succession: 'Take Joshua the son of Nun, a man in whom is the breath (a man who is inspired)' (27:18).

The Heroes or 'Judges'

These were charismatic leaders or warriors aroused in turn by God in the critical circumstances in which Israel was placed, repeatedly and through its own fault, during the 150 years from the occupation of Canaan by Joshua until the insitution of the monarchy.

> Othniel: 'The spirit (breath) of the Lord came upon him. . .' (Judg 3:10).
> Gideon: 'The spirit (breath) of the Lord took possession of Gideon. . .' (6:34).
> Jephthah: 'The spirit (breath) of the Lord came upon Jephthah. . .' (11:29).
> Samson: 'And the spirit (breath) of the Lord began to stir him. . .' (13:25); 'And the spirit of the Lord came mightily upon him and he tore the lion asunder . . . and he had nothing in his hand' (14:6); 'And the spirit (breath) of the Lord came mightily upon him and he went down to Ashkelon and killed thirty men of the town . . .' (14:19).

Saul was the last of the judges and the first of the kings. When the monarchy was instituted, this type of unusual and sudden experience of being seized by the breath-spirit that has been encountered in the Old Testament up to this point ceases, at least in this form. After Saul, who was still living under the régime of such 'happenings' (1 Sam 10:6–13; 11:6), when Samuel anointed the youngest of Jesse's sons, 'the spirit of the Lord came mightily upon David *from that day forward*' (1 Sam 16:13). Something quite definitive, then, began with David, the course of which can be traced through the prophecy of Nathan (2 Sam 7) and the prophecy of Isaiah— 'There shall come forth a shoot from the stump of Jesse and a branch shall grow out of his roots. And the Spirit of the Lord shall rest upon him . . .' (Is 11:1–2)—to Jesus, the 'son of David', as is attested by Matthew's genealogy and the genealogy that Luke (3:31) places after his account of Jesus' baptism. We shall consider this later.

The Prophets

At least since the time of the baptismal creed formulated by Cyril of Jerusalem (*c.* 348), but even in the writings of Justin Martyr and Irenaeus, the Holy Spirit has been characterized in our confessions of faith as the one 'who has spoken through the prophets'. In opposition to Gnosticism and the teaching of Marcion, Christians wanted to stress that the Spirit by whom Jesus had been conceived and who animated the gospel was the same as the

Spirit who acted in the old dispensation.[8] But in the Targums, this Spirit is often called the 'spirit of prophecy' and although it may not have been attributed to a breath of God or an in-spiration during the ninth to the eighth centuries B.C.,[9] the prophetic word was thus attributed during the Deuteronomic period[10] and quite firmly during the exile, especially in Ezekiel (Ezek 2:2; 11:5; see also Is 48:16; 61:1), and then again in post-exilic Judaism (Zech 7:12; 2 Chron 15:1; 20:14; 24:20), in Hellenistic Judaism and in the rabbinical writings.[11] Was the intention perhaps to avoid a rather mechanical portrayal? Certainly Jeremiah never had recourse to an in-spiration of this kind.

Three prophetic books are particularly interesting in this context. They are Isaiah, Ezekiel and Joel. The word *rûaḥ* occurs about fifty times in the book of Isaiah[12] and 46 times in Ezekiel. The first aspect of *rûaḥ* that is expressed in Isaiah is common to the rest of the Bible. What exists in life that is worthy of the name comes from the breath of God. So, for example, the prophet declares: 'The Egyptians are men and not God; their horses are flesh and not spirit. When the Lord stretches out his hand . . .' (Is 31:3). It is God who communicates life. After proclaiming the fall of Samaria, the prophet contrasts its 'fading flower' with the 'crown of glory' that the Lord will be for his people: 'A diadem of beauty to the remnant of his people; and a spirit of justice to him who sits in judgement' (28:5–6).

It is in the midst of storm and danger that Isaiah announces the deliverance of his people and a future of hope—to Ahaz through the prophecy of the Emmanuel (7:10ff.) and to Hezekiah at the time of Sennacherib's invasion (37:21–35; 'And the surviving remnant of the house of Judah shall again take root downwards . . .'). During these dramatic events, Isaiah foretells that 'There shall come forth a shoot from the stump of Jesse and a branch shall grow out of his roots. And the Spirit of the Lord shall rest upon him, the spirit of wisdom and understanding, the spirit of counsel and might, the spirit of knowledge and the fear of the Lord and (he will inspire him with) the fear of the Lord . . .' (11:1ff.).

This is the Messiah. He will receive from the Spirit all the gifts that are necessary to rule according to justice. The result of this will be wonderful—nothing less than paradise regained (see 32:15–18). D. Lys regards it as legitimate to see the promised descendant of David as a new Adam.[13] He finds it surprising that there is no reference to anointing in the text, but says that 'the link between anointing and the spirit cannot fail to be established insofar as the mediator in Is 11 is the king and the one on whom the spirit rests is the Messiah'.

The first Servant song in Deutero-Isaiah—'I have put my Spirit on him' (42:1)—at once raises the important question: Is it a prophetic utterance about the Messiah[14] or is it concerned with Cyrus? If it is in fact, as it would seem to be, concerned with Cyrus, then it is remarkable that it is the breath of God upon him which enables him to reveal and realize God's judgement, in other words, his plan or his justice, for the nations. All those who, in the Old Testament, carried out God's plan with regard to his people were called the servants (*'ebhedh*) of God. They include Abraham (Gen 26:24; Ps 105:6), Moses (Ex 14:31; Num 12:7; Deut 34:5; Josh 1:2, 7; 9:24; 11:15; 1 Kings 8:53; 2 Kings 21:8; Mal 3:22; Ps 105:26; Neh 1:7, 8; 9:14), Joshua (Josh 24:29; Judg 2:8), David (2 Sam 3:18; 7:5, 8; 1 Kings 3:6; 8:66; 11:13; 14:8; 2 Kings 20:6; Is 37:35; Jer 33:21ff., 26; Ps 18:1; 78:70), Elijah (2 Kings 9:36; 10:10), Isaiah (20:3), Zorobabel (2 Kings 9:36; 10:10), the prophets collectively (2 Kings 9:7; Jer 7:25; Amos 3:7) and finally, in Isaiah, the people of Israel (41:8; 42:19; 43:10; 44:1, 2, 21; 45:4; 48:20).[15] Here, however, the nations are involved: Israel has entered the history of the world and its empires, in and through which God also pursues his plan. It is the work of his breath and of that impulse of life and activity which is his Spirit. For Isaiah, the return is a new exodus, and the first deliverance under the leadership of Moses had taken place under the action of the Spirit (the psalm inserted into Is 63:7–14). From the very detailed study made by D. Lys and the less exhaustive one made by J. Isaac, it is clear that there is a continuity and a connection between the movement that God gives to the creatures of the cosmos by his breath and that which he puts into them to establish a personal relationship with him, in other words, between nature and grace.

This universal extension of election of which Israel is the centre is celebrated by Trito-Isaiah in chapters 60 and 61, which are addressed in particular to the exiles of Israel in the solemn declaration: 'The Spirit of the Lord God is upon me; the Lord has made a messiah of me; he has sent me to bring good tidings to the afflicted' (61:1). This messiah is not called Servant, but has several of the aspects of the Servant that are found in chapters 42, 49 and 50 and also has aspects, not of a king, but of a prophet. As we shall see when we consider the New Testament, Jesus himself provided an interpretation of this text: 'Today this scripture has been fulfilled in your hearing' (Lk 4:21).

Isaiah 11, which deals with the king-messiah, goes back to a period when the Davidic monarchy was still in existence in Jerusalem. Ezekiel saw the ruin of Jerusalem that he had foretold and the destruction of the Temple, from which he had 'seen' the Presence depart. He also saw the deportation of the people into Babylonia. The cult and those who celebrated it are dead, but, as Yahweh is more present than ever to his people, his Spirit will re-animate the dead bones and his breath will make living beings of them. He will do this by communicating himself within men's hearts. There are, in this context, the two incomparable chapters of Ezekiel, 36 and 37:

'I will sprinkle clean water upon you and you shall be clean from all your uncleannesses and from all your idols I will cleanse you. A new heart I will give you, and a new spirit I will put within you; and I will take out of your flesh the heart of stone and give you a heart of flesh. And I will put my breath (spirit) within you. . .' (36:25–27).

'Son of man, can these bones live?' And I answered, 'O Lord God, thou knowest'. Again he said to me, 'Prophesy to (pronounce an oracle against) these bones and say to them: O dry bones, hear the word of the Lord. Thus says the Lord God to these bones: Behold, I will cause breath to enter you and you shall live. . . .' So I prophesied (pronounced an oracle) as he commanded me, and the breath came into them and they lived and stood upon their feet (37:3–5, 10).

And finally:

'And I will not hide my face any more from them when I pour out my spirit upon the house of Israel, says (oracle of) the Lord God' (39:29).

The disaster of the invasion and the test of exile, interpreted by the greatest prophets, led to a vision of the Spirit-breath of God as purifying men's hearts, penetrating into them and making them a holy people of God. This was to be a new beginning, a new exodus, a new covenant and a people renewed. This message is proclaimed, for example, in Jer 31:31–34 (although the breath is not mentioned in this text). It is also to be found in the part of Isaiah belonging to the exile: 44:3–5 (verse 3 proclaims a resurrection of the scattered people: 'I will pour water on the thirsty land and streams on the dry ground; I will pour my Spirit upon your descendants and my blessing on your offspring') and 63:11–14. Finally, the same theme occurs, after the return from exile, in Hag 2:5; Zech 4:6; 12:10; and Neh 9:20.

It is a very important step. Through his breath-Spirit, God will be the principle of faithful life and holy life for Israel. But this gift is extended to all peoples in Joel's proclamation of eschatological events made about 350–340 B.C.: 'Afterwards I will pour out my Spirit on all flesh; your sons and your daughters shall prophesy, your old men shall dream dreams and your young men shall see visions. Even upon the menservants and maidservants in those days I will pour out my Spirit' (3:1–2). On the day of Pentecost, Peter was to proclaim that this had in fact happened.

The Wisdom Literature

During the four centuries that preceded Jesus' coming into our world, a body of Jewish writings now known as the Wisdom literature developed. This literature includes Job and the Proverbs (between 450 and 400 B.C.), numerous Psalms, Qôheleth or Ecclesiastes, Sirach or Ecclesiasticus (*c.* 187 B.C.) and, in Alexandria, where the Jews were in contact with Hellenistic thought, Wisdom (*c.* 50 B.C.). The sapiential literature of Hellenized Judaism constitutes a remarkable reflection on Wisdom. In it, Wisdom is brought so close to the Spirit that the two realities are almost identified, at least if they are viewed in their action.[16]

9

This Wisdom comes from God. She is his action for the benefit of his creatures, enabling them to go straight. There is an inclination in God to do good and to desire what is good. Wisdom therefore has a universal extension. In Wis 1:7 and 8:1, she—or the Spirit—even has a cosmic function, similar to the part that Wisdom played in Stoicism in holding the universe together. The real function of Wisdom, however, is to guide men in accordance with God's will. For this reason, she chose especially to reside in Israel, where she formed God's friends and prophets. She is 'the book of the covenant of the Most High God, the law which Moses commanded (us)' (Sir 24:23). The action of Wisdom is therefore very similar to that of the Spirit. They would be identical were it not for the fact that Wisdom does not have what the Spirit has, namely the character of a force or inner energy, the power to transform. C. Larcher has outlined the relationship between Wisdom and the Spirit in the following way:

> The two realities are identified in several ways. Wisdom possesses a spirit (7:22b) or she is a spirit (1:6). She acts in the form of a spirit (7:7b). She also has power at her disposal and the various functions of the Spirit in the Old Testament are attributed to her. She has, for example, a universal cosmic function. She arouses the prophets. She guides mankind and especially the chosen people. Finally, she acts as the great interior master of the souls of men. Wisdom and the Spirit are identified in so many respects that Wisdom appears above all as a sublimation of the part played by the Spirit in the Old Testament. This explains why some of the Fathers of the Church regarded Wisdom as prefiguring, not the Word, but the Holy Spirit.[17]

There was a great deal of reflection about wisdom in the ancient world and in Judaism, then, but it incorporated certain philosophical and especially Stoic ideas only in the book of Wisdom itself.[18] That book presents us with a view of the nature of wisdom: wisdom *is* a spirit who is a friend of men (1:6; cf. Job 32:8). At the very beginning of the book, a number of profound statements are made:

> Wisdom is a kindly spirit (a friend to man) and will not free a blasphemer from the guilt of his words; because God is witness of his inmost feelings, and a true observer of his heart and a hearer of his tongue. The spirit of the Lord has filled the world and that which holds all things together knows what is said (1:6, 7).

This verse has been included in the Church's liturgy as the introit for Pentecost. Later in the book of Wisdom we read:

> In her there is a spirit that is intelligent, holy, unique, manifold, subtle, mobile, clear, unpolluted, distinct, invulnerable, loving the good, keen, irresistible, beneficent, humane (loving to man), steadfast, sure, free from anxiety, all-powerful, overseeing all and penetrating through all spirits that are intelligent and pure and most subtle. For Wisdom is more mobile than any motion; because of her pureness she pervades and penetrates all things. For she is a breath of the power of God and a pure emanation of the glory of the Almighty; therefore nothing defiled gains

entrance into her. . . . Though she is but one, she can do all things and while remaining in herself, she renews all things; in every generation she passes into holy souls and makes them friends of God, and prophets. . . . She reaches mightily from one end of the earth to the other and she orders all things well (7:22–25, 27; 8:1).

Two aspects that were influential in the later theology of the Holy Spirit should be noted here. The first is that the Spirit is to some extent personalized. In the case of Wisdom, this personalization is progressively stressed from Prov 8:22–31 onwards: 'The Lord created me at the beginning of his work . . .'; Sir 1:1–10; 4:11–19; 15:1–10; 24:1–22. Sometimes this personification is no more than a form of literary expression. The strict monotheism of the Jewish religion, however, associated certain realities with God which were God himself but which at the same time represented in God various ways of acting, being or being present (with men): the Shekinah, Wisdom. What is said of this Wisdom in chapters 8 and 9 of the book of Wisdom expresses the *intimate* action of the Spirit of God and can be applied to the Spirit. Wisdom and Breath (Spirit) are often closely connected and do the same thing (see, for example, Wis 1:4–5; 7:22–23; 9:17). They are God for us and with us. Writing about Palestinian Judaism, that is, the apocryphal and rabbinical literature, Erik Sjöberg said:

> The autonomy of the Spirit in Judaism is surprising. In Rabbinic writings the Spirit is often spoken of in personal categories. There are many instances of the Spirit speaking, crying, admonishing, sorrowing, weeping, rejoicing, comforting etc. Indeed, the Spirit can even be said to speak to God. For this reason it has often been thought that the Spirit is regarded in Judaism as a hypostasis, as a personal angelic being. . . . The decisive thing is that man stands here before a reality which comes from God, which in some sense represents the presence of God, and yet is not identical with God. . . . The Holy Spirit is a special divine entity which is sent by God and which acts independently within the limits set by the divine will.[19]

Wisdom also provides us with a very interesting reflection on the very idea of spirit. The spirit is characterized by its subtlety and purity, which enable it to enter everything and everyone and, while remaining unique, to be in everything and everyone as the principle of life, newness and holy conduct.[20] In his *Treatise on the Holy Spirit* (written in 375), Basil of Caesarea described the Spirit as having a nature that is not limited and not subject to change, 'intelligent, infinite in power, unlimited in greatness, not governed by time and the centuries and generous with his own goods'.[21] I am allowing myself to look ahead in quoting a patristic text at this point, but it is important to mark the continuity of thought and to emphasize the promises that are already present in the Old Testament. Even before the book of Wisdom, there are texts such as Ps 139:7–12; Job 28:20–27 (on Wisdom). Nor was it without good reason that oil later became a symbol of the Spirit in the New Testament, the patristic period and the Church's liturgy. What sport and athletics did in the ancient world, cars and machines do in the modern world: they enable us to appreciate the play of this substance that penetrates everywhere, spoils nothing and, on the contrary, facilitates the smooth functioning of each part.

*   *   *

In the Jewish Bible, the Breath-Spirit of God is the action of God. Through that Breath-Spirit, God reveals himself as active in animating and giving life at the level of what we call nature. Through the Breath-Spirit too, God led his people and raised up for them heroes and strong warriors, kings, leaders (such as Moses and Joshua), prophets and finally wise men. The Messiah who had been proclaimed was to bring all these functions together in himself and raise them to a higher level. As for the prophets, there were no more after Zechariah and Malachi.[22]

The 'economy' or God's plan, to which Scripture bears witness, moves forward in the direction of greater and deeper interiority. Eschatology will be the realization of absolute interiority: 'God all in all'. This progress is clear in the Old Testament. It reaches its conclusion in the New Testament, where it is connected with a more perfect revelation and experience of the Spirit. It is possible to establish a progressive commitment and at the same time a more complete revelation of God himself, as Father, Son and Holy Spirit. That is the plan of our creed. Creation is attributed to the Father. That creation is visible and shared. Revelation and redemption are ascribed to the Son and these are universal works inscribed in history. The Spirit is regarded as responsible for sanctification, inhabitation and intimacy and he 'inhabits our hearts'.

NOTES

1. Studies that I have consulted include: P. van Imschoot, 'L'action de l'esprit de Jahvé dans l'Ancien Testament', *RSPT*, 23 (1934), 553–587; *idem*, 'L'esprit de Jahvé source de vie dans l'Ancien Testament', *RB*, new series, 44 (1935), 481–501; *idem*, 'L'esprit de Jahvé et l'alliance nouvelle dans l'Ancien Testament', *ETL*, 22 (1936), 201–226; *idem*, 'Sagesse et Esprit dans l'Ancien Testament', *RB*, new series, 47 (1938), 23–49; E. Schweizer *et al.*, '*pneuma*', *TDNT*, VI, pp. 332–451 [this article was also published separately in English: *Spirit of God* (London, 1960), but references in this present book are to *TDNT*]; F. Büchsel, *Der Geist Gottes im Neuen Testament* (Gütersloh, 1926); E. Haulotte, 'L'Esprit de Yahvé dans l'Ancien Testament', *L'homme devant Dieu. Mélanges H. de Lubac*, I (*Théologie*, 56) (Paris, 1963), pp. 25–36; D. Lys, '*Rûach*': *le Souffle dans l'Ancien Testament* (Paris, 1962). Most of these studies contain ample bibliographies. Specialized studies are noted at the relevant points in the text.
2. J. Isaac, *La révélation progressive des Personnes divines* (Paris, 1960), pp. 103–209; A.-M. Henry, *L'Esprit Saint* (Paris, 1959); T. Maertens, *Le souffle de l'Esprit de Dieu* (Paris, 1959); G. A. Maloney, *The Breath of the Mystic* (Denville, 1974). It is worth noting that 277 times out of the total of 378 that it occurs in the Old Testament, *rûaḥ* is translated in the Greek Septuagint as *pneuma*. In most of the cases where another Greek word is used, the reference is to 'wind'.

3. J. Daniélou, 'L'horizon patristique', originally meant to be included in *Recherches actuelles* (*Le Point théologique*, 1) (Institut Catholique, Paris, 1971), pp. 22–23; the author withdrew this text from publication and I do not know whether it has appeared since then elsewhere. This raises questions with regard to the old catechisms. E. Germain, for instance, quotes Mgr de Harlay's catechism of 1687, in which he answers the question: 'What is God?' with 'He is a spirit'. She comments: 'When the Bible said: God is Spirit, its intention was to declare that God is the only Living Being who did not receive life. He is. But now—since the time of Cartesian idealism—being a spirit means not having a body': *Langages de la Foi à travers l'histoire* (Paris, 1972), p. 90.

4. P is the priestly code or account, which has been dated to after the exile; J is the Yahwistic document, dated to the ninth century, Judah; E is the Elohistic account, dated to the eighth century, Northern Kingdom; D is the Deuteronomistic account, *c*. 620, which is found not only in Deut, but also in Judg, Sam and Kings. This distinction between various documents or accounts must, of course, be accepted with caution and it does not mean that there were no earlier attempts to edit, at least partially.

5. There are many examples besides these in *'pneuma'*, *TDNT*, VI, pp. 361–362.

6. See *ibid.*, pp. 362–367.

7. According to the Priestly tradition, those who made the holy garments (Ex 28:3) or who provided the furnishings for cultic purposes (31:3; 35:31) were given the spirit of God to enable them to do this.

8. See A. Orbe, *La unción del Verbo. Estudios Valentinianos*, III (*Anal. Greg.*, 113) (Rome, 1961), pp. 483–499; H.-J. Jaschke, *Der Heilige Geist im Bekenntnis der Kirche* (Münster, 1976), p. 144 and note 4, which gives references to texts from the first three centuries A.D.; see also pp. 233 ff., where the author discusses this idea in the writings of Irenaeus.

9. Is the 'pneumatophore', the 'man of the spirit', mentioned in Hos 9:7 the same as the 'prophet' in the same verse? They are certainly placed in parallel. The word 'spirit' appears in the Revised Standard Version with a small initial letter. The reference to the spirit of the Lord in Mic 2:3 is possibly a gloss.

10. There is no reference in the Deuteronomistic account itself to the Spirit; but see Num 24:2 (Balaam) and 2 Sam 23:2 (David speaking about himself).

11. See *pneuma*, *TDNT*, VI, pp. 381–383. See also Wis 9:17.

12. In Isaiah, the word *rûaḥ* has three different meanings: the breath of God carrying out his plan of salvation; an anthropological and biological reality; the Spirit of Yahweh (especially in the messianic texts and the songs of the Servant). See R. Koch, 'La théologie de l'Esprit de Yahvé dans le livre d'Isaïe', *Sacra Pagina*, ed. J. Coppens *et al.* (Paris and Gembloux, 1959), I, pp. 419–433.

13. See D. Lys, *op. cit.* (note 1), p. 89, note 1.

14. The Jerusalem Bible thinks this, whereas the French *Traduction Œcuménique* opts for Cyrus. R. Koch, 'Der Gottesgeist und der Messias', *Bib*, 27 (1946), 241–268, 276–403, also interpreted it, pp. 379ff., in the sense of the Messiah, opposing the view that the text had Cyrus in mind. It is also interesting to note that the Ethiopic Book of Enoch attributes the Spirit to the Messiah (49:3).

15. These references, which have all been checked, are taken from Koch, 'Der Gottesgeist', *op. cit.*, p. 384.

16. See, for example, P. van Imschoot, 'L'Esprit de Jahvé et l'alliance nouvelle', *op. cit.* (note 1), 201–220; *idem*, 'Sagesse et Esprit', *op. cit.* (*ibid.*), 23–49; D. Colombo, 'Pneuma Sophias ejusque actio in mundo in Libro Sapientiae', *Studii Biblici Franciscani Liber Annuus*, I (1950–51), 107–160; C. Larcher, *Etudes sur le Livre de la Sagesse* (Paris, 1969), especially pp. 329–414, 'La Sagesse et l'Esprit'; M. Gilbert, 'Volonté de Dieu et don de la Sagesse (Sg 9, 17 sv)', *NRT*, 93 (1971), 145–166.

17. C. Larcher, *op. cit.*, p. 411, with reference, in the case of the Fathers, to J. Lebreton, *Les origines du dogme de la Trinité*, 2nd ed. (Paris, 1928), II, p. 513 (Theophilus of Antioch), pp. 567f. (Irenaeus) and pp. 569–70 (Clementine Homilies).

18. A. M. Dubarle, *Les sages d'Israël* (Paris, 1946); '*pneuma*', *TDNT*, VI, pp. 370–372; G. Verbeke, *L'évolution de la doctrine du pneuma du stoïcisme à S. Augustin. Etude philosophique* (Paris, 1945).

19. '*pneuma*', *TDNT*, VI, pp. 387–388; cf. F. Büchsel, *op. cit.* (note 1), pp. 35, 134.

20. The Breath-Spirit of God leads or conducts believers so that they may carry out his plan. The Exodus is the classical example of this. See also Is 32:15–17; 63:7–14; Ps 143; Neh 9:20–21. Clement of Rome quoted the text of Prov 20:27: 'The spirit of man is the lamp of the Lord, searching all his innermost parts' in this form: 'The Spirit of the Lord is a lamp searching the depths of the heart' (21:2).

21. Basil, *De spir. sanct.* 9; cf. Gregory Nazianzen, *Orat. theol.* V, 29 (*PG* 36, 165).

22. 'The Jewish people believed that they were, from that time onwards (that is, as the Christian event came closer), deprived of the Spirit: "We do not see our signs; there is no longer any prophet and there is none among us who knows how long" (Ps 74:9)'; 'Those righteous men have joined their fathers and the prophets have fallen asleep' (Apoc. Bar. 85:1, 3). The Maccabaean historians and their contemporaries were already conscious of this disappearance of the Spirit (see, for example, 1 Macc 14:41); this tradition of the Spirit is found again in the second century A.D. in the rabbis: 'Since the death of Haggai, Zechariah and Malachi, the last of the prophets, the Holy Spirit has ceased in Israel' (Tosefta of the Talmudic treatise *Sota* 13:2): see J. R. Villalon, *Sacrements dans l'Esprit. Existence humaine et théologie existentielle (Théologie historique*, 43) (Paris, 1977), p. 351. At the time of Jesus, the idea was widespread among the Jews that there would be no more revelation of the Spirit until the eschatological era: see Strack and Billerbeck, IV. 2, pp. 1229ff. See also H. Gunkel, *Die Wirkungen des Hl. Geistes nach der populären Anschauung des apostolischen Zeit und der Lehre des Apostels Paulus*, 3rd ed. (1909), pp. 50ff.; F. Büchsel, *op. cit.* (note 1), pp. 123ff.

2

THE NEW TESTAMENT[1]

[*Note:* in this chapter the numbered notes are collected at the end of each section.]

Because of the chronological order of the New Testament texts, I ought to discuss the evidence provided by Paul first, then that found in Mark and Matthew, followed by that in Luke, both the gospel and Acts, and finally the witness of John. All the New Testament texts, however, including Paul, speak of Jesus as the one without whom everything lacks a foundation (1 Cor 3:11). It is therefore both legitimate and suitable to follow an order of realities rather than an editorial order and, since our knowledge of Jesus Christ comes above all from the gospels, it is also legitimate and suitable to begin with them.

If I were approaching this question purely as a study in exegesis and biblical theology, I would have to write a series of learned monographs. That, however, is not the aim of this book and, in any case, I lack the competence to write such monographs. All that needs to be done here is to make use of the relevant works and with their aid to disengage the meaning of the most important elements in the experience and revelation of the Spirit during the messianic period—the conception, baptism and activity of Jesus, Christian existence according to St Paul, the life of the early Church and the supreme witness borne by John.

*   *   *

THE BAPTISM, CONCEPTION AND LIFE OF JESUS

The Gospels

The Gospel is the communication to men of the fact that God's promises of salvation are fulfilled in Jesus. It opens with John the Baptist's call to conversion and the baptism of Jesus (see Mk 1:1ff.).[2] It is in this framework that Mark sets the 'beginning of the good news'. This is the beginning of the eschatological period characterized by the gift of the Spirit to a people of God with a universal vocation. At his baptism by John the Baptist, Jesus is marked out and dedicated as the one by whose words, sacrifice and activity the Spirit enters the history of mankind as a messianic gift and, at least as

15

arrha or earnest-money, as an eschatological gift. There is no doubt that the Spirit was active before Jesus' coming, under the old disposition. It was by the Spirit that Mary conceived Jesus, whose quality of 'son of God' is mentioned by Luke (1:35), in whose gospel it refers, not to Jesus' pre-existence, but to his conception by the Holy Spirit. Nevertheless neither Matthew nor Luke, both of whom speak of it, connect the fact that Jesus is to act through the Spirit and will finally communicate that Spirit with his birth. Both connect it with his baptism. Before it, Jesus did not appear as someone acting in the power of the Spirit, and his fellow-townsmen in Nazareth saw nothing exceptional in him.[3] The event of baptism cannot therefore be seen simply as a 'manifestation that played a subordinate part in the cycle of infancy'.[4] On the contrary, it opens an entirely new chapter. Jesus was indeed the Son of God and he was filled with the Spirit from the time that he was in Mary's womb. F. Büchsel, however, has noted (p. 167) correctly that a pneumatology inherited from the Old Testament and Judaism is used in the gospels.[5] The Spirit is received by an act of God which expresses his love and brings about a union with him. A first sending of the Spirit— Thomas Aquinas speaks of the 'mission' of the Holy Spirit—made the little Jesus who was brought to life in Mary's womb 'holy' and the 'Son of God' (= Messiah).[6] A new communication or mission was initiated in the event of his baptism, when he was declared the Messiah, the one on whom the Spirit rests, who will act through the Spirit and who, once he has become the glorified Lord, will give the Spirit. If he was consecrated at the time of his baptism to carry out his prophetic ministry, then he was able to pour out the Spirit when he was 'exalted at the right hand of God' (see Acts 2:33).

There is no need for us to examine the texts of each gospel exegetically here. The close unanimity of the witness that they bear is expressed at the same time as their differences. In the gospel of John, for example (1:32–34), Jesus, the Word made flesh, already possesses the Spirit, and the theophany of the Jordan is evidence given to John the Baptist. Jesus is baptized by John in the Jordan. Luke adds that he was baptized after a great number of people and that the Spirit descended while he was praying. The heavens opened and the Spirit descended upon Jesus (according to John, it remained on him) 'in the corporeal form of a dove'.

The dove was not a symbol of the Spirit in the Old Testament or the rabbinical writings.[7] Need we look for a different meaning from that of a pair of wings showing that a gift comes from heaven? The gift of the Spirit to the prophets was sometimes represented by a winged heavenly messenger.[8] The dove was a messenger and the message was given in heavenly words (*bath-qôl*). The dove was, however, a symbol of Israel, the chosen people.[9] It may therefore be a representation or the symbolic presence of that people and of the penitential movement with which Jesus wanted to be at one, since he was the new Adam and represented and embodied the new people of God (Mt 3:14–15). In addition, the titles 'Son of God' and 'Servant' were also applied to the whole people of God.[10] The dove might therefore represent it as the people to whom the Spirit was to come through the Messiah.

In the Christian tradition, the dove was to be the symbol of the Holy Spirit. This is clear from iconographical evidence and from a whole series of texts, including liturgical ones.[11] The part played in Augustine's ecclesiology by *columba* is well known—it is a name for the one, holy Church and for the Holy Spirit.[12]

As in the case of the annunciation to Mary (Lk 1:35), the Word and the Spirit came together. The Word, the testimony of the Father, is addressed to the crowd and to Jesus according to Matthew and Luke, to Jesus according to Mark. In the fourth gospel, John the Baptist testifies that he has seen the Spirit, in the form of a dove, descend and remain on Jesus, but he does not report the heavenly word. 'We see the Dove rest on the Lamb and we hear the Father, who has sent the Spirit, proclaim the beloved Son' (a monk of the Eastern Church, *Contacts*, 41, 1963).

The word is: 'This is my beloved Son, the one whom it has pleased me to choose (= the one with whom I am well pleased)' (Mt 3:17) or 'Thou art my beloved Son. . .' (Mk 1:11). It is not a call, as it would be in the case of the prophets or Paul, but a declaration that echoes in Jesus' mind and it is also the confirmation of a condition that qualifies Jesus in what he is. This word also includes a verse of Ps 2:7, which is a royal, messianic psalm: 'The Lord said to me, "You are my son, today I have begotten you" ', which is the way in which the Father's word is reported, in the so-called Western version, in Lk 3:22. It combines this verse with the first verse of the first Song of the Servant (Is 42:1): 'Behold my servant, whom I uphold, my chosen, in whom my soul delights; I have put my Spirit upon him'. This was the moment when Jesus was called and sent as the Messiah and that Messiah is described as having the characteristics of a prophet, as a king in the line of David and his house ('he shall be my son', 2 Sam 7:14) and also as the Servant. The characteristics of the Servant, called to mind by the reference to Is 42:1, are made explicit in the description of Jesus as the 'Lamb of God, who takes away the sin of the world' (Jn 1:29), the declaration made by Jesus in the synagogue in Nazareth (Lk 4:17–21) and Matthew's commentary on Jesus' healings (11:16ff.).

Jesus himself was fully conscious of being the one 'whom the Father consecrated and sent into the world' (Jn 10:36). This is a particularly difficult point to explain and even to express, since it concerns the growth in Jesus' human knowledge of his consciousness of his own quality and his mission. His baptism, his encounter with John the Baptist, the Spirit's coming to him and the Word that accompanied that coming were certainly all events of decisive importance in making explicit his human consciousness of his quality of the one who was chosen and sent and of the Son of God and the Servant and Lamb of God. There is fairly general agreement now that, because of the hypostatic union, the Word or Son of 'God' is the principle of

Jesus' existence and the metaphysical subject to which his actions are attributed, but that this union leaves the play of his faculties of knowing and willing a matter of his true and full humanity.[13] It is a fact that is borne out in Scripture that Jesus increased in wisdom and favour with God (Lk 2:52), that there were certain things that he did not know, that he may have been mistaken[14] and that he experienced difficulty in obeying his Father perfectly.[15] He carried out his mission from childhood to the cross under the rule of obedience (see Phil 2:6–8; see also Rom 5:19), which means that he was ignorant and not in control of the consequences of his actions. In what terms and how was he, at the level of his human experience, conscious of his ontological quality of the Son of God? The 'categorial' way of expressing and representing this consciousness is made explicit by the experiences, encounters and actions that take place in his life. He understood his mission by carrying it out. On the one hand, he discovered it as something that was already outlined in the Mosaic law, the prophets and the psalms.[16] On the other hand, he carried it out by receiving the miraculous works and prophetic words from his Father and living in obedience to God's will for him: 'In that same hour he rejoiced in the Holy Spirit and said, "I thank thee, Father, Lord of heaven and earth, that thou hast hidden these things from the wise and understanding and revealed them to babes" ' (Lk 10:21).

Jesus' acceptance of baptism by John the Baptist within the plan of fulfilling God's will (see Mt 3:13–15), the new coming of the Spirit to him and the words describing him as the royal Messiah, Servant and 'beloved Son' are all moments of decisive importance at the beginning of the mission that he had to carry out for us. The Spirit then leads him at once into the desert to confront the demon (Mt 4:1; Mk 1:12; Lk 4:1). Jesus' temptation is closely connected with his baptism and the declaration: 'Thou art (This is) my beloved Son'. The words 'If you are the Son of God' are repeated twice by the tempter, but Jesus is also the Servant, whom the Father has chosen to fight and to suffer and die on the cross. His temptation is a test of his obedience to God. We know that it ended in a decisive victory—Satan was bound and Jesus again and again cast him out by the 'finger' or the Spirit of God.[17]

After his baptism and his victory over the tempter, Jesus experienced the presence in himself of the Spirit, whose activity made it possible for him to make the kingdom of God present and therefore to eliminate the reign of the demon. That is also why Jesus was to heal so many people. His healing ministry is on several occasions linked in Matthew with his call to be the Servant (see 8:17 and Is 53:4; 12:15–21 and Is 42:1–4). It is possible to be mistaken about Jesus himself, 'being born in the likeness of men, being found in human form', but it is wrong to blaspheme or sin against the Spirit by not recognizing his work where the Spirit exerts his power.[18] His opponents' wrong and hostile interpretation of his power over evil and the evil one confirmed Jesus in the evidence that he had of working through the Spirit.

18

It would undoubtedly be claiming too much if we were to say that the baptism of Jesus contained the whole doctrine of his substitutive death,[19] but there can be no doubt—and it is stated quite explicitly in Mt 3:15—that Jesus came to be baptized and that he experienced the event with the intention of offering himself and being open to God's plan for him. This plan included firstly the type of the Servant and then the supreme offering of his life (see Heb 10:5–10). Jesus in fact saw his death as a 'baptism' (Mk 10:38; Lk 12:50). He offered himself to God as a spotless victim through the 'eternal spirit', that is, the Holy Spirit.[20] His sacrifice was the consequence of this baptism, and his glory was the consequence of his sacrifice. The baptism of the passion and glory are brought together in his reply to the sons of Zebedee (Mk 10:35ff.), who represent us all. Several exegetes have compared these texts, and their closeness confirms the fact that all those who believe in Jesus are concerned in his baptism, in which his destiny as the Messiah who suffers and is dedicated to glory is involved.[21] We are baptized in his death (Rom 6:3), but we are also baptized by one Spirit into one body (1 Cor 12:13).

It was also as one who was led by the Spirit that had come upon him at his baptism that Jesus undertook his evangelical ministry. All three synoptic gospels show that ministry as beginning with his victorious struggle against the demon. Luke brings together several aspects of Jesus' presence in Nazareth and adds the reading of Isaiah 61:1–2a (and 58:6): 'The Spirit of the Lord is upon me, because he has anointed me to bring good tidings to the afflicted . . .' and the declaration: 'Today this scripture has been fulfilled in your hearing' (4:21). The descent of the Holy Spirit on Jesus at his baptism is described as an anointing, that is, as a prophetic anointing for a mission to proclaim, and as a realization of, the good news of liberation from evil and the evil one.[22] Luke writes of the continuation of this process in the Acts of the Apostles. Pentecost was for the Church what his baptism was for Jesus, that is, the gift and the power of the Spirit, dedication to the ministry, mission and bearing witness.[23] In Acts 10:38–39, for example, we read: 'You know . . . how God anointed Jesus of Nazareth with the Spirit and with power; how he went about doing good and healing all that were oppressed by the devil, for God was with him. And we are witnesses to all that he did. . . .' Acts 4:24–30 is the prayer of the community of Jerusalem. It recalls Ps 2, the messianic psalm from which the heavenly word spoken at Jesus' baptism was taken: 'Thy holy servant Jesus, whom thou didst anoint'. The coming of the Spirit at Jesus' baptism, then, is clearly seen as his anointing for his messianic ministry. That anointing is both royal and prophetic.

The Patristic Tradition

We will leave our exegesis of the New Testament texts at this point and go on to a synthesis of the Tradition and a consideration of the dogmatic implications. Our first task, however, is ecclesiological and for this purpose we will examine a number of patristic statements.

In their attempts to explain the anointing of Christ at his baptism, the Fathers were troubled by three data in the context within which they thought and expressed themselves. The first of these was the climate of Stoic thought, according to which *pneuma* was seen as a force permeating the universe and holding it together, in such a way that it was associated with the *logos*. A cosmic function was ascribed to this *logos* which preceded the part that it played in the economy of salvation. The second datum was the need to maintain that Christ did not begin to be the Son of God and the Christ at the time of his baptism. Justin Martyr insisted on this in his reply to Trypho (*Dial*. 87–88), but he did not make a clear distinction between the Logos and the Pneuma. He also believed that Jesus possessed his power from the moment of his birth and that the descent of the Spirit at his baptism was simply a sign of his messianic quality.[24] The third datum was that certain Gnostics maintained that the Saviour on high descended on Jesus at the time of his baptism and that this was necessary since, in their opinion, his birth in the flesh could only have defiled him.[25]

Irenaeus refuted them firmly and clearly.[26] In an admirable statement, he says that this Jesus, the humanity of the Word, 'insofar as he is God receives from the Father, that is, God, the throne of the eternal royalty and the oil of anointing'. He quotes Ps 45:7–8 in this context and believes that this points to the incarnation.[27] The Spirit, however, had to be given to all of us[28] and that is why it descended on Jesus at his baptism. This happened so that he could communicate the Spirit to us. It was for this reason that the Word became Jesus Christ:

St Matthew says, in connection with the baptism of the Lord: 'The heavens were opened and he saw the Spirit of God descending like a dove and alighting on him; and lo, a voice from heaven, saying, "This is my beloved Son, with whom I am well pleased" ' (3:16–17). It was, after all, not one who claimed to be the Christ who descended on Jesus, and it cannot be claimed that the Christ was other than Jesus. The Word of God, the Saviour of all men and the Lord of heaven and earth—that Word who is, as we have already shown, no other than Jesus—by having assumed a flesh and having been anointed with the Spirit by the Father, became Jesus Christ. As Isaiah said: 'There shall come forth a shoot from the stump of Jesse and a branch shall grow out of his roots. And the Spirit of the Lord shall rest upon him' (11:1–4). Elsewhere Isaiah announced his anointing and the reason why he was anointed: 'The Spirit of the Lord God is upon me, because the Lord has anointed me to bring good tidings to the poor' (61:1–2) . . . . It was therefore the Spirit of God that descended on him—the Spirit of that same God who had, through the prophets, promised to bestow anointing on him so that, receiving ourselves the superabundance of that anointing, we should be saved.[29]

Hippolytus was familiar with the works of Irenaeus and it should not surprise us to read, in his prayer for the consecration of a bishop: 'Pour out that power which comes from you, the sovereign Spirit that you have given to your beloved Son, Jesus Christ; that he gave to the holy apostles who founded the Church in every place'.[30]

There was, then, a lively awareness in the Church of the part played by the baptism of Jesus in the economy of salvation. Basil the Great wanted to show that the Spirit 'was with the flesh of the Lord' and therefore cited Jn 1:33; Lk 3:22 and Acts 10:38, which refer to the anointing at the time of Jesus' baptism.[31] Jesus had been filled and sanctified by the Spirit since the time of his conception, which had brought about the union of a humanity with the person of the eternal Son. He had, however, been 'anointed' by the Spirit at his baptism in order to be the Messiah, the minister of salvation and holiness. It was then that 'he appeared as the man who was able to make others holy'.[32] No other kind of 'anointing' occurs in Scripture.[33]

The Fathers were, however, impressed by the gifts of grace, salvation and deification that were made to humanity by the incarnation of God in the man Jesus. They traced the beginning of the new creation, which was paschal and pentecostal, back to the incarnation as such.[34]

A century after Irenaeus, Methodius of Olympus formulated statements that have been repeated again and again in the East. He said, for example, that through the incarnation, the mortal had been changed into immortal and the passible into impassible.[35] The struggle against Arianism and its by-products, and the necessary but difficult growth of Christological thought led to attempts to trace the saving and sanctifying activity of Jesus Christ back to the personal union of the Word with humanity in Jesus rather than to the descent of the Spirit on Jesus at his baptism. Athanasius,[36] for example, maintained that it was by the incarnation of the Logos that humanity was anointed by the Holy Spirit.[37] A similar view was held by Gregory Nazianzen,[38] Gregory of Nyssa († c. 394),[39] Augustine[40] and Cyril of Alexandria, who said: 'Christ filled his whole body with the life-giving power of the Spirit. . . . It was not the flesh that gave life to the Spirit, but the power of the Spirit that gave life to the flesh.'[41] At the end of the great Christological debates, Maximus the Confessor (580–662) stated that the hypostatic union was the basis of the individual nature of Christ.[42]

In the West, the Fathers expressed this consecration of Christ by the Spirit in terms of the grace of Christ as the Head, which made him the principle of salvation and sanctification for his body.[43] This view was formulated in the twelfth century in the theology of Christ the Head and his capital grace. This theology was very consistently, forcefully and systematically outlined by Thomas Aquinas. It teaches that sanctification by the Spirit and the fullness of grace were acquired from the outset of the hypostatic union and as a necessary consequence of that union. According to the Fathers, the coming of the Spirit in the form of a dove at the time of Jesus' baptism was a sign for John the Baptist.[44] Thomas Aquinas called it a 'visible mission', and such a mission is simply a sign given for the sake of others of an invisible mission that had previously been carried out fully.[45] The question in the *Summa* devoted to Jesus' baptism goes back to a theology that is both analytical and typological, not to say metaphorical, and certainly disappointing.[46]

Thomas derived his Christology from the Greek Fathers,[47] Augustine and the early Scholastic theologians. Möhler, the Roman School and Scheeben also used the same sources in their theological renewal in the nineteenth century. In all these theologies, the Church is linked to the incarnation and the Trinity because of the hypostatic union.[48] This is particularly clear in the case of Scheeben, who, despite his theology of the indwelling of the Holy Spirit, was more systematic. He went so far as to say, for example: 'When the Fathers say that Christ is anointed with the Holy Spirit, this means only that the Holy Spirit has descended into the humanity of Christ in the Logos from whom he proceeds, and that he anoints the humanity of Christ as the pouring out of the unction which is the Logos himself. Only God the Father can be regarded as the efficient principle of Christ's anointing because he alone communicates to the Son the divine dignity and nature which formally anoint the humanity that is assumed to the Son's person. . . . Christ is anointed not merely by divine deputation for the discharge of an office, nor even merely by the pouring out of the Holy Spirit. He is called divine, but not simply as God's friend and representative. He is the true Son of God and truly God.'[49]

Is this a satisfactory argument? Yes, as analytical theology, but as a concrete, historical theology going back to biblical sources, it is disappointing.

The Theology of Heribert Mühlen

Nearly twenty years ago, Heribert Mühlen of Paderborn undertook a wide-ranging renewal of this aspect of Catholic theology.[50] In numerous publications, he has explored the same themes and has developed them continuously and progressively in the following order:

1. The Holy Spirit can be presented in his relationship with the Father and the Son as 'the We in person'. This representation is valid not only at the level of the essential Trinity (the intra-divine level), but also at that of the 'economic' Trinity. In other words, it also applies to the involvement and the revelation of the divine Persons for the benefit of the world and men.

2. The greatest importance has to be attached to the anointing of Christ, at his baptism, by the Holy Spirit.

3. The Church has to be seen not as what Möhler called a 'continued incarnation', a formula that was later accepted by the Roman School, but rather as the presence and activity in the 'Church' of the same personal Spirit that anointed Jesus as the Messiah. The most suitable formula for a dogmatic definition of the mystery of the Church, then, would be 'only one Person, that of the Holy Spirit, in several persons, namely Christ and us, his believ-

ers'. This would 'define' the mystery of the Church as strictly, as precisely and as concisely as the mystery of the Trinity has been 'defined' as 'three Persons in one nature' and the mystery of the incarnation has been 'defined' as 'one Person in two natures'. Of course, the presence (or 'indwelling') and activity involved are a presence and an activity in *persons*, who preserve their freedom, including their freedom to sin, so that there is nothing of an 'incarnation' of the Spirit here in the way there is an incarnation of the Word in Jesus.

4. Mühlen provides another formula for the mystery of the Church, calling it a 'Great I' or a 'corporative personality'. It is not the Great I of the Holy Spirit, but it is the Great I of Christ, since the Spirit is the Spirit of Christ. He is communicated by Christ and he animates the body of Christ.

5. Mühlen has also applied these pneumatological and ecclesiological views to several contemporary movements and in particular to the movement of renewal in the Spirit, which we shall consider later, and to ecumenism. In the case of the latter, it can be used, he claims, either to justify the ecclesiological value of other churches or church communities[51] or to interpret ecumenical activity in the light of a future council (perhaps the next council?), which might be ecumenical in that sense of the word as well and as such an act of unity.[52]

We cannot at this point consider either these contemporary applications of pneumatology or Mühlen's original development of relationships within the Trinity in terms of interpersonal relationships.[53] We shall come back to these questions later. Here, we must limit ourselves to his theology of the anointing of Christ by the Spirit in its connection with the hypostatic union, in other words, the assumption of an individualized human nature by the Person of the Word or Son of God.

Mühlen's interpretation is fortunately quite close to the way in which Scripture speaks, that is, concretely and historically. Whereas 'Christus' was regarded by the Scholastic theologians simply as a proper noun or name that could be replaced equally well by 'Jesus' or 'the Lord', Mühlen gives it its full biblical value of 'the anointed one', in Hebrew *mᵉšîaḥ*, the 'Messiah', a term which points to the three biblical and classical functions of king, priest and prophet. 'Christ', then, is a name describing the part played and the mission carried out by Jesus of Nazareth. The preaching of the apostles and the disciples' confession of faith also point to this affirmation: Jesus is the Christ, the Messiah of God.[54] 'You know', Peter testified, what happened 'throughout all Judea, beginning from Galilee after the baptism which John preached: how God anointed Jesus of Nazareth with the Holy Spirit and with power' (Acts 10:38). I. de la Potterie was therefore able to conclude his study of the anointing of Christ with the words: 'The real and, in one sense, unique context within which the New Testament speaks of the anointing of Christ is that of baptism'. This does not present us with any difficulty if the term 'Christ-Messiah' is understood simply in the sense of a function and a ministry and if no more is attributed to his 'anointing' than the naming and the gifts of the power required for this mission. If, however, what occurred at his baptism was a declaration of this mission—Mühlen speaks of 'promulgation' in this context[55]—then Jesus was destined for it from the beginning. The revelatory and soteriological part played by Christ cannot be separated from what he was constituted to be from the beginning. The author of the Acts calls Jesus the 'Christ-Messiah' from the very beginning. He does this implicitly in the annunciation made to Mary (Lk 1:31–33) and explicitly in the annunciation to the shepherds (2:11) and the assurance given to Simeon (2:26). This has led W. Grundmann to comment that, when Peter proclaims: 'God has made him both Lord and Christ, this Jesus whom you crucified' (Acts 2:36), this is, on God's part, a revelation or manifestation in the quality of Christ-Messiah, even though Jesus was that from the moment of his conception.[56]

What is Mühlen's intention and what does he in fact base on the theology of the Trinity and Scripture? It is not that Christ was not made holy at the moment of his conception. It is rather that this sanctification should not be attributed to the hypostatic union as such, that is, the mission of the Word, but to the Holy Spirit. The mission of the Spirit is the consequence in time—'in the fullness of time'—of his eternal procession 'from the Father and the Son', as the term of their mutual love, first in Mary's womb and then in the Church, whose supernatural existence is connected with the Spirit of Jesus. This view is quite in accordance with the dogmatic explanation of the mystery, which attributes the hypostatic union to the Word, and the *formatio corporis* and the sanctification of the fruit conceived in Mary's womb to the Spirit (see Lk 1:35).[57] This sanctification is the gift, made in absolute fullness, of created graces, a fullness that is evoked by the quality of the Son of God in the absolute sense of the term. This is why Thomas Aquinas spoke of it in this way and quoted Is 42:1, applying the words to the Messiah: 'Behold my servant, whom I uphold, my chosen, in whom my soul delights; I have put my Spirit upon him'. Thomas distinguished two aspects, following one another not in time, but in logic and by nature, the first relating to the assumption of a human nature by the Word and the second to the Spirit who fills that man-God with gifts of grace.[58]

Ought we, then, not to recognize a similar order in the Church and, in these circumstances, make up for what Mühlen has failed to do by stressing the real connection between the Church and the incarnation as such? Was the institution of the Twelve by Jesus (see Mk 3:14) not followed by the sanctification and animation of the apostles by the Spirit of Pentecost? And was the institution of the sacraments and the delivery of the message of the gospel not followed by the making present of those gifts of the covenant by the Spirit? This is a very familiar theme in the patristic tradition (see below, note 2) and we shall return to it later, when we shall see that it can be applied to the theology of the sacraments and in particular to the two-sided sacrament of baptism/confirmation and to the consecration of the eucharistic gifts by the words of institution and the epiclesis. The essential thing is to respect the two missions, of the Word and of the Spirit, on the pattern of the succession which derives from the procession within the Trinity. It goes without saying that we speak of such matters as best we can. . . .

NOTES

1. For this chapter, see, in addition to '*pneuma*', *TDNT*, VI, esp. pp. 396–451; and F. Büchsel, *Der Geist Gottes im Neuen Testament* (Gütersloh, 1926): H. B. Swete, *The Holy Spirit in the New Testament. A Study of Primitive Christian Teaching* (London, 1909); M.-A. Chevallier, *L'Esprit et le Messie dans le bas-judaïsme et le Nouveau Testament* (Paris, 1958); *idem*, *Esprit de Dieu, paroles d'hommes* (Neuchâtel, 1966), pp. 7–17.

2. J. Dupont, ' "Filius meus es tu". L'interprétation du Ps. 2.7 dans le Nouveau Testament', *RSR*, 35 (1948), 522–543; I. de la Potterie, 'L'onction du Christ', *NRT*, 80 (1958), 225–252; C. Cranfield, 'The Baptism of our Lord. A Study of St Mark 1, 9–11', *Scottish Journal of Theology*, 8 (1955/1); A. Feuillet, 'Le baptême de Jésus d'après l'évangile selon S. Marc (1, 9–11)', *CBQ*, 21 (1959), 468–490; A. Légault, 'Le baptême de Jésus et la doctrine du Serviteur souffrant', *SE*, 13 (1961), 147–166; M. Sabbe, 'Le baptême de Jésus. Evangiles synoptiques', *De Jésus aux Evangiles. Mélanges J. Coppens*, ed. I. de la Potterie (Gembloux and Paris, 1967), II, pp. 184–211; H. Mentz, *Taufe und Kirche in ihrem ursprünglichen Zusammenhang* (Munich, 1968); F. Porsch, *Pneuma und Wort. Ein exegetischer Beitrag zur Pneumatologie des Johannesevangeliums (Frankfurter Theologische Studien, 16)* (Frankfurt a. M., 1974), pp. 19–51; J. Bornemann, *Die Taufe Christi durch Johannes in der dogmatischen Beurteilung der christlichen Theologen der vier ersten Jahrhunderte* (Leipzig, 1896); D. A. Bertrand, *Le baptême de Jésus. Histoire de l'exégèse aux deux premiers siècles (Beiträge zur Geschichte der biblischen Exegese, 14)* (Tübingen, 1973).

3. Hence their astonishment (see Lk 4:22; Mt 13:54–56; Mk 6:1ff.). See F. Büchsel, *op. cit.*, pp. 149ff.

4. D. A. Bertrand, *op. cit.*, p. 12.

5. The Holy Spirit is simply the spirit, the powerful breath of God that is creative and gives life and the force by which Jesus performs miracles and drives out demons (see Acts 10:38ff.; Mt 12:28; Lk 11:20). Jesus said: 'The Father who dwells in me does his works' (Jn 14:10). In the New Testament, 'God' is the Father. See K. Rahner, 'Theos in the New Testament' (Eng. tr.), *Theological Investigations*, I (London and Baltimore, 1961), pp. 79–148.

6. What is known as the hypostatic union is, as a 'work *ad extra*', the action of the three Persons and the result of this action is the union in the Person of the Son, the Word. It is, however, the Spirit who, by activating in Mary her capacity as a woman to conceive (and thereby supplying the 23 male chromosomes), produces the human being whom the Son, the Word, unites to himself, and thereby also the 'holy' fact. In this way, Jesus is Emmanuel, God with us, because he was of the Holy Spirit (and conceived by that Spirit). That is, dogmatically and theologically, the meaning of Lk 1:35. See, for example, Thomas Aquinas, *ST* IIIa, q. 32, a. 1, ad 1 and 2 ad 2, in which he explains a saying of 'Jerome's' (in reality, it was not Jerome, but Pelagius, *Libellus fidei ad Innocentium: PL* 45, 1716) and quotes 'John Chrysostom' (the unknown author of the *Opus imperf. in Mat.*, 1:20: *PG* 56, 634) and John Damascene (*De fide orthod.*, c. 2: *PG* 94, 985). The Ottawa edition of the *Summa* gives other references in the same sense to Hugh of Saint-Victor, Peter Lombard and Bonaventure.

7. See 'pneuma', *TDNT*, VI, p. 382. Many suggestions have been made to explain the meaning of the dove: see M. E. Isaacs, *The Concept of Spirit* (London, 1976), pp. 116f.

8. Targum on Is 6. See F. Lentzen-Deis, *Die Taufe Jesu nach den Synoptikern. Literarkritische und gattungsgeschichtliche Untersuchungen* (Freiburg, 1970), pp. 243 ff., 270.

9. See H. Sahlin, *Studien zum dritten Kapitel des Lukasevangeliums* (Uppsala, 1949), pp. 101–105; A. Feuillet, 'Le symbolisme de la colombe dans les récits évangeliques du baptême', *RSR*, 46 (1958), 524–544; F. Lentzen-Deis, *op. cit.*, pp. 181, 265–270; L. E. Keck, 'The Spirit and the Dove', *NTS*, 17 (1970–71), 41–67; F. Porsch, *op. cit.* (note 2), pp. 28–31 (with a very full documentation).

10. See H. Mentz, *op. cit.* (note 2), p. 64.

11. It is forbidden to represent the Holy Spirit in human form: see M. Meschler, *Le don de la Pentecôte* (Paris, 1895), II, p. 226 and note 1. The divine Persons should only be represented by the characteristics for which there is scriptural evidence: see, for example, the decree of the Holy Office, 16 March 1928, *AAS*, 20 (1928), 103. The Holy Spirit could therefore be represented, for example, as a dove, as tongues of fire or as the finger of God (see below, note 17). In the East, adaptations were made to the theological needs of various periods. Representations have included the dove, tongues of fire, light, a luminous cloud or a ray and various human forms, such as the three Magi or Abraham's three visitors (Andrei Rublev). Geometrical shapes have also been used. See T. M. Provetakis, 'To hagion Pneuma eis tēn Orthodoxēn Zōgraphikēn', *To Hagion Pneuma* (Thessalonica, 1971), with 58 illustrations; see also *RHE*, 67 (1972), 675.

12. See my general introduction to Augustine's *Traités antidonatistes*, I, *Bibl. August.*, Vol. 28 (Paris, 1963), pp. 104–109.

13. It is impossible to mention all the books and articles that have been written on this subject since P. Galtier's study in 1939. I would mention only three short bulletins: B.-D. Dupuy, *RSPT*, 47 (1963), 110–116; E. Gutwenger, *Concilium*, 11 (1966), 81–94; B. Sesboué, *RSR*, 56 (1968), 635–666. There are other, more advanced studies which can act as norms for us today. Among the most important of these is K. Rahner, 'Dogmatic Reflections on the Knowledge and Self-Consciousness of Christ' (Eng. tr.), *Theological Investigations*, V (London and Baltimore, 1966), pp. 193–215. C. V. Héris, 'Problème de Christologie. La conscience de Jésus', *Esprit et Vie*, 81 (1971), 672–679 (who criticizes J. Galot and makes a distinction between the metaphysical person and the personality) keeps to Thomistic principles, as does H.-M. Féret, 'Christologie médiévale de S. Thomas et Christologie concrète et historique pour aujourd'hui', *Memorie Domenicane* (1975), pp. 109–141.

14. See A. Vögtle, 'Exegetische Erwägungen über das Wissen und Selbstbewusstsein Jesu', *Gott in Welt. Festgabe für K. Rahner* (Freiburg, 1964), I, pp. 608–667; R. E. Brown, 'How much did Jesus know?' *CBQ*, 29 (1967), 315–345; O. Cullmann, *Salvation in History* (Eng. tr.; London, 1967), esp. pp. 209ff.

15. The agony (*agōn* = struggle), Mt 26:39 and 51; Mk 14:36; Lk 22:42; Heb 2:10 and 13; 4:15; 5:8.

16. The explanation that he gives to the disciples (Lk 24:27 and 44) is based (on infused knowledge, but also) on the circumstances in which the Father has given him the opportunity to verify that he was being spoken of (see, for example, Mt 11:5; Lk 5:17) or on his own prayerful meditation on the Scriptures (see, for example, Mk 12:10; Lk 4:12; 9:22; 20:41ff.).

17. See Lk 11:20 (finger); Mt 12:28 (Spirit); finger of God: Ex 8:19; 31:18; Deut 9:10; Ps 8:3.

18. See my article 'Le blasphème contre le Saint-Esprit (Mt 9, 32–34; 12, 22–32; Mc 3, 20–30; Lc 11, 14–23; 12, 8–10)', *L'Expérience de l'Esprit. Mélanges Schillebeeckx (Le Point théologique*, 18) (Paris, 1976), pp. 17–29; G. Fitzer, 'Die Sünde wider den Hl. Geist', *TZ*, 13 (1957), 161–182.

19. See O. Cullmann, *The Christology of the New Testament* (Eng. tr.; London, 1959), pp. 66–68; A. Légault, *op. cit.* (note 2).

20. Heb 9:14. H. Mühlen defends the interpretation as the Holy Spirit. Swete did not favour this interpretation: *op. cit*. (note 1), pp. 252–253. According to the Syriac Fathers of the fourth century A.D., Aphraates and Ephraem Syrus, Jesus was, at the time of his baptism, consecrated as a priest (deriving his royal quality from his Davidic descent). This priesthood, which was derived from Moses and Aaron (!), was then communicated by John. See R. Murray, *Symbols of Church and Kingdom. A Study in Early Syriac Tradition* (Cambridge, 1975), p. 179.

21. H. Mentz, *op cit*. (note 2), pp. 52 ff.; J. A. T. Robinson, ' "The One Baptism" ', *Scottish Journal of Theology*, 6 (1953), 257–274.

22. I. de la Potterie, *op. cit*. (note 2), who stresses, with Luke, the prophetic mission of Jesus.

23. This traditional idea has been systematically elaborated by J. Lécuyer in his contribution to *Etudes sur le sacrement de l'ordre (Lex orandi*, 22) (Paris, 1957), pp. 167–213, and *Le sacerdoce dans le mystère du Christ (Lex orandi*, 24) (Paris, 1957), pp. 313–338, especially p. 321, with the references in note 1.

24. See A. Houssiau, *La christologie de S. Irénée* (Louvain and Gembloux, 1955), pp. 172ff., 176–180; J. P. Martín, *El Espíritu Santo en los Orígenes del Cristianismo. Estudio sobre I Clemente, Ignacio, II Clemente y Justino Mártir (Biblioteca di Scienze Religiose*, 2) (Zürich, 1971), pp. 213–223.

25. For these ideas and their context, see A. Orbe's enormous work, *La unción del Verbo. Estudios Valentinianos*, III (*Anal. Greg.*, 113) (Rome, 1961); see also F.-M. Braun, *Jean le théologien*, III/I (Paris, 1966), p. 67.

26. Irenaeus, *Adv. haer*. III, 9, 3; 10, 4; 17. 1. For Irenaeus' theology of the anointing of Christ by the Spirit, see A. Houssiau, *op. cit.*, pp. 166–186; H.-J. Jaschke, *Der Hl. Geist im Bekenntnis der Kirche. Eine Studie zur Pneumatologie des Irenäus von Lyon* (Münster, 1976), pp. 148–252, especially pp. 208ff.

27. See *Adv. haer*. III, 6, 1 (*SC* 211, ed. A. Rousseau and L. Doutreleau, p. 67); 12, 7 (pp. 211–213); *Démonstration de la Prédication apostolique (SC* 62; Fr. tr. L.-M. Froidevaux), 47. In §§9 and 53, Irenaeus says that the Spirit of God rested 'on the Son of God, that is to say, the Word, in his coming as a man' (pp. 45 and 114). Did he have the incarnation or the manifestation in the Jordan in mind here or both? See, for example: 'these texts (Rom 14:15; Eph 2:13; Gal 2:13; 1 Cor 8:11) make it sufficiently clear that a "Christ" who was impassible never descended into a "Jesus", but that Jesus, who was the Christ in person, suffered for us and that he fell asleep and was raised again, descended and went up again. That Jesus was the Son of God who became the Son of man. This is moreover what his name indicates, since the name "Christ" means the one who is anointed, the one who anoints and the unction with which he has been anointed. The one who anoints is the Father, the one who is anointed is the Son and he was anointed in the Spirit, who is the unction. As the Word says through the mouth of Isaiah: "The Spirit of the Lord God is upon me, because he has anointed me" (61:1; Lk 4:18)' (*Adv. haer*. III, 18, 3 (*SC* 211, p. 351; *PG* 7, 934)).

28. *Adv. haer*. III, 17, 1, 3 and 4 (*SC* 211, pp. 329, 331: 'That is why this Spirit descended on the Son of God who had become the Son of man—it was in this way, with him, that he became accustomed to dwell in the human race, to rest on men, to live in the work modelled by God'); 3 (pp. 335ff.: 'the dew, which is the Spirit of God, spread over the whole of the earth. It was this Spirit who descended on the Lord, "the Spirit of wisdom and understanding, the Spirit of counsel and might, the Spirit of knowledge and the fear of the Lord" (Is 11:2–3). It is this same spirit that the Lord gave to the Church when he sent the Paraclete from heaven on the whole of the earth'); 4 (pp. 337ff.: 'It was therefore the Spirit who descended because of the "economy" of which we have been speaking').

29. *Adv. haer*. III, 9, 3 (*SC* 211, pp. 107–113).

30. Hippolytus, *Apostolic Tradition*, 3 (verse 215).

31. Basil, *De Spiritu Sancto* XVI, 39 (*PG* 32, 140C; *SC* 17bis (1968), pp. 386 and 387).

32. Cyril of Alexandria, *Comm. in Ioan*. lib. XI, c. 10 (*PG* 74, 549C).

33. See I. de la Potterie, 'L'onction du Christ. Etude de théologie biblique', *NRT*, 80 (1958), 225–252, who says, on p. 250: 'There is no text in the New Testament which refers to an anointing of Christ at the moment of his incarnation. According to the patristic and theological tradition, the hypostatic union is a consecration of Jesus' humanity by his divinity, but this idea cannot be found in any of the New Testament authors.'

34. S. Trooster, 'De Heilige Geest in de Menswording bij de Griekse Vaders', *Bijdragen*, 17 (1956), 117–151, who examined the teaching of Irenaeus, Clement of Alexandria, Origen, Athanasius, Didymus, Gregory of Nyssa, Gregory Nazianzen and Basil. For the anointing at the moment of conception and the hypostatic union, see also S. Tromp, *Corpus Christi quod est Ecclesia*, III: *De Spiritu Christi anima* (Rome, 1960), pp. 237ff. After Nicaea, the part played by the Spirit in the baptism of Jesus was toned down; see J. G. Davies, *The Spirit, the Church and the Sacraments* (London, 1954), pp. 20–26. The Fathers were especially conscious, in the baptism of Christ, of the 'mystery' that was at the foundation of Christian baptism; see P. T. Camelot, *Spiritualité du baptême (Lex orandi*, 30) (Paris, 1960), chapter X, pp. 257–281, which contains deep insights into its reference to the crucifixion, pp. 268f.

35. Methodius, *De res*. 3, 23, 4 (*GCS* 27, 421–422).

36. Athanasius, *Contra Arian*. 2, 61 and 70 (*PG* 26, 277A, 296B); 3, 34 (397B).

37. *Ibid*. 1, 50 (*PG* 26, 117Aff.).

38. Gregory Nazianzen, *Orat*. 10 in the presence of Basil (*PG* 35, 832A).

39. The Logos, becoming merged with the flesh, raised it to the properties of the Logos by the reception of the Holy Spirit that the Logos possessed even before creation: Gregory of Nyssa, *In illud 'Tunc ipse Filius'* (*PG* 44, 1320D); see also *In Cant. Cant., Hom*. 12 (*PG* 44, 1016).

40. Augustine, *De Trin*. XV, 26, 46.

41. Cyril of Alexandria, *Comm. in Ioan*. 6, 64 (*PG* 73, 604); see also *Comm. in Heb*. (*PG* 74, 961B); P. Galtier, 'Le Saint-Esprit dans l'Incarnation du Verbe d'après S. Cyrille d'Alexandrie', *Problemi scelti di Teologia contemporanea* (Rome, 1954), pp. 383–392. See also Cyril's eleventh anathematism: *DS* 262.

42. Maximus the Confessor, *Ambigua* (*PG* 91, 1040C). See also John Damascene, *De fide orthod*. lib. III, c. 3; lib. IV, c. 14 (*PG* 94, 989A and 1161A).

43. Ambrose, *Hexaemeron* 3, 17, 71 (*PL* 14, 186C; in 386–389); Augustine, *Enarr. in Ps*. 123, 1; 136, 22 (*PL* 37, 1640, 1774); *Comm. in Ioan*. 3, 8. (*PL* 35, 1399D), etc.

44. See Augustine, *De Trin*. XV, 26 (*PL* 42, 1093–94); *De Praed. Sanct*. 15, 31 (*PL* 44, 982); Cyril of Alexandria, *Comm in Ioan*. lib. II (*PG* 73, 209A–212D).

45. *In I Sent*. d. 16, q. 1 and 2; III, d. 13, q. 1, a. 2, q. 3, ad 3; *ST* Ia, q. 43, a. 7, ad 6.

46. *ST* IIIa, q. 39. In article 2, Thomas says: 'Christus spirituali baptismate non indigebat, qui a principio suae conceptionis gratia Spiritus Sancti repletus fuit'.

47. See I. Backes, *Die Christologie des hl. Thomas von Aquin und die griechischen Kirchenväter* (Paderborn, 1931).

48. J. A. Möhler, not in *Die Einheit* (1825), but in the successive editions (1832 onwards) of his *Symbolik*: see §36 (for the precise meaning of this, see H. Mühlen, *Una mystica Persona* (below, note 50), pp. 8ff.); see also C. Passaglia, *De Ecclesia Christi* (Regensburg, 1853), lib. III, cc. 1–5 and 41; J. B. Franzelin, *Theses de Ecclesia Christi* (Rome, 1887), Thesis 17, pp. 296ff.

49. M. J. Scheeben, *Mysterien des Christentums* (1865), §51; Eng. tr. *The Mysteries of Christianity* (St Louis and London, 1946), pp. 332–333 [based on 1941 Ger. ed.; not identical with translation here of Fr. tr. (1947), pp. 338–339].

50. H. Mühlen, *Der Heilige Geist als Person. Beitrag zur Frage nach dem Hl. Geiste eigentümliche Funktion in der Trinität bei der Inkarnation und im Gnadenbund. Ich-Du-Wir* (Münster, 1963); *Una mystica Persona. Die Kirche als das Mysterium der heilsgeschichtlichen Identität des Heiligen Geistes in Christus und den Christen* (Paderborn, 1964; refs are to 2nd ed., 1967). He has also written several other, less important works, which add nothing

essential to the theology of these major works. See also, however, *Die Erneuerung des christlichen Glaubens. Charisma-Geist-Befreiung* (Munich, 1974).

51. *Una mystica Persona, op. cit.*, pp. 369ff.; see also my study 'Le développement de l'évaluation ecclésiologique des Eglises non catholiques', *Revue de Droit canonique*, 25 (1975), 168–198, especially 186ff.

52. H. Mühlen, *Morgen wird Einheit sein. Das kommende Konzil aller Christen. Ziel der getrennten Kirchen* (Paderborn, 1974).

53. See, for example, the surveys made by B. Rey in *RSPT*, 49 (1965), 527–533, and A. Paatfort in *Angelicum*, 45 (1968), 316–327.

54. W. Grundmann, F. Hesse, M. de Jonge and A. S. van der Worde, 'chriō', *TDNT*, IX, pp. 493–580 (with a lengthy bibliography); H. Mühlen, *Der Heilige Geist als Person, op. cit.* (note 50), pp. 176ff.

55. *Ibid.*, p 187. Elsewhere, in *Una mystica Persona*, p. 219, Mühlen says: 'This form of activity of the Pneuma in the man Jesus is quite different from his prophetic anointing by the Holy Spirit, which is bestowed on him with others in mind. It is therefore possible to speak of a twofold aspect of the anointing of Jesus in the Holy Spirit—an anointing which reaches him in his own humanity and an anointing which is bestowed on him for others.' But, if this is not a separation, then surely it is at least to make too much of a distinction between the two? Personal grace and capital grace are strictly identical in Christ. See L. Lécuyer, 'Mystère de la Pentecôte et apostolicité de la mission de l'Eglise', *Etudes sur le sacrement de l'Ordre* (Paris, 1957), pp. 193–194.

56. W. Grundmann, 'chriō', *TDNT*, IX, esp. pp. 531–532, 534–535.

57. Thomas Aquinas: 'Filio attribuitur ipsa carnis assumptio, sed Spiritui Sancto attribuitur formatio corporis quod assumitur a Filio': *ST* IIIa, q. 32, a. 1, ad 1. See also above, note 6.

58. See *ST* IIIa, q. 7, a. 13, especially the first and the third reason. See also H. Mühlen, *Una mystica Persona, op. cit.* (note 50), p. 248; the author also quotes the Encyclical *Mystici Corporis* in this sense on p. 252.

ST PAUL[1]

An experience of the Holy Spirit is narrated in the Acts of the Apostles, but it is not combined with any form of teaching. The writings of Paul and John, on the other hand, contain teaching about the Spirit. It would obviously be impossible and in any case out of place to look closely here at all the texts in which the word *pneuma* is used by Paul. (It occurs 146 times, including 117 times in the great early epistles.) We will confine our attention here to the most important and significant uses of the term and deal with them systematically. This treatment is fully justified in the case of the great epistles, since Paul's thought does not reveal any real development.

1. Luke shows the Spirit which anointed Jesus at Nazareth, and especially at his baptism in the Jordan, as having been sent to the Church to animate it and to thrust it forward in its bearing of witness and its mission. Paul, on the other hand, proclaims the Gospel of God, which was promised in the old dispensation and has now become a reality. This Gospel, he claims, concerns God's Son, 'who was descended from David according to the flesh and designated Son of God in power according to the Spirit of holiness by his resurrection from the dead, Jesus Christ our Lord' (Rom 1:3–4; cf. 8:11).

Paul did not know Christ according to the flesh. He was certainly acquainted with the incarnation (see Phil 2:6ff.) and the crucifixion, which was for him the condition of salvation, but, even if he had any knowledge of the Church that came about at Pentecost, he makes no reference to it in his writings. His experience of the Spirit is exclusively and directly related to the event of Easter and to the resurrection and glorification of Jesus as Christ and Lord.

2. This gift of the Spirit, which is dependent on the redemption through the crucifixion, fulfils the promise made to Abraham. This promise is connected with Abraham's faith and is fulfilled, not in the economy of the law, but in that of faith. According to Gal 3, the crucifixion took place 'that in Christ Jesus the blessing of Abraham might come upon the gentiles, that we might receive the promise of the Spirit through faith' (verse 14) This is done 'in Jesus Christ', who is the one 'offspring of Abraham' and who takes us into himself (verses 16ff.), so that we are also 'sons' in him (verse 26) and heirs. Our inheritance as sons is the content of the promise (verses 18 and 29). This is accomplished by faith and when we have been 'baptized into Christ' we shall 'put on Christ' (verse 27).

3. This blessing of Abraham and this Spirit as the object of the promise come from God and also reach the gentiles through preaching, which arouses faith. The Spirit acts first and foremost in this proclamation of the Gospel. Paul here bears witness to his own experience as a 'minister of Christ Jesus to the gentiles in the service of the Gospel of God, so that the offering of the gentiles may be acceptable, sanctified by the Holy Spirit' (Rom 15:16). Paul also bears witness in other letters:

> Our Gospel came to you not only in word, but also in power and in the Holy Spirit. . . . And you became imitators of us and of the Lord, for you received the word in much affliction, with joy inspired by the Holy Spirit (1 Thess 1:5–6; Paul's first epistle).

> My speech and my message were not in plausible words of wisdom, but in demonstration of the Spirit and of power, that your faith might not rest in the wisdom of men, but in the power of God. . . . And we impart this (the gifts of God's grace) in words not taught by human wisdom, but taught by the Spirit, interpreting spiritual truths in spiritual language (1 Cor 2:4–5, 13).

> O foolish Galatians! . . . Did you receive the Spirit by works of the law or by hearing with faith? (Gal 3:2).

God is the absolute principle of the Christian's being. He is the norm and the source. Man has to be open to his activity and to allow the norm and the source to do their work. That work is done through faith. The minister of the word does that work by emptying himself of all his own wisdom so that everything can be from God.

4. By faith and baptism,[2] the believer begins a life in and through the Spirit, serving 'in the life of the Spirit' (Rom 7:6; 8:2). He enters and follows the way of a holy life: 'God chose you from the beginning to be saved through sanctification by the Spirit and belief in the truth' (2 Thess 2:13; 1 Thess 4:7–8; cf. 5:23). This life under the rule of the Spirit is described in Rom 8. It is the life of sons of God: 'For all who are led by the Spirit of God are sons of God. For you did not receive the spirit of slavery to fall back into fear, but you have received the spirit of sonship. When we cry "Abba, Father!" it is the Spirit himself bearing witness with our spirit that we are children of God and, if children, then heirs, heirs of God and fellow-heirs with Christ' (Rom 8·14–17; Gal 4:5–7).

Clearly, our inheritance is eschatological. The Holy Spirit is given to us in the present time as a 'guarantee of our inheritance until we acquire posses sion of it' (Eph 1:14; cf. 4:30). 'He who has prepared us for this very thing (= this future) is God, who has given us the Spirit as a guarantee' (2 Cor 5:5; 2:21–22).

This guarantee or earnest-money is real and fruitful, so long as we make it bear fruit: 'If we live by the Spirit, let us also walk by the Spirit' (Gal 5:25). It is possible, 'having begun with the Spirit', to end 'with the flesh' (Gal 3:3). Paul develops the theme of the struggle between the flesh and the Spirit as a conflict between two choices and two ways of life in the epistles that are concerned with the idea of justification by faith. 'Walk by the Spirit and do not gratify the desires of the flesh, for the desires of the flesh are against the Spirit and the desires of the Spirit are against the flesh; for these are opposed to each other' (Gal 5:16–17; cf. 23–25; Rom 7:5–6; 8:1, 17). Paul also lists the fruits of the flesh and the fruits of the Spirit.[3] The first fruit of the Spirit is love. It is more than simply the first in the order of the list. It is the all-embracing and creative principle and is in fact all. 'He who loves has fulfilled the law' (Rom 13:8). Paul, however, goes even further than this and teaches that the holy life is a communication of the holiness of God. The love of which he speaks is the love of God which 'has been poured into our hearts through the Holy Spirit which has been given to us' (Rom 5:5). This Spirit also makes us sons of God.

The Spirit who made the humanity of Jesus (who was 'descended from David (and from Mary) according to the flesh', Rom 1:3; Gal 4:4) a completed humanity of the Son of God (through his resurrection and glorification, Rom 1:4; Eph 1:20–22; Heb 5:5) does the same with us, who are of the flesh from the moment of our birth, and makes us sons of God, sons in the Son and called to inherit with him and to say after him: 'Abba, Father!' (Rom 8:14–17). The Spirit makes us sons of God in accordance with a truth that the status of adoption, which corresponds to our condition as creatures, situates but does not contradict. As Paul affirms, 'You are sons' (Gal 4:6). In this way, God himself communicates himself to us, makes himself active in us and thus enables us to perform actions of 'Christ in us',

31

which are the actions of sons.[4] This is particularly expressed in the cry invoking the name of God in the form that Jesus himself did it and taught us to do it: 'Because you are sons, God has sent the Spirit of his Son into our hearts, crying "Abba, Father!" ' (Gal 4:6). In a very unpredictable way, in which he continues to be Master, the Holy Spirit 'helps us in our weakness . . . and intercedes for us with sighs too deep for words' (Rom 8:26). In other words, he prays in us. This is not a case of God replacing us. The Protestant fear of a 'mystical' merging together of God and man—a fear that, in certain authors, is almost a morbid obsession—has been fully allayed.[5] God's substance does not take the place of our substance. There is a communication of dynamism or of an active faculty and we continue to act. This is clear from the parallel passage in Rom 8:14–15: 'All who are *led by* the Spirit of God are sons of God. . . . You have received the spirit of sonship and . . . cry, "Abba, Father!" '

This fine distinction is important, because this is a question of what the Fathers of the Church called 'deification'. The biblical texts and, in this context, those of Paul in particular have a power that is inescapable: 'Christ is all in all' (Col 3:11) and he lives in us (see Gal 2:20; Phil 1:21); 'In Christ Jesus you are all sons of God . . . you have put on Christ' (Gal 3:26–27) and finally God will be 'everything to everyone' (1 Cor 15:28). It has to be recognized that we are and will be the subjects of a quality of existence and activities which go back to God's sphere of existence and activity. This is the ultimate content of the promise and the real fruit of the Spirit and the principle of our eschatological life (see 1 Cor 15:44ff.).

5. Our life in Christ—or his life in us—is ecclesial. The Spirit plays a decisive part in building up the Church.[6] 'By one Spirit we were all baptized into one body' (1 Cor 12:13). The Spirit and the body are not opposed to each other—they have recourse to each other.[7] The 'body' of which Paul is speaking here is a visible reality, but it is not a physical or material body. Whoever is united to the glorious body of Christ and is permeated with the Spirit through faith, baptism and the bread and wine of the Last Supper is spiritually—and therefore really—a member of Christ and forms a body with him at the level of the life of a son which promises God's inheritance.[8] The captivity epistles add to this concrete view, which is rather lacking in theoretical structure, a theology of the glorified Christ as the head of the body that is the Church (Eph 1:20–23) and even of Christ as enjoying an absolute cosmic primacy (Col 1:15–20).

The body of Christ formed by believers on earth has to be built up (1 Cor 3:9; Eph 2:20; 4:12). What is built in this way becomes a 'dwelling place of God in the Spirit' (Eph 2:22), a 'spiritual house' (1 Pet 2:5ff.; Phil 3:3), which is a temple where spiritual worship is offered to God. 'Do you not know that you are God's temple and that God's Spirit dwells in you?' (1 Cor 3:16; 6:19; 2 Cor 6:16). This rich and profound theme of the indwel-

32

ling of the Holy Spirit in our bodies and the community that we form is the other side of the balance in a theology affirming God's immanence whilst avoiding confusion. The Spirit can be the principle of communication and communion between God and us and between us and our fellow-men, because of what he is as Spirit—sovereign and subtle, unique in all men and uniting persons without encroaching on their freedom or their inner lives. (See 2 Cor 13:13: *koinōnia tou hagiou pneumatos*; subjective genitive, indicating the communion or 'fellowship' of which the Spirit is the principle.)

Christ is similarly in me and is my life, but he remains himself and I continue to be myself. This indwelling or immanence is expressed in the depth of its intimacy by the fact that the Spirit is said to have been 'sent into our hearts' (see Gal 4:6; 2 Cor 1:22; 3:2, 3; Rom 5:5; cf. 2:29; 8:27; Eph 3:17; 2 Thess 3:5).

Paul also compares the fruit of his apostolate to a 'letter from Christ, written not with ink, but with the Spirit of the living God . . . on tablets of human hearts' (2 Cor 3:2–3).[9] In this image, he compares a ministry of the Spirit and its fruit in the Church with a ministry of writing letters. This gives an eschatological range to the Christian ministry—it reaches the definitive and absolute limit of the communication that God establishes between us and his good things and himself. This means that the minister has to be quite translucent and simply the means of an activity that goes beyond his own power and even the measure of his initial understanding of it.

This ministry of the Spirit is first and foremost something that has to be carried out by the apostle, who lays the foundation (1 Cor 3:10; Rom 15:20). Among the ministers whom God calls or 'places' are the apostles, whom Paul always places first (1 Cor 12:28; Eph 4:11). After these come the 'prophets' and these are followed by different 'gifts', 'ministries', 'ways of acting' or 'ways of working'. These are the terms that are employed as almost equivalent to those used by Paul in reference to the one Spirit, the one Lord or the one God, for example, in 1 Cor 12:4ff. It is, however, mainly to the Spirit that Paul traces back the various gifts which reveal his activity 'for the common good'. This chapter in the first letter to the Corinthians contains a truth and a contemporary value of remarkable importance for the modern Church, and we shall be examining it in depth at a later stage. Here, we shall restrict ourselves to a few paragraphs on the situation in the church of Corinth.

6. The situation in the church of Corinth can be outlined as follows.[10] Corinth was a great and intensely busy town, in which there were many cross-currents. Paul spent eighteen months there. The Christians of Corinth presented a spectacle of abundant vitality. They were 'enriched with all speech and all knowledge' and 'not lacking in any spiritual gift' (1 Cor 1:5, 7). This vitality, however, was full of dangers. Several of these Corinthian Christians believed that they were living in the last age and were therefore

beyond the stage of the difficult struggle between the spirit and the flesh.[11] They all rejoiced in the gifts of the Spirit, but did not care about serving the community or the unity of Christians. This is why there were sects and divisions among them: ' "I belong to Paul"—"I belong to Apollos"—"I belong to Cephas"—"I belong to Christ" ' (1 Cor 1:12), court cases between Christians (chapter 6) and individuals asserting themselves at meetings and even at eucharistic assemblies (11:17ff.). There were also anarchistic tendencies in the Corinthian community in the manifestations of the gifts of the Spirit, the *pneumatika* such as speaking in tongues and prophesying, in which members of the community took such delight.[12] They were intoxicated and almost bewitched by these manifestations of an external kind and, although they continued to ask questions about sexual morality (see, for example, 7:1), they were undoubtedly lax in their behaviour (see chapter 5; 6:12; 10:23).[13]

Paul discussed all this, both at the practical level and at the level of fundamental truths, although he made no attempt to restrain the Corinthians' exuberant manifestations of the Spirit. He insisted, however, that there could be no Church of the Spirit based either on individual inspiration or on a greedy personal enjoyment of the gifts of the Spirit. The apostle traces everything back in the first place to Christ. Christ is the 'all' of Christianity.[14] All the activity of the Spirit goes back to this 'all', which is the criterion of the active presence of that Spirit: 'No one speaking by the Spirit of God ever says "Jesus be cursed!" and no one can say "Jesus is Lord" except by the Holy Spirit' (12:3).

In the second place, he traces everything back to the Spirit himself as the sovereign subject. The Corinthians attached more importance to the gifts of the Spirit which they enjoyed than to the Spirit himself as the transcendent subject who is above all personal 'spiritual experience' and, by his gifts, builds up the Church as the Body of Christ.

In the third place, Paul teaches that the gifts of the Spirit and their use are for the 'common good' (12:7) and the building-up of the Body and that this is done by the diversity of the gifts given according to grace (*echontes de charismata kata tēn charin . . . diaphora*; Rom 12:6). He develops this idea in chapter 12, continuing it in chapter 13, in which he expatiates on charity (we should not allow the lyricism of this chapter to make us forget the critical aspect), and then returns to the *pneumatika* which the Corinthian Christians preferred—speaking in tongues and 'prophesying' (chapter 14).

He provides criteria for the healthy use of these gifts of the Spirit. He stresses that, if the Christian is too attached to his individual and immediate experience of the manifestations of the Spirit, he will place an excessive value on their external and extraordinary forms. In the first place, he maintains, they are not simply gifts among other gifts. They have to be appreciated according to the criterion of the 'common good' and, seen in this light, speaking in tongues is the last in importance. They have to use it as responsible men. This means, in concrete terms, that there are three demands: (a) discipline in the community (14:27–33); (b) the need for others to understand (14:14ff.)—speaking in tongues is not simply a means of self-expression; it is the expression of an intelligible word that is useful to the community; (c) discernment.[15]

We shall consider these questions more closely when we come to discuss the present-day movement of Renewal in the Spirit. At present, however, all that is necessary is to define more precisely the meaning of *charisma* in Paul's writings. With the exception of 1 Pet 4:10, which bears a remarkable resemblance to Paul, this word occurs seventeen times in the New Testament and always in the Pauline letters. For the most part, it is used in 1 Cor and Rom.

A great deal has been written about the charisms. I have myself consulted dozens of books and articles. Very many of them contain two serious defects. On the one hand, there is a false contrast in many of these publications, which is elevated to a false problem, between 'charisms' and 'institution' or institutional functions. This goes back to Harnack, Sohm and Troeltsch.[16] Theological problems of pneumatology and ecclesiology are reduced to the level of the sociology of religion. On the other hand, 'charism' is often regarded as a particular gift of the Spirit representing a special register of activities. (These two defects are, of course, closely linked.) I have myself at times accepted this view, which Chevallier calls the 'theory of charisms'. The same author has also remarked that 'to state, as Paul does here very forcefully, that the charisms *are* gifts of the pneuma has never meant that the *word* charisma *means* "gifts of the pneuma" '.[17]

If these charisms are connected with the Holy Spirit, as they are in 1 Cor 12:4–11, then they must refer in the first place, simply because of their name, to God's *charis* or grace. *Charisma* and *charis* are compared textually in 1 Cor 1:7; Rom 5:15 and 12:6. The last text is particularly illuminating: *echontes de charismata kata tēn charin dotheisan hēmin diaphora*, 'having gifts (charisms) that differ according to the grace given to us'. The charisms are differing gifts depending on one single grace. They are the gifts of salvation and of Christian life (see also Rom 5:15–16; 1 Cor 3:10) and of eternal life (Rom 6:23). As they correspond in the case of each Christian to his vocation, they closely resemble what has been called a 'grace of state', provided the idea of vocation is included in it (see 1 Cor 7:7).[18]

Paul says of these gifts or talents that come from God's grace firstly that they are distributed by the Spirit 'according to his will' and secondly that they are different. He gives several lists which do not coincide exactly with each other and which do not claim to be exhaustive. He says thirdly that the Spirit gives these various gifts 'for the common good', that is, so that they can be used to build up the community of the Church or the life of the Body of

Christ. Fourthly and finally, he raises above all these gifts the gift or charism of love, and puts in their proper place two 'gifts of the Spirit' or *pneumatika* (12:1 and 14:1) which the Corinthians valued very highly: speaking in tongues and prophecy.[19]

This way of understanding the charisms as different gifts of grace for the building-up of the Church (cf. 1 Pet 4:10) is also to be found in the apostolic Fathers,[20] John Chrysostom,[21] the language of the liturgy[22] and at times in the writings of the mediaeval theologians.[23]

Very soon, however, and too often even until quite recently, the charisms were seen as graces—*gratis datae* in the sense of the Scholastic tradition[24]—and even as extraordinary gifts of the kind that works miracles or causes healings. The apologists of the second and third centuries, such as Irenaeus and Origen,[25] Theodore of Mopsuestia and Theodoret at the end of the fourth and during the first half of the fifth centuries[26] tended to think this. Leo XIII at the end of the nineteenth century spoke of extraordinary and miraculous gifts when he spoke of charisms.[27] It was at this period too that German Protestant critics emphasized the fallacious contrast and even opposition between free charisms and institutional functions.[28] Most Catholics rejected this opposition, but unfortunately all too often accepted a contrast and a state of tension between charism and office.[29] This was all the more difficult to avoid in view of the fact that history pointed to the existence of tension between free inspiration and the institution, as we shall see later. A place has to be made for this in any true ecclesiology, but it is important not to let it influence Paul's teaching about charisms so much that it changes the real meaning of those gifts according to the apostle.

These charisms, in the sense in which Paul uses them, have made a remarkable return to modern Catholic theology. Pius XII spoke about them in the encyclical *Mystici Corporis*.[30] The Second Vatican Council recognized their value and gave them an important theological place.[31] Since then, in conjunction with a renewed theology of ministries, including that of the bishop and the priest, they have been reintroduced into ecclesiology as gifts or talents placed by the Spirit at the service of the building-up of the community and the Body of Christ.[32]

We do, however, still have further work to do in order to give the charisms their full place. Let me do no more than simply point to an essay by W. C. van Unnik, in which he explains the meaning of the liturgical formula: 'The Lord be with you—And with your spirit'.[33] This, the author claims, can be compared with statements made by Paul in Gal 6:18; Philem 25; 2 Tim 4:22. The words do not simply mean: 'And with you', which would be no more than an exchange of religious wishes helping to create the spiritual space of the celebration. They mean more than this. The formula 'The Lord is (be) with . . .' is frequently used in the Old Testament and it is often concerned with an action that has to be done according to God's plan and is connected with the presence of the Spirit in the one who has to perform this action. In the New Testament and early Christianity, the Spirit is particularly active in prayer and the worshipping assembly.[34] In the brief dialogue between the minister and the community recorded by Hippolytus (*Apostolic Tradition*, 4; 7; 22; 26), the presence of the Spirit has to be ensured so that the liturgical action can take place; hence the words: The Lord be with you, gifted as you are for that purpose with the charism of the Spirit. According to the Fathers, the necessary charism was conferred on the priest at ordination. Nothing, however, takes place automatically, and every spiritual activity requires an epiclesis.[35]

7. The Pneuma and Christ:

(a) The Pneuma, as given to us, relates entirely to Christ. Paul was so dedicated to Christ and so full of him that he was able, as Büchsel has pointed out (*op. cit.* (note 1 below), p. 303), to present what constituted his life without even mentioning the Spirit. It is a question of believing and then of confessing, with one's lips and in one's life, that 'Jesus is Lord' (Rom 10:9). It is the Spirit that enables us to do that: 'No one speaking by the Spirit of God ever says "Jesus be cursed!" and no one can say "Jesus is Lord" except by the Holy Spirit' (1 Cor 12:3)—this is a most important text and we shall be returning to it later.

The Spirit makes it possible for us to know, recognize and experience Christ.[36] This is not simply a doctrinal statement. It is an existential reality which comes from a gift and involves us in our lives. There is no 'Body of the Holy Spirit'—there is a 'Body of Christ'. Is the Spirit not the Spirit of Christ (Rom 8:9; Phil 1:19), the Spirit of the Lord (2 Cor 3:17) and the 'Spirit of his Son' (Gal 4:6)? Irenaeus pointed out that the Spirit brought about the *communicatio Christi* (or *commutatio*, as Sagnard writes), that is, the intimacy of union with Christ.[37] As regards the content of a work of the Spirit as opposed to a work of Christ, it is neither autonomous nor different.

(b) It has often been stressed that very many effects have been attributed either to Christ or to the Spirit and that the formulae 'in Christ' and 'in the Spirit' are indiscriminately applied to both.[38] It is not difficult to find a number of examples:

So that in him (Christ) we might become the righteousness of God (2 Cor 5:21)	Righteousness and peace and joy in the Holy Spirit (Rom 14:17)
Justified in Christ (Gal 2:17)	Justified in the name of the Lord Jesus Christ and in the Spirit of our God (1 Cor 6:11)
Those who are in Christ Jesus. . . . If Christ is in you (Rom 8:1, 10)	But you are not in the flesh, you are in the Spirit, if the Spirit of God really dwells in you (Rom 8:9)

Rejoice in the Lord (Phil 3:1)	Joy in the Holy Spirit (Rom 14:17)
The love of God in Christ Jesus (Rom 8:39)	Your love in the Spirit (Col 1:8)
The peace of God . . . will keep your hearts and your minds in Christ Jesus (Phil 4:7)	Righteousness and peace and joy in the Holy Spirit (Rom 14:17)
Sanctified in Christ Jesus (1 Cor 1:2, 30)	An offering . . . sanctified by the Holy Spirit (Rom 15:16; cf. 2 Thess 2:13)
Speaking in Christ (2 Cor 2:17)	Speaking by the Spirit (1 Cor 12:3)
Fullness of life in him (Christ) (Col 2:10)	Filled with the Spirit (Eph 5:18)
One body in Christ (Rom 12:5)— baptized into Christ (Gal 3:27)	By one Spirit we were all baptized into one body (1 Cor 12:13)
In whom (Christ) the whole structure . . . grows into a holy temple in the Lord (Eph 2:21)	Becoming a dwelling place of God in the Spirit (Eph 2:22)

In several texts, Christ and the Spirit are combined in the same statement: 1 Cor 6:11; 12:13; Rom 9:1.

It is important, however, to go further and consider four other texts:

The Gospel concerning his Son, who was descended from David according to the flesh and designated Son of God in power according to the Spirit of holiness by his resurrection from the dead, Jesus Christ our Lord (Kyrios) (Rom 1:3–4).[39]

The first man Adam became a living being (= an animal being endowed with life); the last Adam became a life-giving spirit (= a spiritual being giving life) (1 Cor 15:45).

If the Spirit of him who raised Jesus from the dead dwells in you, he who raised Christ Jesus from the dead will give life to your mortal bodies also through his Spirit which dwells in you (Rom 8:11).

This Jesus God raised up. . . . Being therefore exalted at the right hand of God and having received from the Father the promise of the Holy Spirit, he has poured it out (Acts 2:32–33).

These texts raise us to the eschatological level. Paul reveals the fantastic perspective at the end of time: 'When all things are subjected to him, then the Son himself will also be subjected to him who put all things under him, that God may be everything to everyone' (1 Cor 15:28). The means of achieving this, however, is for Jesus to be glorified in his humanity, in such a way that he has a humanity and an activity of the Son of God and that these are assumed by a divine condition.[40] It is the Spirit, as the content and the end of the Promise and therefore as an eschatological gift, who establishes 'Jesus', that is, Christ in his crucified humanity, in his condition as the 'Son of God in power' and as Kyrios. The Spirit permeates him and makes him a *Pneuma zōopoioun*, a spiritual being giving life. It is therefore not difficult to understand why Paul attributes activities and consequences in the Christian life either to Christ or to the Spirit, to such an extent that he apparently identifies the two.

(c) He says in fact: 'When a man turns to the Lord, the veil is removed (from the eyes of Moses' disciples). Now the Lord is Spirit and where the Spirit of the Lord is, there is freedom' (2 Cor 3:16–17). Ingo Hermann has devoted a whole monograph to a study of this text.[41] He dismisses those interpretations that claim that the Spirit is the Lord (since the Lord is Christ) or the Lord (Jesus) is made of spirit as of substance. The statement, he believes, has to be understood in the sense of existential experience. In other words, we experience the Lord Jesus as Spirit, or what we experience as Spirit is in reality the Lord Jesus glorified. As a whole, exegetes are in agreement that there is no identification in Paul between the Lord and the Pneuma and that the two are not confused in his writings. The evidence of this is that Paul speaks, in the text considered here, of the 'Spirit of the Lord': 'The distinction made in verse 17b between *kurios* (Lord) and *pneuma* shows clearly that the two persons are not identified in verse 17a, but that the mode of existence of the *kurios* is defined by the word *pneuma*. In speaking of *pneuma kuriou*, Paul is defining his mode of existence and pointing to the power in which he is coming forward to meet his community.'[42] The apostle, then, is pointing to the sphere of existence and activity of the glorified Lord. That sphere is the eschatological and divine sphere of the Spirit. This means that, from the functional point of view, the Lord and his Spirit perform the same work, but in the duality of their rôles.

There are some forty ternary and even Trinitarian formulae in Paul's writings, but there are no precise dogmatic statements about the Trinity of persons in a unity of substance. In any attempt to consider the question at the level and in the categories of the Trinitarian dogma (and the Christological dogma!) it is necessary to go back firstly to the biblical datum (John) of consubstantiality and circumincession, according to which the divine Persons are in each other,[43] and secondly to the idea of the raising of Jesus' humanity by his glorification to the quality of Lord and Son of God in power. I have already said a little about this.

8. The possible personality of the Spirit is discussed by Büchsel in part of chapter XVI of his book (see note 1 below). The Spirit is not a simple force in Paul's writings, but God himself insofar as he is communicated, present and active in others. The Spirit is God as love that is active in us (Rom 5:5). Is it

possible to go further than this and find indicators pointing in the direction of a personality of the Spirit in this Trinitarian manifestation and communication of God? In the following passage, V. Warnach (*op. cit.* (below, note 1), pp. 185–186) recognizes these indicators and gives them the greatest possible importance:

> There are many passages which give us the sense of a personality that is unique to the divine Pneuma who 'searches . . . even the depths of God' (1 Cor 2:10ff.) or is 'sent into our hearts' (Gal 4:6). The Pneuma enters actively into the history of salvation or, in what he enables us to know of God's will to save us (1 Cor 2:10–14), establishes a 'fellowship' between God and ourselves and between us and our fellow-men (2 Cor 13:13). The Pneuma also 'bears witness with our spirit that we are children of God' (Rom 8:16) and cries in us: 'Abba, Father!' (Gal 4:6). Finally, the same Pneuma also intercedes for us with God (Rom 8:26ff.).
>
> These are texts which cannot be understood as purely figurative and which must indicate that a subject acting in this way must be an autonomous, free person. This personal character is particularly obvious in 1 Cor 12:11, in which Paul shows the Spirit distributing the gifts of grace 'as he wills'. Paul also sees the divine Pneuma as a person when he speaks of his dwelling in believers (1 Cor 3:16; 6:19). God is present in the Pneuma as he is present in the Son, because he is God himself (1 Cor 3:16; cf. 14–25). As the Spirit 'which is from God' (1 Cor 2:12), he is a gift to us (Rom 5:5), not as a thing, but as someone who gives, since, in the Pneuma, God gives himself (1 Thess 4:8).
>
> Finally, the triadic formulae in which the Pneuma is presented as equal to God (*ho Theos* = the Father) and Christ (see especially 1 Cor 12:4–6; 2 Cor 13:13) do not point to a simple community of activity, but indicate an equality of three Persons in being.

NOTES

1. Very many books and articles have been written on this subject, but I will mention only H. B. Swete, *The Holy Spirit in the New Testament* (London, 1909), I, chapters IV-VI, pp. 169–253; F. Büchsel, *Der Geist Gottes im Neuen Testament* (Gütersloh, 1926), chapters XIII–XVII, pp. 267–451; E. Schweizer, '*pneuma*', *TDNT*, VI, esp. pp. 415–437; P. Gächter, 'Zum Pneumabegriff des hl. Paulus', *ZKT*, 53 (1929), 345–408; H.-D. Wendland and V. Warnach have published under the same title 'Das Wirken des Hl. Geistes in den Gläubigen nach Paulus', *Pro Veritate. Ein theologischer Dialog. Festgabe L. Jaeger und W. Stählin*, ed. E. Schlink and H. Volk (Münster and Kassel, 1963), pp. 133–156 and 156–202; M.-A. Chevallier, *Esprit de Dieu, paroles d'hommes. Le rôle de l'Esprit dans les ministères de la parole selon l'apôtre Paul (Bibl. théol.)* (Neuchâtel, 1966), with an extensive bibliography.
2. 1 Cor 1:13f. shows that baptism accompanies accession to faith, even if Paul regarded himself as a minister of faith rather than as a minister of baptism. See also Gal 3:27; 1 Cor 6:11; 12:13; Rom 6:3; Tit 3:5–7; Col 2:12.
3. Gal 5:19–23; 2 Cor 6:6; Rom 6:19–22; 8:6, 12, 14, 17, also 15, 13; Eph 5:9. It is also in this context that those passages in which Paul speaks of 'a spirit of . . .' revelation, wisdom

(Eph 1:17), gentleness (1 Cor 4:21), faith (2 Cor 4:13) and adoption (Rom 8:15) should be situated. See Swete, *op. cit.* (note 1), p. 234.

4. See Phil 2:5, which can be translated literally as 'This think in you which also in Christ Jesus'.

5. E. Schweizer stresses the fact that Paul expressed himself in Greek categories and therefore substantially, but that he thought in biblical and Semitic ways and therefore 'forcefully' or dynamically: '*pneuma*', *TDNT*, VI, pp. 424–432. This dynamism of God is in the Christian and is a part of him, but it does not come from him or from his own being; *ibid.*, pp. 428, 439 note 731, 441. In addition to the prayer that the Spirit makes us utter, there is also the prayer that he himself utters in us: see K. Niederwimmer, 'Das Gebet des Geistes, Rom. 8. 26', *TZ*, 20 (1964), 252–265.

6. This question has unfortunately been very little studied by exegetes. There is nothing about it, for example, in E. Schweizer's article '*pneuma*' in *TDNT*. It has aroused more interest among Catholic scholars, but these have been mainly dogmatic theologians, who have approached it from the angle of the mystical Body, rather than exegetes.

7. G. Martelet, 'Le mystère du corps et de l'Esprit dans le Christ ressuscité et dans l'Eglise', *Verbum Caro*, 45 (1958), 31; P.-A. Harlé, 'Le Saint-Esprit et l'Eglise chez S. Paul', *ibid.*, 74 (1965), 13–29.

8. The body of Christ permeated by the Spirit: Rom 1:4; 1 Cor 15:45; see also Phil 3:21; union with the body of Christ: 1 Cor 6:15–17; Col 3:1–4; baptism: 1 Cor 12:13; body and cup of the Last Supper: 1 Cor 11:23–29. See also P. Benoît, 'Corps, Tête et Plérôme dans les épîtres de la captivité', *RB*, 63 (1956), 5–44; also republished in *Exégèse et Théologie* (Paris, 1961), II, pp. 107–153.

9. See M.-A. Chevallier, *op. cit.* (note 1), Parts I and II; K. Prümm, *Diakonia Pneumatos: Der Zweite Korintherbrief als Zugang zur apostolischen Botschaft. Auslegung und Theologie*, II: *Theologie des 2. Korintherbriefes*, 2 vols (Rome, 1960 and 1962).

10. F. Büchsel: see below, note 13; L. Cerfaux, *L'Eglise des Corinthiens* (Paris, 1946); M.-A. Chevallier, *op. cit.*, pp. 22ff., 171ff.

11. Hence such statements as 1 Cor 4:8: 'Already you are filled! Already you have become rich! Without us you have become kings!'; 4:10: 'We are fools for Christ's sake, but you are wise in Christ. We are weak, but you are strong. You are held in honour, but we in disrepute'; 1:7: 'So that you are not lacking in any spiritual gift, as you wait for the revealing of our Lord Jesus Christ'.

12. *Pneumatika*: 1 Cor 12:1; 14:1. I have here followed M.-A. Chevallier's exegesis, *op. cit.*, pp. 148, 167, 172ff. Hence: 'Since you are eager for manifestations of the Spirit, strive to excel in building up the Church' (14:12); 'Come to your right mind' (15:34).

13. F. Büchsel devoted chapter XV, pp. 367–395, of his book (see note 1 above) to Paul's 'pneumatic' adversaries at Corinth. He saw them as 'inflated' with pride (the word *phusioun* occurs six times in 1 Cor) and intoxicated with freedom, although love was the supreme value. These adversaries were, Büchsel believed, Christians who had come from Judaism. They were not Judaizers, as in Galilee, but 'pneumatic' Christians. Those who 'belonged to Christ' (1:12) appealed, Büchsel thought (p. 392), to the Christ of goodness and anti-legalism. This, of course, is Büchsel's own interpretation.

14. 1 Cor is addressed to 'the church of God which is at Corinth, to those sanctified in Christ Jesus'. Christ, then, is the only foundation (3:11); he is all to us (1:30–31; 10:4; 15); he is the judge (4:4–5). We are his (3:23); we live in him and from him (1:9; 4:15–17; 6:11). He is Christ crucified and our wisdom is the wisdom of the cross (1:23ff; 2:2). The spiritual man is the man who has 'the mind of Christ' (2:16).

15. See 1 Cor 12:1–3, 10; 14:29; 2 Thess 5:15–22. For these three demands, see M.-A. Chevallier, *op. cit* (note 1), pp. 181ff. For the second, see also G. Sauter, 'Gewissheit oder vergewissernde Sicherung? Zum Verhältnis von Geist und Vernunft', *Erfahrung und Theologie des Heiligen Geistes*, ed. C. Heitmann and H. Mühlen (Hamburg and Munich, 1974), pp. 192–213.

16. See U. Brockhaus, *Charisma und Amt. Die paulinische Charismenlehre auf dem Hintergrund der frühchristlichen Gemeindefunktionen* (Wuppertal, 1972); M.-A. Chevallier, *op. cit.* (note 1), pp. 210–213.
17. *Ibid.*, p. 155.
18. This is fundamentally M.-A. Chevallier's explanation, *op. cit.*, pp. 139ff.; see also O. Kuss's disciple J. Hainz, *Ekklesia, Structuren paulinischer Gemeinde-Theologie und Gemeinde-Ordnung* (Regensburg, 1972), pp. 333–335, 338; H. Conzelmann, '*charisma*', *TDNT*, IX, pp. 402–406; B. N. Wambacq, 'Le mot "charisme" ', *NRT*, 97 (1975), 345–355. A.-M. de Monléon writes, in 'L'expérience des charismes, manifestations de l'Esprit en vue du bien commun', *Istina*, 21 (1976), 340–373, on p. 342: 'The word charisma . . . has a great breadth of meaning. With perhaps a special emphasis on the gratuitous nature of the gift, it points to the whole gift of grace made by God (Rom 5:15–16), from eternal life (6:23) to healing (1 Cor 12:30) and from the grace given in marriage (7:7) to the ministry (1 Tim 4:14).'
19. This is Chevallier's way of interpreting the *pneumatika*, *op. cit.*, pp. 148, 167; it is also Hainz's.
20. See the references in Chevallier, *op. cit.*, pp. 164ff.
21. See A.-M. Ritter, *Charisma im Verständnis des Joannes Chrysostomos und seiner Zeit. Ein Beitrag zur Erforschung der griechisch-orientalischen Ekklesiologie in der Frühzeit der Reichskirche* (Göttingen, 1972); cf. G.-M. de Durand, *RSPT*, 59 (1975), 460–464.
22. See, for example, the phrases *carismata coelestia* and *carismata gratiarum* in prayers of the period and the formulae 136 and 137 in G. Manz, *Ausdrucksformen der lateinischen Liturgiesprache* (Beuron, 1941), pp. 96–97.
23. I am thinking here of a text such as that by William of Auxerre: 'credidit Abel Christum fore plenum charismatibus . . . et ita per fidem in ipsum fluxit aliquid de plenitudine Christi sicut in nos per fidem': *Summa Aurea* lib. III, tr. 1, c. 4, sol. ad obj. Of all the charisms discussed by Paul, the Fathers and the mediaeval theologians believed that those of knowledge and wisdom were of permanent value in the Church: see S. Tromp, *Corpus Christi quod est Ecclesia*, III: *De Spiritu Christi anima* (Rome, 1960), pp. 342ff.
24. Even M. Zerwick does this in his excellent *Analysis philologica Novi Testamenti Graeci*, under Rom 12:6; 1 Cor 12:1; 14:1; in the last two places, he even identifies *pneumatika* and *charismata*.
25. See M.-A. Chevallier, *op. cit.* (note 1), p. 165; S. Tromp, *op. cit.* (note 23), pp. 336ff.
26. See A.-M. Ritter, *op. cit.* (note 21).
27. According to the Encyclical *Divinum illud munus* of 9 May 1897 on the Holy Spirit, 'Charisms are only extraordinary gifts obtained by the Holy Spirit in exceptional circumstances and destined above all to prove the divine origin of the Church. They do not form part of the structure of the Church, which is founded exclusively on the authority of the apostles, which is ordinarily the instrument that is both sufficient and adequate to satisfy everything that calls for the building up of the Church and the Church's life.' See also the letter *Testem Benevolentiae* of 22 January 1899 to the Archbishop of Baltimore.
28. See above, note 16.
29. The full history of this has still to be written. I will only mention a few important recent publications: J. Brosch, *Charismen und Ämter in der Urkirche* (Bonn, 1951); *idem*, 'Amt und Charisma', *LTK*, 2nd ed., I (1957), cols 455–457; I. Gomá Civit, *Ubi Spiritus Dei, illic Ecclesia et omnis gratia* (Barcelona, 1954); García Extremeño, 'Iglesia, Jerarquía y Carisma', *La Ciencia Tomista*, 89 (1959), 3–64; P. Rodríguez, 'Carisma e institución en la Iglesia', *Studium* (1966), pp. 489ff.
30. 17 and 47: *AAS*, 35 (1943), 200 and 215. See also D. Iturrioz, 'Carismas. De la encíclica "Mystici Corporis" al Concilio Vaticano', *Estudios Eclesiásticos*, 30 (1956), 481–494. The editor of the encyclical, S. Tromp, produced a 'systematic' study of the charisms: *op. cit.* (note 23), pp. 295–326.
31. See especially *Lumen Gentium*, 12 and *Apostolicam Actuositatem*, 3. See also H. Schür-

42

mann, 'Les charismes spirituels', *L'Eglise de Vatican II* (*Unam Sanctam*, 51b) (Paris, 1966), pp. 541–573; D. Iturrioz, 'Los carismas en la Iglesia. La doctrina carismal en la Const. "Lumen Gentium" ', *Estudios Eclesiásticos*, 43 (1968), 181–233; G. Rombaldi, 'Uso e significato di "Carisma" nel Vaticano II', *Greg*, 55 (1974), 141–162.

32. See my bulletins and those of H.-M. Legrand, the reviews of journals and the tables in the last ten years of *RSPT*, especially C. R. de Dias, H. Küng, G. Hasenhüttl, H. Mühlen, A.-M. Ritter etc.

33. W. C. van Unnik, 'Dominus vobiscum: The Background of a Liturgical Formula', *New Testament Essays. Studies in Memory of T. W. Manson*, ed. A. J. R. Higgins (Manchester, 1959), pp. 270–305.

34. In prayer: Rom 8:15ff., 26; 1 Cor 14:14ff., 25; Eph 5:18. In the assembly: *Apostolic Tradition*, 31, 35; *Didache* X, 7; Hermas (M. Dibelius, *Der Hirt des Hermas* (1928), Excursus, pp. 517ff., on pneumatology).

35. Van Unnik, *op. cit.*, pp. 273, 299, note 21, quotes John Chrysostom, *In 2 Tim.*, *Hom.* 10, 3 (*PG* 62, 659), and Theodore of Mopsuestia, *Commentary on the Lord's Prayer and on the Sacraments of Baptism and the Eucharist* (ed. A. Mingana, Cambridge, 1933), pp. 90ff.

36. And Christ enables us to know the Father: see Irenaeus, *Dem.* 7; *Adv. haer.* IV, 25, 5; V, 36, 2 (*PG* 7, 1035, 1223; ed. W. W. Harvey, II, 216, 429).

37. *Adv. haer.* III, 24, 1 (*PG* 7, 966; Harvey, II, 131; F. Sagnard, *SC* 34, pp. 398–401). A. Rousseau and L. Doutreleau (*SC* 311, pp. 471, 472) have restored *communicatio* and translated it as 'communion with Christ'.

38. A. Deissmann has given very many examples, including some that are not very convincing: *Paul* (Eng. tr; London and New York, 1926), p. 140. It is interesting in this context to note that the wisdom of the disciples when on trial is attributed to Christ in Lk 21:12–15 and to the Holy Spirit in Mt 10:18–20 and Mk 13:10–12.

39. See J. Dupont, 'Filius meus es tu. L'interprétation du Ps II, 7 dans le Nouveau Testament', *RSR*, 35 (1948), 522–543; M.-E. Boismard, 'Constitué Fils de Dieu (Rm 1, 4)', *RB*, 60 (1953), 5–17; M. Hengel, *Jésus, Fils de Dieu* (*Lectio divina*, 94) (Paris, 1977), pp. 98ff.

40. See, for example, E. Schillebeeckx, *Christ the Sacrament of Encounter with God* (London and New York, 1963), esp. pp. 13ff., 33f., 65f.; my own *Un peuple messianique* (Paris, 1975), pp. 35ff.; W. Thüsing, *Per Christum in Deum. Studien zum Verhältnis von Christozentrik und Theozentrik in den paulinischen Hauptbriefen* (Münster, 1965).

41. Ingo Hermann, *Kyrios und Pneuma. Studien zur Christologie der paulinischen Hauptbriefe* (Munich, 1961). C. F. D. Moule has taken up a very similar position in '2 Cor 3, 18ᵇ', *Neues Testament und Geschichte. Oscar Cullmann zum 70. Geburtstag*, ed. H. Baltensweiler and B. Reicke (Zürich, 1972), pp. 231–237. The identification is not at the ontological level, but, in the Christian experience, the same thing is expressed by 'Spirit of God', 'Spirit of Christ' and 'Christ'.

42. E. Schweizer, '*pneuma*', *TDNT*, VI, p. 419, with references. See also F. Büchsel, *op. cit.* (note 1), p. 409 (dynamic unity); M.-A. Chevallier, *op. cit.* (*ibid.*), pp. 95ff. (the spirit of the Kyrios introduces the Kyrios into the heart of man); B. Schneider, *Dominus autem Spiritus est* (Rome, 1951); L. Cerfaux, *Christ in the Theology of St Paul* (Eng. tr.; New York/ Edinburgh and London, 1959), pp. 284ff., esp. 293–296; J.-R. Villalon, *Sacrements dans l'Esprit* (Paris, 1977), pp. 286ff. I have not read J. D. G. Dunn, '2 Cor III, 17 "The Lord is the Spirit" ', *JTS*, new series, 21 (1970), 309–320. For the patristic and the modern interpretations, see J. Lebreton, *Les origines du dogme de la Trinité*, I (5th ed., Paris, 1919), pp. 567ff.; K. Prümm, 'Die katholische Auslegung von 2 Kor 3.17 in den letzten vier Jahrhunderten', *Bib*, 31 (1950), 316–345, 459–482; 32 (1951), 1–24.

43. See Jerome, *Epist.* 18, 4 (*PL* 22, 363); Cyril of Alexandria, *Comm. in Ioan.* lib. IX (*PG* 74, 261); L. Malevez, *NRT*, 67 (1945), 403–404; F. Malmberg, *Ein Leib, ein Geist* (Paderborn, 1960), pp. 150, 163.

SAINT LUKE: ACTS [1]

All the evangelists stress the existence of a dynamic continuity between Christ and the Church.[2] This continuity is the fulfilment of what God had promised from the beginning in accordance with his plan of grace.[3] It is especially noticeable in Luke's Acts, in which it appears under the sign of the Holy Spirit. This Spirit, who, according to Luke, brought Jesus to life in Mary's womb, also brings the Church into the world. The same Spirit who sent Jesus on his mission after his anointing in baptism also animates the apostolate 'from Jerusalem to the ends of the earth'. The central episode in this history is the gentiles' entry into the Church as sanctioned by the council which met at Jerusalem. Together with Cornelius and his family and the gentiles converted by Paul on his missions, they became the people of God. In other words, the *ethnē* became *laos* (Acts 15:14). The 'nations'— terrestrial realities of the 'flesh'—became a people—a reality of the economy of salvation.

In Acts, the Holy Spirit is the dynamic principle of the testimony that ensures the spread of the Church. This is why he appears at Pentecost, which undoubtedly marks the beginning. Luke's account incorporates a tradition that interpreted the event in the light of the values experienced at the Jewish feast of Pentecost. This was a festival of the harvest, the first-fruits of which had been offered on the day after the Passover. The two feasts were thus linked as feasts of the gift of the Law.

A knowledge derived from the Qumran texts, the readings used in the Jewish liturgy of the festival, and the texts of the Book of Jubilees and Philo Judaeus provides a good foundation for the theme of Pentecost as the feast celebrating the giving of the Law on Mount Sinai. On this basis, important comparisons can be made.[4] The tablets of the Law, for example, were written by the 'finger of God' (Ex 31:18). The same 'finger of God' is also used by Luke for the Holy Spirit (Lk 11:20).

Just as the new sanctuary is simply Jesus Christ who is open to all nations, the new Law is the Spirit bearing witness to Jesus for and in all peoples. The sign of tongues prophesies the catholicity of witness. The apostles (possibly all the disciples?) speak the tongues of other peoples and announce in those languages the marvels of God. The Fathers of the Church, many exegetes and probably Luke himself regarded this miracle of the Spirit as a reversal of the scattering of Babel (Gen 11:1–9).[5] It is not simply an extension or a universalization. The distinctive aspect of the Spirit is that, while remaining unique and preserving his identity, he is in everyone without causing anyone to lose his originality. This applies to persons, peoples, their culture and their talents. The Spirit also makes everyone speak of the marvels of God in his own language.[6]

To begin with, Christians celebrated Pentecost simply as the end of an Easter of fifty days. The mystery of Easter was conceived as a whole and included the resurrection, the glorification (ascension) and the life of sons of God communicated by the Lord by the sending of his Spirit. It was not until the end of the fourth century that each element of this great single mystery was celebrated separately.[7] Pentecost did not thereby become a feast (of the Person) of the Holy Spirit.[8] There is in fact no feast of the Persons of the Trinity. Pentecost was and is a paschal feast. There is one single liturgical cycle, which is Christological and paschal. What is celebrated is the making present, through faith and the sacrament and in praise and thanksgiving, of the Christian mystery as such.

According to Acts, the part played by the Spirit is that of making present and spreading the salvation that has been gained in and through Christ and to do this by bearing witness. This salvation is always attributed to Christ. It is communicated 'in the name' of Christ, that is, in his power.[9] It is always Christ who acts. The Spirit animates his disciples so that they proclaim him. He guides them in the witness that they bear and is even concerned with the details of their movements and journeyings.[10] 'The Acts describe Christ's saving activity as it takes place in the communities. The communication of the Spirit to the disciples is therefore not a total replacement of Christ, but rather a transmission of his prophetic mission (in the full sense of the word), which consists of being the one who proclaims the message of God. . . . It is possible to say that Christ transmits to his apostles the presence of the Spirit that he received in the Jordan.'[11]

The Spirit intervenes at every decisive moment in the carrying out of God's plan to save. As Swete has noted, Pentecost did not simply give the apostles once and for all an understanding of the universal nature of the call to faith. This understanding was only gained after some time and several fresh interventions. There is, in other words, a history of the coming of the Spirit. In accordance with his plan (see 1:8), Luke refers to a series of various kinds of Pentecosts: in Jerusalem (2:4, 25–31), in Samaria (8:14–17), in the event which begins the missionary adventure with Cornelius and the 'Pentecost' at Caesarea (10:44–48; 11:15–17) and even the episode in Ephesus (19:1–6). A sign indicating the intervention of the Spirit is given at each of these important moments. This sign is a giving of praise to God in tongues and 'prophesying'.[12]

Jesus had proclaimed the coming of the Spirit as the gift of a power that would make witnesses who were full of confidence (parrēsia[13]) and as a baptism, not with water, but with the Holy Spirit (1:5; 11:16). The Twelve themselves and the 120 disciples mentioned by Luke seem never to have received baptism by water, except possibly from John the Baptist.[14] They were, as it were, plunged in the Spirit, who came upon them. From that time onwards, they practised a baptism of water in the name of Jesus, that is, in reference, through faith, to his saving Passover and his power as Lord.[15] This baptism was accompanied by the gift of the Spirit. All the texts point to a connection between the two. Apart from the case of Cornelius, in which the

Spirit had an absolute initiative, the gift of the Spirit follows the baptism of water, although the baptismal rite does not appear as the direct means (or rather the instrumental cause) of that gift.[16] Sometimes another rite is the instrument of the gift of the Spirit. This rite is usually the apostolic laying-on of hands (see 8:16; 19:5–7). One is, however, bound to ask whether the gift of the Spirit which figures in the Acts of the Apostles, where it is said to be the same as that given at Pentecost (11:17), is that of the Spirit as the principle of interior personal sanctification, or of the Spirit as the principle of dynamic testimony accompanied by a confidence that is borne out by the experience of speaking in tongues.

One is prompted to ask this question by the difference, as stressed by G. Haya-Prats, for example, between Acts and Paul.[17] The explanation that Haya-Prats gives for this is based on P. Gächter's summary. In the first place, Acts describes the intervention of the Spirit in the growth of the Church outwards, whereas Paul considers that intervention as it concerns each member inwardly. In the second place, in Acts, the activity of the Spirit is charismatic and the normal experience of any Christian, whereas for Paul that activity is as much the object of faith as it is of experience and he is aware of the fact that many Christians do not have that experience. In the third place, Christ sends his Spirit, according to Acts, to this disciples so that his work will be carried out. According to Paul, on the other hand, the Spirit realizes each Christian's being in Christ individually.

It is, of course, true to say that Luke does not provide a theology of the effects and fruits of the Spirit in the life of the Christian as Paul does ('Christ in us'), but that he shows the dynamism of faith and the growth of the Church. Even when he says that Christ gives the Spirit (2:33), it is still in the line of mission and prophecy (2:17ff.), not in that of the new life. Both were proclaimed in the Old Testament (the one in Joel 3, for example, and the other in Ezek 36:26ff.; Jer 31:31–34). Luke is firmly orientated in Acts towards mission, but is it really possible to separate the disciples' impulses for mission and the 'spiritual' life in this way? Is this not a question of letting the theme in the text predominate over the reality? It has been said, quite correctly, that the famous summary which describes the life of the Church (Acts 2:42) and the *koinōnia* (communion or 'fellowship') mentioned in that summary do not explicitly refer to the Holy Spirit. From the point of view of the reality of the situation, however, Acts 2:42 may well reflect the life of the Church as it emerged from Pentecost. If the Church was sent out into the world by the event of the Spirit, did the Spirit not animate its inner life as he animated its external life? Is there not a danger of saying that Luke has an Old Testament understanding of the Spirit, even a partial one? He may well be close to such a view, but can his understanding be reduced to that level?

Is the Holy Spirit, even with the article (in Greek), and repeated at that (before the noun and before the adjective), in Luke *the Person* of the Holy Spirit? We cannot attribute to the evangelist the explicit statement of the

46

dogma of the Second Ecumenical Council (Constantinople I, in 381). All the same, Luke certainly goes beyond the Old Testament stage, at which 'God' gives his breath. At certain times, the Spirit acts himself in the Acts of the Apostles.

It is therefore possible to agree with Haya-Prats' statement at the end of his section 11 (pp. 82–90): 'A remarkable development in the direction of a personalization of the Holy Spirit that goes beyond a merely literary personification can be discerned in the Acts of the Apostles. The author's repeated attribution of definite and important interventions in the history of salvation to the Holy Spirit would seem to indicate that the Spirit was regarded in practice as the subject of such attribution and therefore as in some way different from Yahweh, even though the problem of such a distinction is not posed as such.'

NOTES

1. In addition to H. B. Swete, *The Holy Spirit in the New Testament* (London, 1909), pp. 63–109, and the article '*pneuma*', *TDNT*, VI, esp. pp. 404–415, the following can be consulted: H. von Baer, *Der Heilige Geist in den Lukasschriften (BWANT, III/3)* (Stuttgart, 1926); G. W. H. Lampe, 'The Holy Spirit in the Writings of Luke', *Studies in the Gospels. Essays in Memory of R. H. Lightfoot*, ed. D. E. Nineham (Oxford, 1955), pp. 145–200; J. H. E. Hull, *The Holy Spirit in the Acts of the Apostles* (London, 1967); J. Borremans, 'L'Esprit Saint dans la catéchèse évangélique de Luc', *Lumen Vitae*, 25 (1970), 103–122; E. Rásco, 'Jesus y el Espíritu, Iglesia e "Historia": Elementos para una lectura de Lucas', *Greg*, 56 (1975), 321–367; G. Haya-Prats, *L'Esprit force de l'Eglise. Sa nature et son activité d'après les Actes des Apôtres (Lectio divina* 81) (Paris, 1975), with a very full bibliography.

2. This is very clear in the ecclesiological gospel of Matthew with its missionary conclusion. For John, see O. Cullmann, *The Johannine Circle* (Eng. tr.; London, 1976), esp. pp. 14f. For Mark, apart from 16:15ff., the summary 1:14–15 combines the mission of the Church and the ministry of Jesus: see *Traduction Œcuménique de la Bible*, note w; J. J. A. Kahmann, *Bijdragen*, 38 (1977), 84–98.

3. The Spirit = the Promise: Lk 24:49; Acts 1:4; 2:33; Gal 3:14; Eph 1:13. It is clear from the last two texts that the Spirit is the fulfilment of the promise made to Abraham insofar as it concerns all nations and comes to them through the apostolic word. See also Col 1:25.

4. See R. le Déaut, 'Pentecôte et tradition juive', *Spiritus*, 7 (1961), 127–144 or *Assemblées du Seigneur*, 51 (1963), 22–38; R. Cabié, *La Pentecôte. L'évolution de la Cinquantaine pascale au cours des cinq premiers siècles (Bibl. de Liturgie)* (Tournai and Paris, 1965); J. Potin, *La fête juive de la Pentecôte*, 2 vols (*Lectio divina*, 65) (Paris, 1971); K. Hruby, 'La fête de la Pentecôte dans la tradition juive', *Bible et Vie Chrétienne*, 63 (1965), 46–64; G. Haya-Prats, *op. cit.* (note 1), pp. 185ff. and notes, pp. 280ff.; E. Schweizer, '*pneuma*', *TDNT*, VI, pp. 410–411, who says: 'It is far more probable, however, that already in the pre-Lucan period the concept of the new covenant, of the renewal of the giving of the Law for world-wide Judaism, strongly influenced the account of the first coming of the Spirit. Undoubtedly pre-Christian are [the Book of Jubilees] and Philo's account of the divine voice at Sinai which evokes a special sound in each individual soul, turns into flame, and passes like a *pneuma* through a trumpet, so that it is heard by those both near and far off, and the sound goes forth even to the ends of the earth. . . . If even before 70 Pentecost was

regarded as the end of the passover which celebrates the exodus from Egypt, and if already in Deut 4:10, 9:10, 18:16 LXX the day of the giving of the Law is called *hē hēmera tēs ekklēsias* [the day of the assembly], such an interpretation is natural.'

5. We could add to the patristic references given in the conciliar decree *Ad Gentes Divinitus*, 4, with regard to this striking theme. See also the various liturgies (the Syrian and the Leonine liturgies especially) and the following exegetes: L. Cerfaux, 'Le symbolisme attaché au miracle des langues', *ETL*, 13 (1936), 256–259 (= *Recueil Lucien Cerfaux*, II, pp. 183–187); J. G. Davies, 'Pentecost and Glossolalia', *JTS*, new series, 13 (1952), 228–231. There may not be any allusion in the account in Acts to Babel, but there is certainly one to the rabbinical theology of the universal intelligibility of the Torah.

6. See, for example, H.-M. Legrand, 'Inverser Babel, mission de l'Eglise', *Spiritus*, 63 (1970), 323–346.

7. This was one of the most important discoveries made by the liturgical movement. See *Les questions liturgiques et paroissiales* (June 1925: Kreps); *ibid*. (1948), 60; *ibid*. (1949), No. 208; *ibid*. (1958), 101–131; D.-R. Pierret, *Ami du Clergé* (1935), 278ff.; J. Daniélou, *Bible et Liturgie* (Paris, 1951), pp. 249ff.; my own *La Pentecôte* (Chartres, 1956; Eng. tr. in *The Mystery of the Church* (London, 1960)); R. Cabié, *op. cit.* (note 4). The scholarly studies of O. Casel are indispensable; see especially *Jahrbuch für Liturgiewissenschaft*, 14 (1938), 1–71. Equally important are G. Kretschmar's studies: see especially *Zeitschrift für Kirchengeschichte*, 66 (1954–55), 209–253.

8. See Leo XIII, encyclical *Divinum illud munus* of 9 May 1897.

9. See Joel 3:5, included in Peter's address, Acts 2:21ff.; 4:12, 29–31; 16:18 (hence 19:13).

10. See Acts 16:6, 7 (verse 10 speaks of a vision); 19:1; 20:3 in the text of Codex D; 19:21; 20:22, 23; 21:4, 11.

11. See Haya-Prats, *op. cit.* (note 1), p. 52.

12. Speaking in tongues: 2:4, 11; 10:46; 19:6; prophesying: 2:17; 11:27; 20:23; 21:4, 11.

13. See Acts 2:29; 4:13, 29; 4:31; 14:3. See also Haya-Prats, *op. cit.*, pp. 102ff.

14. The question of the baptism of the apostles troubled Tertullian: *De bapt.* 12 and 13 (*SC*, 35, pp. 85–86). Clement of Alexandria, in a treatise that has been lost, but for a fragment (ed. O. Stählin, *GCS* III, p. 196) quoted by John Moschus, reports a legendary story: see H. A. Echle, 'The Baptism of the Apostles. A Fragment of Clement of Alexandria's Lost Work "Ipotyposeis" in the Pratum Spirituale of John Moschus', *Traditio*, 3 (1945), 365–368. John Moschus' imaginative account, according to which Jesus baptized Peter, who baptized Andrew, who in turn baptized James and John, was not entirely without foundation. His quotation from Clement of Alexandria's lost work can be found in the *Pratum Spirituale*, 176: *PG* 87/3, 3045. From the theological point of view, it is possible to think that contact with Jesus was, for the apostles, equivalent to baptism; the same applies, in exceptional cases, to the righteous: see O. Rousseau, 'La descente aux enfers. Fondement sotériologique du baptême chrétien', *RSR*, 40 (1952), 273–297. Paul, on the other hand, was baptized: see Acts 9:18.

15. 'In the name of' (*eis to onoma*) has a note of finality and indicates that the baptized person enters into the redemption of the Son, the effectiveness of the Spirit and communion with 'God': see H. Bietenhard, '*onoma*', *TDNT*, V, pp. 270ff. There are many texts mentioning baptism in the name of Jesus: see, for example, Acts 2:38; 8:12; 8:16; 8:37 (Western text); 10:48; 16:15, 30ff.; 19:5; 22:16. H. von Campenhausen has gone against the opinion of most exegetes and historians in favour of the liturgical existence of a baptism 'in the name of Jesus' and has shown that a formula of baptism is not indicated in the texts: 'Taufen auf den Namen Jesu', *Vigiliae Christianae*, 25 (1971), 1–16. See also H. de Lubac, *La foi chrétienne. Essai sur la structure du Symbôle des Apôtres* (Paris, 2nd ed., 1970), pp. 72ff.; I. Crehan, *Early Christian Baptism and the Creed* (London, 1950).

16. See 2:38; 8:15–17; 19:5, 6. H. von Baer, *op. cit.* (note 1), p. 180, believed that baptism of water and baptism of the Spirit were the same. H. Mentz, *Taufe and Kirche* (Munich, 1960), pp. 71, note 139, 75, 93, regarded baptism in the Spirit as baptism of water given on

the basis of faith in the kerygma of Jesus Christ. E. Haenchen, *Die Apostelgeschichte* (Göttingen, 14th ed., 1965), pp. 83–84, thought that baptism was the ordinary means of giving the Spirit. Haya-Prats, *op. cit.* (note 1), pp. 132–138, however has shown that, in Acts, the Spirit does not appear to be given by means of the baptism of water. I shall be dealing with baptism of the Spirit in Volume II.

17. Haya-Prats, *op. cit.*, pp. 28, 117–129, 206. Haya-Prats' quotation from Gächter will be found on p. 241, note 17. See also E. Schweizer, '*pneuma*', *TDNT*, VI, pp. 409–410; and E. Trocmé, 'Le Saint-Esprit et l'Eglise d'après le livre des Actes', *L'Esprit Saint et l'Eglise. L'avenir de l'Eglise et de l'Œcuménisme* (Paris, 1969), pp. 19, 27, 44.

THE JOHANNINE WRITINGS[1]

Jesus appears in the fourth gospel firstly as the one who gives the Spirit and then, in the discourses of the last evening, as the one who proclaims the sending of the Paraclete.

1. *Jesus gives the Spirit*

In the first place, he has the Spirit. Jn 3:34 can be translated either as: 'He whom God has sent utters the words of God, who gives (him) the Spirit not by measure' or as: '. . . and (he) gives the Spirit not by measure'. The first translation exalts Christ, who is word and who reveals God in comparison with the prophets.[2] This translation is in accordance with the testimony of John the Baptist: 'I saw the Spirit descend as a dove from heaven and it remained on him' (Jn 1:32). In addition, it makes the whole verse coherent—the fact that Jesus utters the words of God and does his work is based on his having received the Spirit without measure.

Jesus speaks of the Spirit in his dialogue with Nicodemus: 'Unless one is born of water and the Spirit, he cannot enter the kingdom of God. That which is born of flesh is flesh and that which is born of the Spirit is spirit. . . . The wind blows where it wills and you hear the sound of it, but you do not know whence it comes or whither it goes; so it is with everyone who is born of the Spirit' (3:5–6, 8).[3] The fact that the words 'of water and' do not come from Jesus' words to Nicodemus (at a time when they could only have called to mind the baptism of John the Baptist) does not detract in any way from the text as we have it or the fact that it refers to Christian baptism. We are not told that baptism confers the Spirit, but that, with the Spirit, it causes birth from on high or 'of God' (1:13; 1 Jn 3:9; 5:1), that is, the birth that introduces man into the kingdom of God. The Spirit is active in the whole of the process that leads to faith; he enables man to confess faith and to live by it.

In the dialogue with the Samaritan woman, Jesus says: 'Everyone who drinks of this water will thirst again, but whoever drinks of the water that I shall give him will never thirst; the water that I shall give him will become in him a spring of water welling up to eternal life' (4:13–14). The Spirit is involved here and Jesus gives him. The Spirit is described as the one who urges and animates the believer on to eternal life, in the way in which water coming from higher ground makes water rise to the same level. What we have here is 'living water', that is, a current or stream going from God the source to God the ocean without shores or banks. Jesus also says elsewhere: 'He who believes in me shall never thirst' (6:35). In other words, Christ also gives (eternal) life through faith in him (see also Jn 3:36; 5:21, 40; 6:33, 35; 10:10; 20:31). As in the Pauline writings, then, Christ and the Spirit both carry out the same work of salvation.

We must now consider another passage in the fourth gospel:

> (7:37) On the last day of the feast (of Tabernacles), the great day, Jesus stood up (in the Temple) and proclaimed (in a loud voice), 'If anyone thirst, let him come to me and let him drink (38) who believes in me. As Scripture has said, "Out of his heart shall flow rivers of living water".'(39) Now this he said about the Spirit, which those who believed in him were to receive; as yet the Spirit had not been given, because Jesus was not yet glorified.

This way of punctuating this passage is widely accepted nowadays. The 'rivers of living water' flow from the heart of the Messiah, not from the believer, who is invited to come and drink.[4] The situation is clearly indicated—it is at the feast of Tabernacles, when the priests went every morning to draw water from the spring of Siloam. They brought it back to the Temple singing the Hallel (Ps 113–118) and the verse from the book of Isaiah (12:3): 'With joy you will draw water from the wells of salvation', and poured it out as a libation on the altar of sacrifice. This was a purification rite and at the same time a prayer for the autumn rains. In the Bible and for the Israelites, however, the symbolism of the water was very rich in several ways, in that it pointed to purification and life or fertility. It also pointed to the Law, the word of God and the wisdom that these brought (Is 55:1ff., 10–11) and, in connection with the memory of the water from the rock in the desert during the exodus, an eschatological announcement of a new miracle (Isaiah) or a fertility flowing from the Temple in the form of living water from a spring. The people of God had experienced or were to experience this water. Jesus applies the promise of this water to himself. In the gospel of John, he is the temple (2:21) from which the prophet Ezekiel saw life-giving waters flowing (47:1–12; see also Rev 21:22; 22:1).[5] We have, then, a second image of the Spirit. He is not only the wind or breath—he is also water (see, for example, Is 44:3ff.; Ezek 47:1–12; in the Johannine writings, Rev 22:1, 17). In the East especially, water is what enables seed to produce life. It also quenches the thirst and purifies (baptism!).

What were Jesus' listeners able to understand of the appeal that he was making to them? The symbolism of the water was sometimes applied to the Spirit,[6] but it was not common or at once intelligible. Jesus claimed to fulfil all these images in himself and John, understanding this, says explicitly: 'He said this about the Spirit'. Various suggestions have been made to determine the passage or the passages in Scripture to which Jesus was referring. It is probable that there were several passages with a related meaning or intention—those concerning the Rock, those referring to the Temple and also those on the Torah as a source of life. Jesus claimed to be the truth of all these passages.

John adds to this passage: 'As yet the Spirit had not been given, because Jesus was not yet glorified'. Obviously this does not mean that the Holy Spirit did not exist at that time. The evangelist himself says elsewhere that not only Jesus, but also the disciples had (the) Spirit already.[7] There are also other examples in which a formula of this kind should clearly not be understood in an exclusive or negative sense.[8] The Johannine affirmation corresponds to the statement made by Luke or Paul, namely that the gift of the Spirit relating to the messianic period is made by Jesus glorified and raised to the state of Lord.

It is true that John speaks of a certain glory of Jesus that his disciples can perceive in the signs that he performed (see Jn 2:11; 12:4, 40; 18:28; cf. 1:14), but he insists again and again that Jesus' glorification is closely connected with his Passover and even more closely with his Passion (see Jn 12:23, 27–28; 13:31–32, 17:1; cf. 3:14; 12:32). Jesus' glory was not a worldly glory derived from the appreciation of men because of success according to the criteria of the world. It was a glory that he, as the only Son, had from the Father (1:14) by his obedience and his carrying out of his plan.[9] This included the cross, and the cross was followed by the resurrection and the glorification. As he was approaching his Passion, Jesus said: 'Now is the Son of man glorified and in him God is glorified; if God is glorified in him, God will also glorify him in himself and glorify him at once' (13:31–32). Later, he said: 'Father, the hour has come; glorify thy Son . . . . And now, Father, glorify thou me in thy own presence with the glory which I had with thee before the world was made' (17:1, 5). The glorification governing the sending of the Spirit by Jesus consists in his heavenly glory or his divine glory as the Son being communicated to his humanity as offered and sacrificed. John envisages this, in the book of Revelation, in the form of a Lamb standing and sacrificed (Rev 5:6). He shares his throne with God, and a river of living water flows from this throne (22:1). Later, we read: 'Let him who is thirsty come; let him who desires take the water of life without price' (22:17; cf. 21:6).

This is a description of the consummation in the heavenly Jerusalem. But what is there between the crucifixion and the glory? The giving of the Spirit by Jesus is indicated in the fourth gospel in four ways:

(a) John uses a phrase that is peculiar to him to speak of Jesus' death. Whereas Matthew says that he 'yielded up his spirit' (*aphēken to pneuma*;

51

27:50) and Mark (15:37) and Luke (23:46) say that he 'breathed his last' or 'expired' (*exepneusen*), thus using quite ordinary terms that have no theological intention, John says that Jesus 'bowed his head and gave up (handed over) his (the) spirit' (*klinas tēn kephalēn paredōken to pneuma*; 19:30). Jesus, in the fourth gospel, 'breathes out' over Mary and John, who are, as the Church, at the foot of his cross, and thus hands over the spirit. It is, of course, not possible to say that this is the Holy Spirit. John shows that the Holy Spirit is given on the evening of Easter (20:22). At the symbolic level, which is endowed in John's gospel with such intense significance, however, there is clearly a very close connection between the gift of the Spirit and Jesus' self-sacrifice. The phrase used in the gospel clearly expresses this connection and also translates what has already been said in 7:39 and 16:5–7. Several of the Church Fathers saw it in this light[10] and certain exegetes agree with this interpretation.[11] This is, finally, a further example of a term with a double intention of the kind that John liked to use. Jesus breathes his last breath and, through his death, which he willingly accepts, hands over the Spirit to his disciples.

(b) John speaks of the lance or spear thrust into Jesus' side or breast when he has just breathed his last breath 'and at once there came out blood and water' (19:34). F.-M. Braun believes that the water here symbolizes the Spirit and that John regarded this as the fulfilment of the anouncement made in 7:38–39.[12] The terms, however, are not exactly the same. In Jn 19:34, the word *pleura*, 'side' or 'chest', and not *koilia*, 'bosom' or 'belly', is used and there is no question of 'rivers of living water'. There is also no really close parallel with 1 Jn 5:6–8, since the Spirit is explicitly linked with the water in the latter text, whereas in Jn 19:34 the water does not mean the Spirit. It is, however, not possible to doubt that the text has a deep and important meaning, since it is clear that John or his disciple bears very solemn witness to this. This lends serious credibility to the tradition that has persisted since the time of Tertullian that the water and blood flowing from the side of Christ who had fallen asleep in death symbolizes the birth of the Church taken from the new Adam, just as Eve had been taken from the side of the first Adam who had similarly fallen asleep (see Gen 2:33). This is, according to this tradition, an affirmation of the unity of mankind expressed in the duality of man *and* woman and therefore in the duality of Christ *and* his Church. The Church, however, is taken from Christ and especially from his Passion. On the other hand, we should retain the exegetically more satisfying explanation given by both the Fathers and the Scholastics, that is, that the water and blood point to the two most important sacraments, baptism and the Eucharist, through which the Church is built up.[13]

(c) In John, Jesus promises another Paraclete. This teaching is only found in the fourth gospel. It is so important that the following sub-section is devoted entirely to it.

(d) The paschal gift of the Spirit to the Eleven (Thomas being absent) plays an important part in the Johannine account. Jesus says:

> 'Peace be with you. As the Father has sent me, even so I send you.' And when he had said this, he breathed on them and said to them, 'Receive the Holy Spirit. If you forgive the sins of any, they are forgiven; if you retain the sins of any, they are retained' (20:21–23).

Scholars have referred to the 'Johannine Pentecost', which is not the exact equivalent of the Pentecost described in the Acts.[14] According to the fourth gospel, Jesus was still not fully 'glorified' and had 'not yet ascended to the Father' (see verse 17). He had risen, but was still for a time with his disciples, where they were, although he was to take them to where he would be and return to them, at the same time sending his Spirit to them from the Father (15:26).[15]

Jesus communicates the Holy Spirit, but not the Paraclete, whom he had promised in Jn 14 and 16. The Spirit is not given personally (there is no article preceding *pneuma hagion*), but as a force that corresponds to the mission that is communicated.[16] This mission is, to be sure, superhuman and is the continuation of the mission of Christ himself, who was sent by the Father (see 17:18; 13:20). It has to be carried out here on earth in the Church in the time following the ascension, a Church in which there will always be sin. (This is clear from the first Johannine epistle.[17]) Jesus brought about and still brings about purification and remission of sins (Jn 1:29; 1 Jn 1:7, 9; 2:1–2; 3:5; 4:10). As the victim of propitiation, he communicates his breath to the apostles as energy active in the Church for the forgiveness of sins. This is, as it were, a beginning of this promised gift of another Paraclete. We must now turn to this promise and the wide-ranging mission of the Paraclete.

2. *The Promised Paraclete*

Jesus speaks explicitly in the fourth gospel of the Spirit in this context and sometimes of the 'Spirit of truth' (Jn 14:17; 15:26; 16:13). I prefer to keep to the simple Greek term 'Paraclete' (*Paraklētos*) as both Jerome and the Jews themselves did (*p^eraqlît*), because there is no suitable word in our language which adequately renders all the values of the Greek word: defender, counsel for the defence, helper, comforter (this word is used by both Swete and J. G. Davies; Luther used the German word *Tröster*), assistant, lawyer, advocate, solicitor, counsellor, mediator and one who exhorts and makes urgent appeals. All these meanings are present in the Greek *Paraklētos*.[18] With one exception, the term is used exclusively in the Johannine writings, where it occurs five times.

There are five passages in the farewell discourses (Jn 14–16 and 17) that are concerned with the Paraclete-Holy Spirit. The first is 14:16–17, where Jesus promises 'another Paraclete' who will be—and is already—with the disciples and in them. In the second text (14:26), we are told that the Paraclete will teach and recall to mind. The third passage is 15:26–27 (he will bear witness to Jesus). The fourth text (16:7–11) describes how he will establish the guilt of the world and the fifth (16:13–15) points out that he will lead the disciples into the fullness of truth. These passages have to be re-read and re-examined in detail. It is not possible to go into detailed exegesis here, but, in the absence of this, the survey that is provided by F. Porsch (*op. cit.* (note 1 below), pp. 237ff.) is rather meagre, but it is very instructive. It is given in translation below and followed by a brief elucidation.

THE RELATIONSHIP OF THE PARACLETE

(a) *with the Father*

He will give him (at the prayer of Jesus): 14:16.

He will send him (in Jesus' name): 14:26; cf. Lk 24:49. 'In Jesus' name' points to his value and importance in the economy of salvation (Porsch, pp. 90, note 47, 256). It also means that the Son, precisely as the Son, plays an active part in sending the Spirit in close association with the Father (I. de la Potterie, *op. cit.* (note 1 below), pp. 90–91).

The Spirit 'proceeds' from the Father: 15:26.

The Spirit will take (or receive) from what is Christ's, but also from what is the Father's: 16:14ff.

(b) *with the Son*

With regard to Jesus, the Spirit is the other Paraclete: 14:16.

He will be given (at the prayer of Jesus): 14:16.

He will be sent (in his name): 14:26.

He will teach the disciples and recall to their minds all that Jesus has said to them: 14:26.

He will bear witness to Jesus: 15:26.

He will glorify Jesus because he will take (receive) from what is his: 16:14, and he will communicate it to the disciples.

He will point out (say) what he hears (of Jesus): 16:13.

The glorified Jesus will send him: 15:26; 16:7.

Jesus' departure is presupposed at the coming of the Spirit: 16:7.

(c) *with the disciples*

They know him because he dwells with them: 14:17.

He will be with them for ever: 14:16.

He will be in them: 14:17.

He will teach them and recall to their minds all that Jesus has said to them: 14:26.

He will be given to them: 14:16.

He will be sent to them: 15:26; 16:7.

He will come to them: 16:7, 13.

He will guide them into all the truth: 16:13.

He will communicate (or unveil) all that is to come: 16:13, or all that he will receive from Jesus.

(d) *with the world*

The world neither sees him nor knows him and therefore cannot receive him: 14:17.

He will confound the world with regard to sin, righteousness and judgement: 16:8.[19]

THE NATURE, CHARACTERISTICS AND ACTIVITY OF THE PARACLETE

(a) *His relationships with the Pneuma (the Spirit)*

He is the Spirit of truth; he is the Holy Spirit.

(b) *He is the subject of the following actions*

He dwells with the disciples: 14:17; he will be in them: 14:17.
He comes: 16:7ff.; 16:13.
He receives what is Jesus': 16·14ff.
He proceeds from the Father: 15:26.
He listens (hears): 16:13.
He teaches: 14:26.
He calls to mind: 14:26.
He communicates (makes known): 16:13ff.
He speaks (reveals): 16:13.
He glorifies (Jesus): 16:14.
He guides into all the truth: 16:13.
He bears witness: 15:26.
He convinces of sin: 16:8.

(c) *He is the object of the following actions*

He is given: 14:16.
He is sent: 14:26; 15:26; 16:7.
He is neither seen nor known: 14:17.
He is not received: 14:17.

THE CLOSE CONNECTIONS BETWEEN THE PARACLETE AND JESUS
PARALLEL ACTIVITIES

There are far more statements about these connections than there are about the relationships between the Paraclete and the Father. The Paraclete should therefore be seen above all in his relationship with Jesus. It should be clear from the following conspectus how close this is. (G. Bornkamm (see note 18 below) should also be consulted in this context.)

The Paraclete	*Jesus*
given by the Father: 14:16	3:16
is with and in the disciples: 14:16ff.	3:22; 13:33; 14:20; 14:26
the world cannot receive him: 14:17	1:11; 5:53 (12:48)

The Paraclete	Jesus
it does not know him; only believers know him: 14:17	14:19; 16:16ff.
sent by the Father: 14:26	see chapters 5, 7, 8, 12
teaches: 14:26	7:14ff.; 8:20; 18:37
comes (from the Father into the world): 15:26; 16:13, 7	5:43; 16:28; 18:37
bears witness: 15:26	5:31ff.; 8:13ff.; 7:7
confounds the world: 16:8	(3:19ff.; 9:41; 15:22)
does not speak of himself; speaks only what he has heard: 16:13	7:17; 8:26, 28, 38; 12:49ff.; 14:10
glorifies (Jesus): 16:14	cf. 12:28; 17:1, 4
unveils (communicates): 16:13ff.	4:25 (16:25)
guides into all the truth—he is the Spirit of truth: 16:13	cf. 1:17; 5:33; 18:37; 14:6

The fact that the Spirit is the subject of a number of actions, that he is, after Jesus, 'another Paraclete' (14:16) and that the masculine form of the demonstrative is used in the text, even after the neuter word *Pneuma*,[20] clearly means that certain personal characteristics are attributed to him.[21] It is, however, probably impossible to draw any direct conclusions from the fourth gospel regarding the dogma of the Trinity. The evangelist says, it is true, that the Spirit proceeds from the Father: *ekporeuetai*, but *para tou patros*, 'from near the Father', not *ek* (15:26). He also says: 'he will take from what is mine', *ek tou emou lēmpsetai*, since 'all that the Father has is mine' (16:14, 15). The context, however, is one of a communication of truth, not one of eternal existence preceding the economy of salvation.[22] Of course, the Father is the first and absolute origin, both of the Spirit and of the Word. The relationships between the Paraclete and Christ are also extremely close in the economy of salvation. The revelation of the Father, as the source of faith and love, must be experienced by the disciples in a hostile world and in faithfulness to that revelation. This is the function of the Spirit-Paraclete, the Spirit of truth. He continues, after Jesus' departure, to do Jesus' work, that is, to welcome by faith the one who is sent by the Father to reveal the Father and to keep his words and his commandments. He enables us to bring about the new relationship between Jesus and his own after Jesus has withdrawn his tangible presence from us. This takes place in the baptism of water, the offering of flesh and blood and the keeping and the living penetration of Jesus' words. I. de la Potterie has shown in his very detailed studies that the part played by the Spirit relates to faith, which forms the living substance of our relationship with Jesus. F. Porsch has also pointed, in his equally detailed and exact book, to a constant relationship between the Spirit-Paraclete and the word of Jesus, especially in the life of the disciples and within the framework of the struggle in which they are engaged. The Spirit does not invent or introduce a new and different economy. He gives life to the flesh and words *of Jesus* (6:63). He recalls those words to mind and penetrates the whole truth: 'He will not speak on his own account, but whatever he hears he will speak. . . . He will glorify me'. According to Swete, Jesus is the way (*hē hodos*) and the Spirit is the guide (*ho hodēgos*) who enables man to go forward on that way (p. 162).

3. *The Spirit in the Disciples and in the Time of the Church*

The evangelist and the circle of his disciples belonged to a Church in which the Spirit was active. Their particular place was probably in Syria; they certainly lived and wrote in a Church which knew of the activity of Paul and the history recounted in Acts. The Spirit aroused in them a feeling of communion, by reason of which they were, through faith and love, in God, who was in them: 'By this we know that we abide in him (God) and he in us, because he has given us of his own Spirit' (1 Jn 4:13; cf. 3:24; Jn 14). The Spirit acts in the first place in order to make them believe that the Son was sent in human flesh and to make them know and to confess him. This involves their loving as he loved (1 Jn 4:14ff.; 3:23).

In order to achieve this, the Spirit adds his testimony to that of Jesus, who was sent from the Father in human flesh, and that testimony is made present in the Church by baptism and the Eucharist:

> This is he who came by water and blood, Jesus Christ, not with the water only, but with the water and blood. And the Spirit is the witness, because the Spirit is the truth. There are three witnesses, the Spirit, the water and the blood, these three agree (1 Jn 5:6–8).

An intention to oppose Cerinthus, who made a distinction between the Christ of baptism and the Christ of the Passion, and even to oppose Docetism, by affirming the elements of which man is made in his mother's womb, water and blood,[23] can be recognized in the above passage. If, however, the whole text is seen as part of the entire Johannine witness, it is easy to recognize in it the coming of Jesus in the water, through his baptism, his coming through the blood of his Passion, and the Spirit, given to us thanks to both comings. John is not, however, thinking simply of the historical and unique events of the baptism and the sacrificial death of Jesus. As O. Cullmann has pointed out,[24] in accordance with the intention of his gospel, the evangelist saw Jesus' gestures as the inauguration and institution of what was to take place in the Church in a sacramental form. Because of this, the Spirit acts in the one who hears the testimony in order to arouse faith in him; he then acts in or with the sacraments (for baptism, see Jn 3:5; for the Eucharist, see 6:27, 63). He also similarly acts in the word, with which he is, as John shows, constantly united (6:63) and in the worship that true worshippers give to God (4:23–24).[25]

The time of the Church is essentially a time of mission, bearing witness and kerygma. It is a remarkable fact that all the gospels end with the sending of the apostles on their mission and with the gift of the Holy Spirit, at least in the case of Luke and John (see Mt 28:15; Mk 16:15; Lk 24:47ff.; Acts 1:8; Jn 17:18; 20:20). In John, the Spirit is essentially the Spirit of truth and, as such, he bears witness to Christ together with the apostles.[26]

Throughout the time of the Church, there are disciples. The Spirit guides them in a knowledge of the whole truth and even announces or communicates to them what is to come (see 16:13). While they were still accompanying Jesus and still saw and heard him, the disciples had both faith and a lack of faith. They also had above all a lack of understanding. The Spirit will bring to mind the teachings of Jesus and will bring to maturity in them a testimony which will not be simply a repetition of material facts, but a communication and an understanding of their meaning.[27]

John admits that he understood the meaning of Jesus' words and actions only after his departure (see 2:22; 12:16; 14:26) and the whole of his gospel illustrates this gradual deepening of understanding after Easter. What we have here is simply the fullness of the Christian mystery and the economy of salvation resulting from the life and the passover of Christ. 'The things that are to come' means that the calling to mind of what Jesus said is accompanied by an unfolding of new responses in what is new in history. The Spirit takes the realization of the Christian mystery forward in the history of mankind. This is in accordance with the nature of the testimony as contained in Scripture—as R. Asting has shown, it is 'directed forward', *vorwärtsgerichtet*.

All believers are concerned in this. John writes to them: 'You have been anointed by the Holy One and you all know. . . . The anointing which you received from him abides in you and you have no need that anyone should teach you; as his anointing teaches you about everything . . .' (1 Jn 2:20, 27). According to the context, this 'anointing' is received from Christ and it consists of the word of Jesus assimilated in faith and subject to the action of the Holy Spirit.[28] In the book of Revelation, Jesus' testimony is called the 'spirit of prophecy' (19:10).[29] The 'prophets' occupy an important place in it,[30] whereas, in the Johannine writings, there is no reference to the 'charisms' and the 'spiritual gifts' that abounded in Corinth. Despite all tribulations, it is essential to preserve the 'testimony of Jesus' (1:2; 12:11; 17:6; 19:10; 20:4) and to resist the 'false prophet' who serves the idolatrous ambition of the beast (13; 16:13; 19:20; 20:10). The Spirit does not reveal himself. He appears in relation to Jesus. He is communicated by Jesus and intervenes with the churches—the Church—to warn them and to bring them back to the truth.[31] In them, he is constantly an inspiration from Jesus and an aspiration towards Jesus the Lord: 'The Spirit and the Bride say, "Come" '

(22:17). This, then, in a situation of tribulation and distress, is the struggle of faith, which corresponds to what the gospel and the first epistle of John tell us.[32]

The fourth gospel is remarkably coherent in its teaching about the Spirit. What it says about the Spirit relates entirely to the testimony given to Jesus and Jesus is entirely related to the Father. The passage that provides the best summary of this mystery is undoubtedly the meditation that the evangelist added to the testimony of John the Baptist:

> He who comes from above is above all; he who is of the earth belongs to the earth and of the earth he speaks; he who comes from heaven is above all. He bears witness to what he has seen and heard, yet no one receives his testimony; he who receives his testimony sets his seal to this, that God is true. For he whom God has sent utters the words of God, for it is not by measure that he gives the Spirit. . . . He who believes in the Son has eternal life . . . (3:31–36).

Jesus comes from heaven, from eternity. At his baptism, John the Baptist bears witness: 'He was before me. . . . I have borne witness that this is the Son of God' (1:30, 34). John baptizes him and sees the Spirit, as a dove, descend from heaven and remain on him, declaring: 'It is he who baptizes with the Holy Spirit' (1:33). The man Jesus, the Word made flesh, who shows a humanity that is so much a part of this earth that it is often denounced (see Jn 6:30, 42; 7:27ff.; 5:18; 10:33), lives, in that humanity, totally in reference to the Father, so that he is entirely from him, for him and towards him (*pros ton Theon*: 1:1; 1 Jn 1:2). He is the one who is sent. He is the revelation of the Father and the communication of eternal life. It is enough to cling to him through faith and to practise love. In order to achieve this, Jesus, before leaving our earth corporeally, sent his Spirit as living water into believers, as the Paraclete to make their faith and their testimony firm and as one who is jointly effective in the word, the water of baptism, the Eucharist, bearing witness, the ministry of reconciliation: in a word, as the one who does his work, the task that he received from the Father, in the time of the Church. 'I will pray the Father and he will give you another Paraclete, to be with you for ever . . . the Paraclete, the Holy Spirit, whom the Father will send *in my name*' (14:16, 26).

This deeply Trinitarian Johannine view of the Christian mystery inspired the thinking of the earliest Fathers of the Church—Ignatius of Antioch in 107,[33] Justin about 150[34] and Irenaeus about 180 A.D.[35] It has also been a constant theme in the liturgy: to the Father (who gives absolute life), through Christ, in the Spirit. There are so many pronouncements made by the Fathers during the classical period that it would be impossible to refer to them all. Reference may, however, be made to several of the documents of the Second Vatican Council, which re-established links with this great tradition.[36]

NOTES

1. See, for example, H. B. Swete, *The Holy Spirit in the New Testament* (London, 1909), pp. 129–168 (Jn) and 267–279 (Jn and Rev); F. Büchsel, *Der Geist Gottes im Neuen Testament* (Gütersloh, 1926), chapter XIX, pp. 485–511; E. Schweizer, *'pneuma'*, *TDNT*, pp. 437–444 (Jn), 448–449 (1 Jn) and 449–451 (Rev); I. de la Potterie, various studies in *La vie selon l'Esprit. Condition du chrétien (Unam Sanctam,* 55) (Paris, 1965); F.-M. Braun, *Jean le théologien*, III: *Sa théologie*, 2 vols incorporating earlier articles (Paris, 1966 and 1972), especially II, pp. 37–56, 139–169, 180–181; F. Porsch, *Pneuma und Wort* (Frankfurt, 1974), with a bibliography containing some 700 titles.

2. The prophets had the Spirit only in a certain measure: see Strack and Billerbeck, II, p. 132. The interpretation that Jesus gave the Spirit (to the community) also has its supporters, including M.-J. Lagrange. It ensures a certain coherence with the rest of the fourth gospel: see 7:38–39; 19:34; 14:26; 15:26; 16:14; 20:22.

3. See P. van Imschoot, 'Baptême d'eau et baptême d'Esprit', *ETL*, 13 (1936), 653–664; F.-M. Braun, 'Le baptême d'après le 4ᵉ évangile', *RThom*, 48 (1948), 358–368 and *op. cit.*, II, pp. 139, 145; J. Guillet, 'Baptême et Esprit', *Lumière et Vie*, 26 (1956), 85–104; I. de la Potterie, ' "Naître de l'eau et naître de l'Esprit". Le texte baptismal de Jn 3, 5', *SE*, 14 (1962), 417–443, included in *op. cit.* (note 1), pp. 31–63, with full bibliography; Porsch, *op. cit.* (note 1), pp. 83–135.

4. Swete, *op. cit.* (note 1), pp. 142ff., still has the earlier punctuation. See, however, Braun, *op. cit.* (note 1), II, pp. 50–56; Porsch, *op. cit.*, pp. 53–81; H. Rahner, 'Flumina de ventre Jesu. Die patristische Auslegung von Joh VII, 37–39', *Bib*, 22 (1941), 269–302, 307–403; J.-E. Ménard, 'L'interprétation patristique de Jean VII, 38', *Revue de l'Université d'Ottawa, Section spéciale*, 25 (1955), 5*–25* (Origen believed that it referred to Christ, with reference to the rock in the desert, but then applied it to the Christian); J. Daniélou, 'Le symbolisme de l'eau vive', *RSR*, 32 (1958), 335–346; M.-E. Boismard, 'De son ventre couleront des fleuves d'eau vive', *RB*, 65 (1958), 523–546; P. Grelot, the same title and the same journal, 66 (1959), 369–374; A. Feuillet, 'Les fleuves d'eau vive de Jn VII, 38', *Parole de Dieu et sacerdoce. Etudes présentées à Mgr Weber* (Tournai and Paris, 1962), pp. 107–120; P. Grelot, 'Jean VII, 38: Eau du Rocher ou Source du Temple', *RB*, 70 (1963), 43–51.

5. Miracle of a new exodus: Is 35:6ff.; 41:13–20; 43:20. Water from the rock in the exodus: Ex 17:1–7; Num 20:1–3; Ps 78:16–20; 114:8; Is 48:21–22. Water flowing from the Temple: Ezek 47:1, 8–12; Zech 13:1; 14:8–9; Joel 4:18; Ps 46:5. See also J. Bonsirven, *Le judaïsme palestinien au temps de Jésus-Christ* (Paris, 1976), I, p. 432; A. Jaubert, *Approches de l'Evangile de Jean* (Paris, 1976), pp. 80, 140–146; my own *The Mystery of the Temple* (Eng. tr.; London, 1962), pp. 75–77. The following texts were included in the readings of the synagogue during the feast of Tabernacles: Is 43:20; 44:3; Jer 2:13; Zech 14:8; Deut 7:11–15; see Braun, *op. cit.* (note 1), II, p. 52.

6. Swete, *op. cit.* (note 1), p. 144, note 2 (talmudic texts); Strack and Billerbeck, II, p. 434; Porsch, *op. cit.* (note 1), pp. 63–65.

7. See 6:63; 14:17. Before Jesus' glorification, there is a mixture of faith and weak faith or understanding: see Porsch, *op. cit.*, p. 67.

8. Büchsel, *op. cit.* (note 1), p. 495, note 4, quotes texts here where a negation is at once compensated for by an affirmation: Jn 8:15–16; 3:32–33; 5:31; 6:63, 51. 16:12, contrasted with 15:15, could also be added to this list.

9. See Jn 5:36, 41, 44; 7:13; 8:50, 54; 12:43. See also Michael Ramsey, *The Glory of God and the Transfiguration of Christ* (London, 1949).

10. See Irenaeus, *Adv. haer.* IV, 31, 2 (*PG* 7, 1069–70); V, 1, 1 (*PG* 7, 1121). Caesarius of Arles, *Sermo* 40, 4 (*PL* 39, 1825) and Gregory the Great, *Moralia XXXV*, 8, 18 (*PL* 76, 759) compared Christ giving life to the Church on the cross by the seven gifts of the Spirit with Elijah leaning over the dead child and breathing seven times into him.

11. See Porsch, *op. cit.* (note 1), pp. 327ff.
12. F.-M. Braun, 'L'eau et l'Esprit', *RThom*, 49 (1949), 5–30; *idem*, *op. cit.* (note 1), I, pp. 167ff.
13. I have personally collected more than a hundred pieces of evidence of the symbols of the Church or the sacraments. See S. Tromp, 'De nativitate Ecclesiae ex corde Iesu in cruce', *Greg*, 13 (1932), 489–527; J. Daniélou, *Sacramentum Futuri* (Paris, 1950), pp. 37ff., 172; H. Barré, *Bulletin de la Société française d'Etudes mariales*, 13 (1955), 61–97; E. Guldan, *Eva-Maria* (Cologne and Graz, 1966), pp. 33ff., 46ff., 75, 173ff. For the East (and especially the liturgy of the Eastern Church), see J. Ledit, *La plaie du côté* (Rome, 1970).
14. See Swete, *op. cit.* (note 1), pp. 165–168; Porsch, *op. cit.* (note 1), pp. 341–378. *La Pentecôte johannique (Jean XX, 19–23; Ac II)* is the title of a book by Mgr Cassien Besobrasoff (Valence, 1939).
15. See Jn 14:3 and M. Ramsey's commentary, *op. cit.* (note 9), pp. 73, 23, 26, 28.
16. See Swete, *op. cit.*, p. 166; Porsch, *op. cit.*, p. 343.
17. See 1:8–10; 2:1ff., 12; 5:16. See also Porsch, *op. cit.*, pp. 361ff
18. For the word, see J. Behm, *'paraklētos'*, *TDNT*, V, pp. 800–814; J. G. Davies, 'The Primary Meaning of parakletos', *JTS*, new series, 4 (1953), 35–38; Porsch, *op. cit.*, pp. 227ff. D. Betz believed that the word was derived from *parakalein* and that it had a Jewish origin, having the meaning of bearing witness in front of a tribunal: see his *Der Paraklet* (Leiden and Cologne, 1963). See also H. M. Drion, 'L'origine du titre de "Paraclet": à propos d'un livre récent', *SE*, 17 (1965), 143–149. C. K. Barrett, 'The Holy Spirit in the Fourth Gospel', *JTS*, new series, 1 (1950), 1–15, thought, however, that the word was related to *paraklēsis*, 'exhortation'. For an exegesis of the Johannine texts, see Porsch, *op. cit.*, pp. 215–324; Swete, *op. cit.*, pp. 148–164; F. Mussner, 'Die johanneischen Parakletssprüche und die apostolische Tradition', *BZ*, 5 (1961), 56–70; I. de la Potterie, *op. cit.* (note 1), pp. 85–105; R. E. Brown, 'The Paraclete in the Fourth Gospel', *NTS*, 13 (1967), 113–132; G. Bornkamm, 'Der Paraklet im Johannes-Evangelium', *Geschichte und Glaube. Erster Teil. Gesammelte Aufsätze*, III (Munich, 1968), pp. 68–89; G. Johnston, *The Spirit-Paraclete in the Gospel of John* (Cambridge, 1970), reviewed by E. Malatesta in *Bib*, 54 (1973), 539–550.
19. See T. Preiss, 'La justification dans la pensée johannique', *Hommage et Reconnaissance. Recueil . . . K. Barth* (Neuchâtel and Paris, 1946), pp. 100–118; M.-F. Berrouard, 'Le Paraclet, défenseur du Christ devant la conscience du croyant (Jo XVI, 8–11)', *RSPT*, 33 (1949), 361–389; Porsch, *op. cit.*, pp. 275–289. This text is concerned with Jesus' trial, which continues in history: the Spirit will convince the world that it has sinned and still sins in its rejection and condemnation of Jesus, that Jesus' cause was just, that God declared it to be just when he raised him up and glorified him and finally that the unbelieving world and the demon that inspires that world have already been judged and declared guilty.
20. For *ekeinos*, see 14:26; 15:26; 16:8, 13.
21. These have been underestimated by certain authors, including, for example, G. Johnston, *op. cit.* (note 18). See, however, apart from E. Malatesta, *op. cit.* (*ibid.*): J. Goitia, 'La noción dinámica del pneuma en los libros sagrados', *Estudios Bíblicos*, 16 (1957), 115–159; R. E. Brown, *The Gospel according to John*, II (Garden City, N.Y., 1970/ London, 1971), esp. App. V.
22. See Porsch, *op. cit.* (note 1), pp. 273, 300ff.
23. This interpretation was suggested by G. Richter, 'Blut und Wasser aus der durchbohrten Seite Jesu', *Münchener Theologische Zeitschrift*, 21 (1970), 1–21. For Cerinthus and Gnosticism, see F.-M. Braun, *op. cit.* (note 1), I, p. 169; II, p. 148.
24. O. Cullmann, *The Johannine Circle* (Eng. tr.; London, 1976). See also Braun, *op. cit.* (note 1), II, pp. 148–149, 150–154; R. Brêchet, 'Du Christ à l'Eglise. Le dynamisme de l'Eglise dans l'évangile selon S. Jean', *Divus Thomas*, 56 (1953), 67–98; A. Feuillet, 'Le temps de l'Eglise d'après le IVe évangile et l'Apocalypse', *M-D*, 65 (1961/1), 60–79.

25. I. de la Potterie, in the article quoted below, note 28, has pointed out that, in Jn 5:8, the Spirit is put before the water and the blood; he arouses faith, the anointing of faith that is nourished in the sacraments of baptism and the Eucharist. For this exegesis, see also W. Nauck, *Die Tradition und der Charakter des ersten Johannesbriefes* (Tübingen, 1957), pp. 147–182, 2nd excursus: 'Geist, Wasser und Blut'. A. Jaubert, *op. cit.* (note 5), pp. 147–154, has pointed to possible different meanings and has emphasized the sacramental meaning. In this context, he mentions the Syrian custom of anointing (the Spirit) before administering the sacraments of entry into the Church, namely baptism and the Eucharist.

26. Jn 15:26–27; Acts 5:32. The testimony of the Spirit is linked with that borne by the witness of the life and resurrection of Jesus: Acts 1:8, 21–22; 2:32; 3:15; 4:13; 10:39, 41; 13:31.

27. For the nature of this testimony, see G. Marcel, 'Le témoignage comme localisation de l'existentiel', *NRT* (March 1946), 182–191; J. Guitton, *La pensée moderne et le catholicisme*. VI: *Le problème de Jésus et les fondements du témoignage chrétien* (Aix-en-Provence, 1948), pp. 153–164, 174ff.; idem, *Jésus* (Paris, 1956), pp. 193–217. For the exegesis of this theme, see R. Asting, *Die Verkündigung des Wortes im Urchristentum. Dargestellt an den Begriffen 'Wort Gottes', 'Evangelium' und 'Zeugnis'* (Stuttgart, 1939), pp. 666–698; I. de la Potterie, 'La notion de témoignage dans S. Jean', *Sacra Pagina*, ed. J. Coppens *et al.* (Gembloux and Paris, 1959), II, pp. 193–208; A.-M. Kothgesser, 'Die Lehr-, Erinnerungs-, Bezeugungs- und Einführungsfunktion des johanneischen Geist-Parakleten gegenüber der Christusoffenbarung', *Salesianum*, 33 (1971), 557–598; 34 (1972), 3–51; H. Schlier, The Holy Spirit as Interpreter according to St John's Gospel' *Communio* (Eng. ed.), 2 (1973), 61–67; F. Porsch, *op. cit.* (note 1), pp. 67, 262ff., 289ff. and, for the 'things to come', p. 298. Finally, F. Mussner, *The Historical Jesus in the Gospel of St John* (Freiburg and London, 1967), pp. 59–67, is worth consulting, but J. Beutner's monograph, *Martyria. Traditionsgeschichtliche Untersuchungen zum Zeugnisthema bei Johannes* (Frankfurt, 1972), which is largely lexicographic, goes technically further than our question.

28. See I. de la Potterie, 'L'onction du chrétien par la foi', *Bib*, 40 (1959), 12–69, reissued in *La vie selon l'Esprit, op. cit.* (note 1), pp. 107–167. John's text is also cited in the conciliar Constitution *Lumen Gentium*, 12.

29. This text was quoted by the Second Vatican Council to illustrate the prophetic function of believers (*Lumen Gentium*, 35) and their priestly mission (*Presbyterorum Ordinis*, 2).

30. See 1:3; 10:7; 11:3, 18; 16:6; 18:20, 24; 22:6, 9. John himself prophesied as one seized by the Spirit: 1:10; 4:2.

31. The seven letters to the churches came from Christ, but six of them end with 'what the Spirit says to the churches'. The 'seven spirits' (1:4; 4:5) are the Spirit in his fullness. Jesus possesses them (3:1) and he gives living water (21:6; 22:1, 17).

32. Jn 16:8–11; 1 Jn 2:18–19, 22; 4:1 (false prophet); Rev 4:14 and *passim*.

33. Ignatius' imagery is derived from architecture: Eph 9:1.

34. Justin Martyr, *1 Apol.* LXV and LXVII on the Eucharist.

35. Irenaeus, *Adv. haer*. IV, 20, 5 and 34, 5; V, 36; *Dem.* 7 (*SC* 62, pp. 41–42: the whole of this text would be worth quoting here).

36. Dogmatic Constitution *Lumen Gentium*, 51; Decree *Ad Gentes divinitus*, 2.

PART TWO

IN THE HISTORY OF CHRISTIANITY

1

THE EXPERIENCE OF THE SPIRIT
IN THE EARLY CHURCH[1]

The apostles 'set out, filled with the assurance of the Holy Spirit, to proclaim the good news of the coming of the kingdom of heaven'.[2] In the beginning, the Church saw itself as subject to the activity of the Spirit and filled with his gifts. In the Church's understanding of itself, this was how the glorified Lord exercised his authority over the Church. 'As the hand moves over the zither and the strings speak, so does the Spirit of the Lord speak in my limbs and I speak through his love.'[3]

The charism that is most frequently discussed is prophecy. The *Didache* gives an important place to the ministry of prophets, provides criteria that enable its authenticity to be determined[4] and at the same time observes that those 'bishops' and deacons who are 'worthy of the Lord . . . carry out the ministry of prophets and teachers' (XV, 1). In the middle of the second century A.D., Justin Martyr claimed that prophecy and charismatic gifts still existed in the Church.[5] They would, it was believed, accompany the Church throughout the whole of its history until the end.[6]

The community at Corinth had been given a number of rules by Paul for the correct use of the *pneumatika* and, in the same way, Clement of Rome, in his epistle of *c.* 95 A.D., reminded the Corinthians of the 'abundant outpouring of the Holy Spirit' on them (II, 2; see also XLVI, 6) and gave them this rule: 'Let each one of us respect in his neighbour the charisms that he has received' (XXXVIII, 1). This was the same as saying 'respect your presbyters'. Prophecy declined to some extent in the early Church, at least in the form of more or less ecstatic mental exaltation, but this was not, as Harnack believed, because the canon of scriptures had been established, but rather because of an increasing emphasis on the authority of the bishops.[7] This does not imply a contrast between the 'charismatics' and the hierarchical ministers, still less an opposition, since the ministers were themselves charismatic. Ignatius of Antioch, for example, claimed that he called out his essential message under the action of the Spirit,[8] Polycarp of Smyrna was called a 'teacher who was both an apostle and a prophet'[9] and Melito of Sardis was said to 'live entirely in the Holy Spirit'.[10] That is why the increasing affirmation of the part played by the bishops did not in any way minimize the charismatic life of the Church. They were spiritual men in the sense in which Paul described them (1 Cor 2:10–15). Later, Irenaeus spoke of them in the same way: 'Those who have received the pledge of the Spirit and who behave correctly in everything are rightly called by the Apostle spiritual men'.[11] Elsewhere, he speaks of the obedience owed to the presbyters who have received 'with their succession to the episcopate, the certain charism of truth, according to the pleasure of the Father'.[12] This is the tradition which ended by applying this text of spiritual anthropology to authority in the ✓ Church,[13] the bishop being regarded as a spiritual man, endowed with charisms of the Spirit and especially with those of knowledge and teaching.

It was because of this abundance of charisms and the important part played by them in the Church—especially the charism of 'prophecy'—that Montanus received a sympathetic hearing when he first began to 'prophesy' about 172:

> It was at this time that the disciples of Montanus, Alcibiades and Theodotus began to acquire a reputation as prophets in the Phrygian region. The very many other wonders that had been worked up to that time in several churches by the divine charism persuaded many to believe that the wonder-workers were also prophets.[14]

The disciples of the Montanist sect were received more and more favourably: 'You have a duty to welcome the charisms!'[15] A serious crisis arose in the Church. The teachings and practices of the Montanists spread so rapidly that when the martyrs of Lyons were in prison in 177, their chief concern was the 'peace of the churches'. It was at this time that the first synods met. From 202 onwards, Tertullian was increasingly drawn towards the Montanists, finding an answer to the reasons which had at first deterred him from a Church in which women prophesied. The Montanists, however, were very ascetic and practised severe fasting. . . . The Catholics criticized both the ways in which the Montanist prophets expressed themselves—by convulsions, cries and the suspension of judgement, for example—and the manner of life and biased attitudes of these new prophets. They claimed, for example, that God spoke in them, that they were the living recipients and even the incarnation of the Paraclete[16] and that eschatological fulfilment and the descent of the heavenly Jerusalem were near at hand. There was, in their teaching, a notable connection between, on the one hand, an appeal to prophecy, sectarian protest and a call to ascetic practice and, on the other, a strong eschatological expectation, often with reference to Joel 3:1–5: 'I will pour out my spirit on all flesh; your sons and daughters will prophesy . . . before the great and terrible day of the Lord comes'.[17]

This 'new prophecy' had to be rejected by the Catholic Church, but a rejection of this kind was dangerous if it meant bulding up the life of the Church without charisms and without the Holy Spirit. This danger did not, however, materialize. Irenaeus, whom the Christians of Vienne and Lyons had sent in 177 to the Bishop of Rome, Eleutherus, to discuss with him the new prophetic movement, testified in 180 to the existence in the Church of miraculous charisms[18] and wrote, about ten years later, that 'we know that, in the Church, many of our brothers have prophetic charisms and, by virtue of the Spirit, speak all the languages, reveal, for the good of all men, all secrets and expose the mysteries of God. The Apostle calls them spiritual men, not through tearing and repressing their flesh, but through sharing the Spirit and only because of that.'[19] Similar statements are made again and again later. Miltiades' has already been mentioned (see above, p. 65, and below, note 6). In 248, Origen wrote: 'Among Christians, there are always marks of that Holy Spirit who appeared in the form of a dove. They drive out evil spirits, bring about cures and predict certain events according to the will of the Logos.'[20] In 375, Epiphanius of Salamis added to a quotation of the Montanists' claim regarding the 'duty to welcome the charisms' that 'the holy Church of God also welcomes them, but (in the Church) they are truly charisms, authenticated by the Holy Spirit and coming to the Church from the prophets, the apostles and the Lord himself'.[21]

It is important to mention here the place occupied by visions, warnings and suggestions attributed to the Spirit in the early Church. Cyprian said, for example, of a council held at Carthage in the spring of 252: 'It has pleased us, under the inspiration of the Holy Spirit and according to the warnings given by the Lord in many clear visions. . .'.[22] The life of Cyprian himself is studded with supernatural visions and warnings.[23] The early Church believed that its life was guided by God—not simply by his Word, but also by the inspirations and indications that he gave again and again. It is worth recalling Rudolf Sohm's arguments and his supporting documentation in this context.[24] In the same way, the long series of texts attributing the forces and influences in the life of the Church to an *inspiratio* or a *revelatio* are also worth consulting.[25] This is what we would now call the development of dogma and the teachings of the Church's councils, their canons, the decisions of the Church's teaching authority and the understanding of Scripture. It was the Spirit who disclosed the 'spiritual meaning' of Scripture and it was important to obtain a view of that meaning that would be worthy of the Spirit.[26]

There was, then, only one Church, which was both corporeal and spiritual, hierarchical and pneumatic, institutional and charismatic. As a Montanist, Tertullian made a sharp contrast between the Church of the Spirit and the Church of the bishops,[27] but this was based on a sectarian ecclesiology: the true Church ought, he believed, to be known by the sign of ecstasy.[28] Others would have said that it should be known by the sign of glossolalia. Those who expressed the Catholic Tradition situated the Spirit firmly within the Church. In his refutation of the Alogi, who, in their opposition to the Montanists, suppressed the gospel of John with its emphasis on the promise of the Paraclete, Irenaeus reaffirmed both the gospel and the prophetic Spirit.[29] At the end of Book III of his great work *Against Heresies*, he exalted the Spirit as the principle giving life to the Church and faith:

(Faith) is received from the Church and kept by us; it always makes us young again and, under the influence of the Spirit, like a costly drink contained in a precious vase, even renews the vase that holds it. The Church is entrusted with this gift of God, just as God entrusted breath to the flesh that he fashioned so that all members receive life from it. In this gift the intimacy of the gift of Christ, that is to say, the Holy Spirit, is contained. God established in the Church the apostles, the prophets, the doctors and all the other effects of the working of the Spirit in which those who do not run to the *ecclesia* do not share. . . . Where the Church (*ecclesia*) is, there is also the Spirit of God and where the Spirit of God is, there are also the Church and all grace. And the Spirit is truth.[30]

This Church is the Church Irenaeus knew, the Church of the succession of presbyters and of an assembly of brothers in communion with the faith of the apostles. He recognized that this Church and the Spirit conditioned each other and did so, as it were, at two different but interdependent points of entry. It was for this reason that he stressed not only that where the Spirit is there is also the Church, but also that where the Church is there is also the Spirit. The whole of the history we have to cover and the whole of the theology we must outline are contained within this dialectical tension which is too divine for us to be able to break it without betraying some aspect of it.

Hippolytus and Clement of Alexandria were writing at the same time as Tertullian. According to Hippolytus, the Holy Spirit ensured that the tradition of the apostles would be preserved.[31] The same Spirit refuted heresies and was handed on in the Church, in which there was not only a succession of ministers, but also a kind of succession or transmission of the Spirit.[32] This Church was to be found in the local assembly in which instruction was given by teachers. At least twice, Hippolytus insisted: *Festinet autem et ad ecclesiam ubi floret spiritus*—'Let us hasten to the assembly, where the Spirit produces fruit' (*Apos. Trad.* 31 and 35).

Clement called the Church of the Lord a 'spiritual and holy choir' and a 'spiritual body' (*sōma pneumatikon*) about 210, because 'the one who clings to the Lord is one spirit with him and a spiritual body'.[33] Cyprian's contemporary, Novatian, before his schism in 251, wrote one of the finest theological or ecclesiological statements about the Holy Spirit:[34]

(That Spirit, who enabled the disciples not to fear, in the name of the Lord, either the powers of the world or its torments) gives similar gifts, like jewels, to the Bride of Christ, the Church. He causes prophets to appear in the Church, instructs the Church's teachers, encourages tongues, obtains power and health, works wonders in the Church, brings about the discernment of spirits, helps those who govern the Church, inspires the Church's councils and dispenses the other gifts of grace. In this way, he perfects and completes the Church of Christ everywhere and in all things.

The same Spirit, in the form of a dove, came and remained with the Lord after his baptism, dwelling fully and totally in him, without any kind of limitation. He was then dispensed and sent out in superabundance so that the others might receive from him a pouring out of graces, the source of every gift of the Holy Spirit dwelling in Christ, in whom the Holy Spirit lives in great profusion. This is what was said in prophecy by Isaiah: 'The Spirit of the Lord shall rest upon him. . .' (11:2–3) and in the name of the Lord himself: 'The spirit of the Lord is upon me. . .' (61:1; Lk 4:17–19) and by David: 'Therefore God, your God, has anointed you with the oil of gladness above your fellows' (Ps 45:7).

Did the situation change—for the worse—after the peace of Constantine? It is true that the favour given to the Church by Constantine and his successors brought a certain relaxation. The fourth-century Fathers bear witness to this and complain of it.[35] The extraordinary and more or less miraculous charisms undoubtedly seem to have become rare at this time.[36] The monastic movement has often been represented as the successor of the martyrs and as a protest in favour of an eschatological form of Christianity that was opposed to the secular spirit of the age and against a Church that was too powerful, carnal and worldly. It is, of course, true that, as a way of life and an approach to reality and even in the form of authority that it favoured, monasticism was an original spiritual power that was relatively independent of what Tertullian called the Church of the bishops. In the course of our survey of the Church's history and the Holy Spirit, we shall encounter quite frequently evidence of this kind of duality with its resulting tension. It would, however, be historically incorrect, and it would also do injustice to the ideal, to speak of a complete dichotomy.

In the first place, many bishops were in fact monks or at least men who had been educated within the framework of the religious life and who had retained the attitudes and behaviour encouraged by that way of life. Many examples spring at once to mind: Basil the Great, John Chrysostom, Augustine, Martin of Tours, Germanus of Auxerre, Patrick, Eucherius of Lyons, Faustus of Riez, Lupus of Troyes, Caesarius of Arles, Martin and Fructuosus of Braga, Gregory the Great, Augustine of Canterbury, and Leander and Isidore of Seville. The hierarchy, as we term it, acting as the minister of the Spirit, drew its strength from its close and living relationship with monachism.[37] The bishop as the father of Christians and the monastic founder have the same quality of 'men of God', who are animated by the Spirit and in whom the Spirit dwells.[38] The term *vir Dei* or 'man of God' is the classic name for the man in whom the active presence of the Spirit is made manifest and who is filled with the Spirit. The virtue of God rests on him, animates him, acts through him and often goes beyond the limits of what is ordinary because of a discernment of spirits, a power over souls, prophetic lights and the gifts of knowledge. Such a man, in other words, has thaumaturgic abilities.

One cannot fail to recognize these qualities in such men as Martin of Tours (†397) and Patrick (†460). Did they not form part of a tradition? Patrick himself wrote in his autobiographical *Confession*:

I am bound to the Spirit and it is not I, but the Lord who asked me to come (§ 43).

Was it without God or according to the flesh that I came to Ireland? Who drove me here—bound by the Spirit—to see no one who was related to me? (Letter No. 10).

Once again I saw him praying in me and I was as it were inside my body and I heard him praying over me, that is, over the inner man, and he was praying powerfully there, with groans. And during the whole of that time I was dumbfounded and astonished and I wondered who it was praying in me, but at the end of the prayer he spoke as if he was the Spirit, and so I woke up and recalled that the Apostle had said: 'The Spirit helps us in our weakness; for we do not know how to pray as we ought, but the Spirit himself intercedes for us with sighs too deep for words' (§25–26).[39]

A disciple, Gildas (†570), wrote: 'May he speak for me, he who alone is true—the Holy Spirit'[40] and 'May the *sancti vates* reply for us, today as in the past, since they were the mouth and the organ of the Holy Spirit'.[41]

NOTES

1. H. Weinel, *Die Wirkungen des Geistes und der Geister im nachapostolischen Zeitalter bis auf Irenäus* (Freiburg, 1899); G. Bardy, *La théologie de l'Eglise de S. Clément de Rome à S. Irénée (Unam sanctam*, 13) (Paris, 1945), pp. 128–156.
2. Clement of Rome, *Cor* XLII, 3. In the Acts of the Apostles, the apostles seem to be moved by the Spirit (see W. Mundle, 'Das Apostelbild der Apostelgeschichte', *ZNW*, 27 [1928], 36–54) as are, in a more general way, all those who are engaged in building up the Church: Stephen (Acts 5:8; 7:55), Barnabas (11:24), Paul (13:9), etc. Thomas Aquinas' idea of the apostles was that of persons who were permeated with and fashioned by the Spirit; see A. Lemonnyer, 'Les Apôtres comme docteurs de la foi d'après S. Thomas', *Mélanges thomistes* (Le Saulchoir, 1923), pp. 153–173.
3. *Odes of Solomon*, VI, in Syria, c. 90 A.D. These odes bear witness to great joy through the action of the Spirit.
4. See *Didache*, XI, 8–12; XIII. Similar criteria, based on manner of life, are contained in the *Shepherd of Hermas*, which appeared in the middle of the second century: see especially chapter 43 (Precept XI). For the important part played by prophecy in the apostolic and the sub-apostolic periods, see P. de Labriolle, *La crise montaniste* (Paris, 1913), pp. 112–123.
5. Justin, *Dial*. 82; G. Bardy, *op. cit.*, p. 132. For the gifts of the Spirit, see *Dial*. 39, 2–5; 88, 1.
6. Miltiades, an opponent of Montanism, quoted by Eusebius, *Hist. Eccl.* V, XVII, 4.
7. See J. L. Ash, 'The Decline of Ecstatic Prophecy in the Early Church', *ThSt*, 37 (1976), 227–252.
8. Ignatius, *Philad.* 7.
9. *Mart. Polycarpi*, XVI, 2.
10. See Eusebius, *Hist. Eccl.* V, 24, 2, 5, quoting Polycrates.
11. Irenaeus, *Adv. haer.* V, 8, 2 (*PG* 7, 1142; ed. W. W. Harvey, II, p. 339); IV, 33 (*PG* 7, 1072ff.; Harvey, II, p. 256).
12. *Adv. haer.* IV, 26, 2 (*PG* 7, 1053; Harvey, II, p. 236). For the interpretations of this text, see my *L'Eglise une, sainte, catholique et apostolique* (*Mysterium Salutis*, 15) (Paris, 1970), p. 210, note 73.
13. See A. M. Koeniger, 'Prima sedes a nomine iudicatur', *Beiträge zur Geschichte des christlichen Altertums und der byzantinischen Literatur. Festgabe A. Ehrhard* (Bonn, 1922), pp. 273–300.

14. Eusebius, *Hist. Eccl.* V, III, 4; Fr. tr. P. de Labriolle, *Les sources de l'histoire du Montanisme. Textes grecs, latins, syriaques* (Fribourg and Paris, 1913), p. 68; *idem, La crise montaniste, op. cit.* (note 4); R. A. Knox, *Enthusiasm* (Oxford, 1950), pp. 25–49; H. Kraft, 'Die altkirchliche Prophetie und die Entstehung des Montanismus', *TZ*, 11 (1955), 249–271. For the latest stage in research into this subject, see F. Blanchetière, 'Le montanisme originel', *RSR*, 52 (1978), 118–134, and 53 (1979), 1–22.

15. In Epiphanius, *Panarion*, XLVIII, 1: see P. de Labriolle, *La crise montaniste, op. cit.*, p. 136.

16. P. de Labriolle, *La crise montaniste, op. cit.*, pp. 130ff. For an appeal to the fourth gospel and the book of Revelation, see pp. 190ff.

17. P. de Labriolle, *ibid.*, p. 541. In note 1, this author quotes Priscillian. A recent book on the latter is H. Chadwick, *Priscillian of Ávila. The Occult and the Charismatic in the Early Church* (Oxford, 1976). Priscillian, who was the Bishop of Avila from 381 until 385, was in favour of asceticism and encouraged charismatic prophetism among men and women. He was accused of sorcery and Manichaeanism and was tortured and executed by order of the emperor at Trier in 385. St Martin protested against this use of constraint.

18. Irenaeus, *Adv. haer.* II, 32, 4: 'It is impossible to say how many charisms the Church receives throughout the whole world from God in the name of Jesus Christ who was crucified under Pontius Pilate'.

19. *Adv. haer.* V, 6, 1 (*PG* 7, 1137; Harvey, II, p. 334). To complete Irenaeus' testimony, it is worth quoting once again his *Adv. haer.* III, 11, 9, against Marcion: 'Those people who maintain that there are false prophets and who use it as an excuse to reject the Church's grace of prophecy are very unfortunate, since they behave like men who, because of people who act as hypocrites, even refrain from having relationships with their brothers' (see A. Rousseau and L. Doutreleau, *SC* 211, p. 173); see also IV, 20, 6 (*SC* 100, p. 642). In the *Demonstration of the Apostolic Preaching*, the same author writes: 'Others do not accept the gifts of the Holy Spirit and reject the prophetic charism by which man, when he is watered, bears God's life as a fruit' (*Dem.* 99; Fr. tr. L.-M. Froidevaux, *SC* 62, p. 169). What was most necessary and most permanent in the Church for Origen was the charism of discernment (*In Num.*, Hom. XXVII, 11; ed. W. A. Baehrens, p. 272). This was so even when 'most of the other charisms have ceased' (*In Prov.* c. 1; *PG* 13, 25A). See also I. Hausherr, *Direction Spirituelle* (see note 38 below), p. 46.

20. Origen, *Contra Cels.* I, 46.

21. *Panarion*, XLVIII, 1; see P. de Labriolle, *Les sources, op. cit.* (note 14), 88, p. 115. It is not certain whether Epiphanius was referring here to undisputed contemporary facts.

22. Cyprian, *Ep.* LVII, 5 (ed. W. von Hartel, p. 655).

23. See A. von Harnack, 'Cyprian als Enthusiast', *ZNW*, 5 (1902), 177–191; A. d'Alès, *La théologie de S. Cyprien* (Paris, 1922), pp. 77–83.

24. See my 'Rudolph Sohm nous interroge encore', *RSPT*, 57 (1973), 263–294.

25. See my *Tradition and Traditions* (Eng. tr.; London and New York, 1966), Part One, Excursus B, pp. 119–137, which deals with the permanence of *revelatio* and *inspiratio* in the Church and provides a bibliography. Among dozens of texts, the following, taken from the Council of Carthage (256 A.D.) is worth noting: '(Deus) cuius inspiratione ecclesia eius instruitur' (*Sent.* 28; Hartel, p. 447).

26. See the works of H. de Lubac, *Histoire et Esprit. L'intelligence de l'Ecriture d'après Origène* (Paris, 1950), pp. 104ff., 295–335 and *passim*; and *Exégèse médiévale. Les quatre sens de l'Ecriture*, 4 vols (Paris, 1959–1964).

27. Tertullian, *De pud.* XXI, 17–18 (after 217); see also K. Adam, *Der Kirchenbegriff Tertullians* (Paderborn, 1907).

28. *Contra Marc.* IV, 22 (in 207–208).

29. Irenaeus, *Adv. haer.* III, 11, 9 (*PG* 7, 890; Harvey, II, pp. 50–51; *SC* 34, pp. 203ff.).

30. *Adv. haer.* III, 24, 1 (*PG* 7, 966; Harvey, II, p. 131; *SC* 34, pp. 399ff.). A. Benoît has given this explanation of Irenaeus' text: 'Because the Spirit is given to the Church, Irenaeus was

able to say that where the Spirit was there was the Church. And since there is only one Church, he was able to reverse the statement and say that where the Church was there was also the Spirit': see *L'Esprit Saint et l'Eglise* (Paris, 1969), p. 133. It is, however, important to define the content of the term 'Church' as used by Irenaeus. The Church was, for him, what contained the faith handed down from the apostles by the succession of ministers and made present and renewed again and again by the Spirit. This Church was the whole Church, but also the Church made concrete in the local community. P.-M. Gy understands this passage to refer to the *ecclesia*, i.e. the local assembly in which it is necessary to share in order to participate in the gifts of the Spirit: see his 'Eucharistie et "ecclesia" dans le premier vocabulaire de la liturgie chrétienne', *M-D*, 130 (1977), 19–34, especially 31.

31. In the Prologue to the *Apostolic Tradition*, written in 215 and continuing a treatise on the charisms, Hippolytus ends with these words: 'The Holy Spirit conferring on those whose faith is correct the perfect grace to know how those who are at the head of the Church must teach and preserve everything' (Fr. tr. B. Botte, *SC* 11, p. 26).

32. *Philosophoumena* I, *Praef*. 6 (after 222): 'No one will dispute all this (the teaching of the philosophical sects)—only the Holy Spirit handed down in the Church. The apostles were the first to receive the Spirit and they communicated it to those whose faith was correct. We, who are their successors, who share in the same grace of the priesthood and teaching and who are considered to be the guardians of the Church, do not close our eyes and do not suppress our words. . . . Each one of us will fulfil our tasks in our own time and we shall share in all the graces that the Holy Spirit will grant to us.'

33. Clement of Alexandria, *Strom*. VII, 14 (*PG* 9, 522; ed. O. Stählin, p. 62).

34. Novatian, *De Trin. lib*. XXIX (*PL* 3, 943–946; L. Y. Fausset, *Cambridge Patristic Texts* (1909), pp. 105–111).

35. See the references in my *Vraie et fausse réforme dans l'Eglise*, 2nd ed. (Paris, 1969), pp. 155–156.

36. John Chrysostom made a connection between the gift of tongues, which was, in his opinion, at an end, and the crude nature of the earliest Christians: see his *Hom*. 3, 4, on the Acts of the Apostles; 'the time of miracles is over', *Hom*. 40, 2, on the Acts: see P. Rancillac, *L'Eglise manifestation de l'Esprit chez S. Jean Chrysostome* (Dar Al-Kalima, Lebanon, 1970), pp. 124, 142; A.-M. Ritter, *Charisma im Verständnis des Joannes Chrysostomus und seiner Zeit* (Göttingen, 1972). A more certain faith has no need of external signs: *In 1 Cor. Hom*. 29, 12, 1 (*PG* 61, 239); *Hom*. 1 on Pentecost, 4; cf. Gregory the Great, *Mor. in Job* XXXIV, 3, 7 (*PL* 76, 721A-C).

37. See O. Casel, 'Die Mönchesweihe,' *Jahrbuch für Liturgiewissenschaft*, 5 (1925), pp. 1–47.

38. See O. Casel, 'Benedikt von Nursia als Pneumatiker', *Heilige Überlieferung. Festgabe I. Herwegen* (Münster, 1938), pp. 96–123; B. Steidle, ' "Homo Dei Antonius". Zum Bild des "Mann Gottes" im Alten Mönchtum', *Antonius Magnus Eremita, 356–1956* (*Studia Anselmiana*, 38) (Rome, 1956), pp. 148–200; A. Mandouze, *Saint Augustin. L'aventure de la raison et de la grâce* (Paris, 1968, pp. 168ff.; P. Rousseau, 'The Spiritual Authority of the "Monk-Bishop". Eastern Elements in Some Western Hagiography of the Fourth and Fifth Century', *JTS*, new series, 22 (1971), 380–419. For monks in the early Church, see I. Hausherr, *Direction spirituelle en Orient autrefois* (*Or. Chr. Anal.*, 144) (Rome, 1955), pp. 39–55: 'Spirituel'.

39. Translation based on Fr. tr. of Patrick's *Confession* and the letter to Coroticus by G. Dottin, *Les livres de saint Patrice* (Paris, 1908). See also J. Chevalier, *Essai sur la formation de la nationalité et les réveils religieux au Pays de Galles des origines à la fin du sixième siècle* (Lyons and Paris, 1923), pp. 396ff.

40. Gildas, *De Excidio Britanniae*, c. 62.

41. *ibid*., c. 37.

2

TOWARDS A THEOLOGY AND A DOGMA
OF THE THIRD PERSON

There is no lack of comprehensive histories and detailed monographs on this subject.[1] It would be presumptuous and even foolish to try to provide in a few pages a worthwhile outline of the development of this quite complex teaching and the various forms that it has taken in the course of its history. All that can be done here is to present a number of aspects of reflection about the Christian experience of the Spirit in the Church.

In a well-known text, Gregory Nazianzen, who died in 390 after having been Patriarch of Constantinople, pointed to the gradual progress of the revelation of the mystery of God through the Old Testament to the New and in Christian reflection itself:

> The Old Testament preached the Father openly and the Son more obscurely, while the New revealed the Son and hinted at the deity of the Spirit. Now the Spirit dwells in us and reveals himself more clearly to us. For it was not right, while the deity of the Father had still not been confessed, to preach the Son openly and, before the deity of the Son had been acknowledged, to force us to accept the Holy Spirit—and I speak too boldly here—into the bargain. . . . (It was much more suitable that) by gradual advances and, as David said, by partial ascents, moving forward and increasing in clarity, the light of the Trinity should shine on those who had already been given lights (*Orat. XXXI Theol.* V, 26).[2]

Although several important expressions of this doctrine were known at the beginning, they were insufficient and they were not accepted everywhere. For Hermas, for example, about 148–150, the Holy Spirit was the Son of God.[3] Justin Martyr, writing at the same period, also seems to identify, in an inadequate way, the Pneuma and the Logos. Even more surprising is the confusion that exists in writings (wrongly) attributed to Cyprian, in Lactantius and in a creed attributed to the Council of Sardica (343).[4] From about that time onwards, however, a Trinitarian faith was confessed in the celebration of baptism. When exactly did Christians begin to baptize 'in the name of the Father, of the Son and of the Holy Spirit'? This was certainly being done at the time when Matthew was editing his gospel, but were the words that he attributed to the risen Lord spoken by Jesus? Exegetes think not and have given various reasons for their conviction.[5] The Trinitarian affirmation, however, was generally accepted from the time of St Paul. It is found in its

Matthaean form in the *Didache* (VII, 1) and in Justin.[6] In Irenaeus, it is expanded into a confession of faith containing a form of catechesis:

> In the first place, (faith) urges us to remember that we have received baptism for the remission of sins in the name of God the Father and in the name of Jesus Christ the son of God incarnate who died and rose again and in the Holy Spirit of God.[7] . . . That is why, when we are born again, baptism takes place through these three articles and gives us the grace of new birth in God the Father by means of his Son in the Holy Spirit.[8]

In the East, orthodox teachers reacted against the heresy of Macedonius and the Pneumatomachi[9] or 'enemies of the Holy Spirit'. These believed that the Spirit was a power or an instrument of God that had been created in order to act in us and the world. They therefore remained, in their idea of the Spirit, at the level of 'economy' and did not reach the level of 'theology', that is to say, what, at the level of God himself and in his being, is the presupposition of a deifying activity in man. Among those who reacted against this heresy were Athanasius, Basil of Caesarea and Gregory Nazianzen. In his *Letters to Serapion*, written between 356 and 362, Athanasius concluded from the baptismal formula that the Spirit shared the same divinity as the Father and the Son in the unity of the same substance.[10]

Basil (†379) resumed Athanasius' argument and developed the traditional position still further. On 5 (or 7) September 374, the feast of St Eupsychus, at Caesarea in Cappadocia, he pronounced this doxology: 'Glory to the Father, with the Son, with the Holy Spirit'. Criticized for this ambiguous innovation, since the usual form of the doxology, which Basil also used, was 'Glory to the Father, through the Son, in the Holy Spirit', he wrote a treatise on the Holy Spirit in 374–375.[11] In it, he showed that his new doxology was justified by Scripture and tradition. His argument followed the pattern that it had taken in several letters written at about the same time,[12] namely that it is necessary to be baptized according to the form that has been received, to believe as one has been baptized and to praise God as one believes. Basil avoided calling the Spirit explicitly God, just as Athanasius had avoided this. He did so for two reasons. The first is that, when one speaks of God, one has to remain faithful to the terms defined in Scripture and the second is that it is better to adapt oneself to the weakness of those whom one is combating and to make it easy for them to be converted by not providing an opportunity for a new cavil. An affirmation that the Spirit is worthy of the same honour and the same adoration as the Father and the Son is, however, a confession that the three are of the same substance and a way of confounding the Pneumatomachi, just as the Arians had been confounded by the faith expressed at Nicaea.

One hundred and fifty bishops met at the Council convoked at Constantinople by the emperors Gratian and Theodosius I and completed the Nicene Creed by adding an article on the Holy Spirit in the tradition of Basil and Athanasius. According to this so-called Niceno-Constantinopolitan Creed of 381, the Spirit was neither 'God' nor 'consubstantial' with the Father and the Son, but was the 'Lord and life-giver, proceeding from the Father, object of the same worship and the same glory with the Father and the Son'.[13] In a letter sent in the course of the following year to Pope Damasus and other Western bishops, the bishops, meeting again at Constantinople, set out the work of the Council by using the words *ousia mia, aktistō kai homo-ousiō kai sunaidiō triadi*, 'one substance, the uncreated Trinity, consubstantial and eternal'.[14] That, then, is our faith, proclaimed every Sunday in the Creed that comes from Athanasius, Basil and the 150 Fathers of the Council of Constantinople. At about the same time, Pope Damasus also formulated the same faith. In 374, he expressed it in his letter *Ea gratia* to the Eastern bishops and in 382 (the most commonly accepted date) he convoked a synod at Rome, which formulated exactly the same faith as that of the Fathers of Constantinople in 24 canons.[15]

Seen in the perspective of the Eastern Fathers, but also in the light of our present understanding, this affirmation is concerned not only with the truth of God, but also with the truth about man and his absolute destiny. If the Spirit is not God in substance, then we cannot be truly deified, Athanasius declared in 356.[16] Gregory Nazianzen repeated this in 380, with reference to the baptismal formula.[17] With or without reference to baptism, this argument about our sanctification is common to all the Fathers, but especially to the Greek Fathers, who claimed that the Holy Spirit is God, because he carries out what only God can carry out.[18]

It was, however, in the West, thanks especially to Tertullian (†222–223), that the vocabulary and therefore the concepts used in the Christian confession of faith were fully developed, even though Tertullian's theology remained, in the long run, unsatisfactory.[19] He also referred to baptism, in which we confess our faith in the Spirit as a 'third' in one God.[20] He was responsible for what have been called 'those well-known terms *Trinitas*, *tres personae* and *una substantia*, which he formulated and which became commonplaces in the dogma of the Trinity, and for such imaginative expressions as *Deum de Deo* and *lumen de lumine*, which we still use in confessing our faith'.[21]

The Latin terms *substantia* and *persona* used by Tertullian were readily intelligible, although the second expresses the rôle played and tends to favour the modalism. (In Tertullian, it has the juridical meaning of 'responsible individual'.) The Greek word *hupostasis* was translated literally into Latin as *sub-stantia*: for the Latin Fathers, substance was the same as essence. In the final anathema of Nicaea, *ousia* and 'substance' were also identified, but this was done by calling the latter 'hypostasis'.[22] At a local council at Alexandria in 362, the Cappadocians meant by 'hypostases' the specific characters of the divine persons and spoke of one substance, *ousia*, or nature, *phusis*, in three hypostases or three persons, *prosōpois*. Jerome

75

was quite confused by this.[23] Nonetheless, this vocabulary was finally recognized by the Second Council of Constantinople in 553.[24] It was difficult to find words that were adequate to express a mystery—that of God in his most intimate being—which transcends all created intelligence and understanding. Hilary of Poitiers, one of the great early authors writing about the faith, apologized for having to speak about this question and said that heresy obliged him *illicita agere, ardua transcendere, ineffabilia loqui*—'to do what is not permitted, to rise to the heights and to express what is inexpressible'.[25] The mystery of the Trinity of God is undoubtedly a principle of life, contemplation and praise, but the theological study of the Trinity consists to a great extent of a reflection about the vocabulary and the grammar used to express it; as will also be the case in the *Summa* of a mystic like Aquinas. Now, however, we must return to our special theme, the Spirit.

The struggle against and the victory over the Pneumatomachi seem to have had an influence on two liturgical developments. The first of these is the epiclesis or invocation of the Holy Spirit over the bread and wine. This epiclesis certainly existed already. (See, for example, the anaphora of Hippolytus, and *Catechesis* V, 7 of Cyril of Jerusalem, dating from 348–349; *SC* 126, p. 155.) It gained more and more ground towards the middle and end of the fourth century and subsequently, when the anaphoras of Serapion and Basil of Caesarea, the *Catechesis* of Cyril of Jerusalem or his successor John, and the liturgy attributed to John Chrysostom appeared. We shall be considering the problem of the epiclesis from the liturgical and theological points of view in Volume III. Secondly, whereas the early Christians celebrated the single mystery of salvation and the new life gained and communicated by Christ during the fifty days beginning with Easter, they began, in the course of the fourth century, to make a distinction between the feasts of the Resurrection, the Ascension and Pentecost.[26] Accounts of pilgrimages to Jerusalem detail the separate feasts; there was a wish to give liturgical solemnity to dogmas defined in opposition to heresies. Pentecost was certainly never a feast *of the Holy Spirit*, The mysteries of the Word made man were celebrated and the divine persons were not isolated—the Spirit was 'co-adored and conglorified with the Father and the Son'. This does not mean that Christians did not pray to him as a separate Person, in the same way that they prayed to Christ. According to J. A. Jungmann, this practice was favoured by reaction against the Arians.

No attempt is made here to provide a history of the pneumatological dogma. Certain Fathers have, of course, to be mentioned in this context. These include Hilary of Poitiers (†367), Cyril of Jerusalem (†386), Didymus the Blind (†c. 398), Ambrose (†397), who wrote a treatise *De Spiritu Sancto*, in which he developed the orthodox doctrine of the Tri-unity of God and the divinity of the third Person, and finally Cyril of Alexandria (†444). It is also important to speak of Syrian Christianity and to include Antioch and, at Edessa or Nisibis, Ephraem Syrus (†373), who was called the 'lyre of the Holy Spirit'.[27] In this Syrian tradition, which was for the most part expressed in lyrical verse and especially in hymns, the Church, together with the orientation of its ministries, its sacramental life and the fulfilment of its mission as expressed in Mt 28:18–20, is linked not so much to the incarnate Word as to the Spirit of Pentecost. It is the Spirit that brings the Church to birth and acts in the three sacraments of initiation—baptism, chrismation and the Eucharist. The epiclesis is here an invocation that the reality of the resurrection may be brought about in the celebrating community.

In 393, Augustine (354–430), who was at the time still a simple priest, presented his treatise *De fide et symbolo* to a local council. In it, he said:

> Many books have been written by scholarly and spiritual men on the Father and the Son. . . . The Holy Spirit has, on the other hand, not yet been studied with as much care and by so many great and learned commentators on the scriptures that it is easy to understand his special character and know why we cannot call him either Son or Father, but only Holy Spirit.[28]

From that time onwards, Augustine became intensely interested in the theology of the Holy Spirit. His ideas on this subject are found scattered throughout the whole of his later work, but they are most fully developed in *De Trinitate*, which he began in 399 and did not finish until 419. In this treatise, he reflects about the whole of the Trinitarian mystery at a depth and breadth that are unequalled elsewhere.[29] We shall deal only with what concerns the Holy Spirit. Augustine has an original doctrine of the third Person and the part played by that Person in our lives, the powerful simplicity of which we do not want to betray because of the recurrent constraints of space.

Oddly enough, Augustine had at first criticized his idea of the Spirit, at least in the form in which he met it, in his treatise of 393,[30] but he had other encouraging reasons for pursuing the theme. Thirty years previously, Marius Victorinus, whose conversion had impressed him and to whom he owed his knowledge of the 'books of the Platonists', had written:

> Adesto, sancte spiritus, patris et filii copula.
> Tu cum quiescis, pater es, cum procedis, filius,
> In unum qui cuncta nectis, tu es sanctus spiritus.

> Help us, Holy Spirit, you who connect the Father and the Son!
> When you are resting, you are the Father; when you proceed, the Son;
> in binding all in one, you are the Holy Spirit.[31]

Augustine takes as his point of departure the fact that some attributes are common both to the Father and to the Son; these neither contrast them nor

77

distinguish them. Are goodness and holiness, then, the Holy Spirit? Augustine hardly dares to say this;[32] they are the properties of essence. Augustine, however, does not accept this essence or common nature as his starting-point to go on to the Persons. One only has to read his work to set aside this popular idea, which is still encountered here and there. The Bishop of Hippo is firmer and more precise in his commentary on Jn 16:13, a whole section of which he includes in his *De Trinitate*.[33] The Father, he says, is only the Father of the Son and the Son is only the Son of the Father, but the Spirit is the Spirit of both. According to Mt 10:20 and Rom 8:11, he is the Spirit of the Father and, according to Gal 4:6 and Rom 8:9, he is the Spirit of the Son (that is, of Christ). Although he is quite distinct, the Spirit is therefore what is common to the Father and the Son. He is their shared holiness and their love. The unity of the Spirit is established by the bond of peace:

> Whether he is the unity of the other two Persons or their holiness or their love (*charitas*), whether he is their unity because he is their love, and their love because he is their holiness, it is clear that he is not one of the two (other Persons). . . . The Holy Spirit is therefore something that is common to the Father and the Son, whatever he is. This communion, however, is both consubstantial and coeternal. If the term 'friendship' is suitable, then let us use it, but it would be more exact to speak of 'charity'. . . . They are therefore no more than three: the one loving him who has his being from him, the other loving him from whom he has his being, and that love itself. And if that love is nothing, how can God be Love (see 1 Jn 4:8 and 16)? And if he is not substance, how can God be substance?[34]

Augustine insists on the unity of substance and therefore also on equality in that substance. It is not hard to imagine how difficult it was for him to make an effective transition from the essential to the 'notional', that is, to the 'personal' level. In fact, God is charity (or love), but, Augustine asks, 'Is it the Father who is charity, is it the Son, is it the Holy Spirit or is it the Trinity?' He also asks the same question with regard to the other attributes that are at once common to the three Persons and unique to the Father (*memoria*) or the Son (*intelligentia*). 'It is important to recognize that the Persons—all three and each one separately—possess these perfections, each one in his own nature' (*De Trin*. XV, 17, 28). There is a general or essential meaning and a distinctive or personal meaning with which the terms Love (Charity) and Spirit are used. 'God' is Spirit (Jn 4:24), the Father is Spirit and the Son is Spirit. In some scriptural texts, however, the term Love is applied to the Holy Spirit and Augustine mentions and explains 1 Jn 4:7–19 and Rom 5:5 in this context (*De Trin*. XV, 17, 31). There are also other places in Scripture where the same word is used either in a general sense or in a limited and particular sense; 'the Law' or 'Prophet' are examples of this (*De Trin*. XV, 17, 30).

God is Spirit, the Father is Spirit and the Son is Spirit. Just as both are called and each one is called 'Spirit', the same word can also be applied, Augustine believes, to the one who is not one of them, but in whom is manifested *communitas amborum*, the 'community of both' (*In Ioan. ev.* XCIX, 7). Being common to both, the Spirit receives as his own the names that are common to them: 'Spirit' and 'Holy' (*De Trin*. XV, 19, 37).

The Spirit, then, is Spirit and Love of the first two Persons. He must therefore be said to proceed from those Persons, but in the first place from the Father, since the Son derives his being from the Father, although he is also, with the Father, the origin of the Spirit.[35] Augustine cites several texts in Scripture which show that the Spirit also proceeds from the Son. One is Jn 20:22: 'He breathed on them and said to them: "Receive the Holy Spirit" '. Two others are taken from Luke: 6:19 and 8:4–6: 'Power came forth from him'. Augustine gives various examples showing that this *virtus* is the Spirit. He also quotes Jn 15:26, 17:15 and 5:26. It is clear, then, that there is, for him a continuity between 'economy' and 'theology'; this conviction is a characteristic of his Trinitarian theology. For him, the *Filioque* is an obvious necessity, as it was also for Ambrose, who had quite explicitly affirmed it though his theology of the Trinity had been so inspired by the Greek Fathers that he even took whole sections from their writings.

Augustine also discusses Jn 15:26: *qui de Patre procedit*, 'who proceeds from the Father', but does not find it a difficulty. Jesus, he claims, said this in the sense in which he said: 'My teaching is not mine, but his who sent me' (Jn 7:16). He provides an admirable commentary on the latter text (*In Ioan. ev.* XCIX, 8 and 9; cf. *De Trin*. XV, 27, 48). This goes back to the Spirit proceeding in the first place (*principaliter*) from the Father, since the Father gave the Son life in him and the power to communicate that life. Augustine sums up his teaching in the following way:

> According to Holy Scripture, this Holy Spirit is neither only the Spirit of the Father nor only the Spirit of the Son, but is the Spirit of both. Because of this, he is able to teach us that charity which is common both to the Father and to the Son and through which they love each other.[36]

It is clear that the images that Augustine used for the Trinity continued to preoccupy him throughout his treatise. The third term employed in Books VIII to XV of *De Trinitate* is *amor* (or *voluntas*).[37] Although he sees the Spirit as a mutual love (*invicem*), he does not apply the idea of friendship in a special way to the theology of the Trinity. He is clearly not deceived by the value of psychological images, and dissimilarities occur in his writing together with similarities (*De Trin*. XV, 21, 40ff.). Images are nonetheless useful theological tools which he does not hesitate to employ, because they help to point to the difference between the procession of the Word and that of the Spirit and between 'being begotten' and 'proceeding'.[38]

Augustine frequently calls the Holy Spirit 'Gift (of God)'[39] and refers in this context to Scripture (Acts 2:37–38; 8:18–20; 10:44–46; 11:15–17; Eph 4:78). It is true that the Spirit is only 'given' when there are creatures who are capable of 'possessing' and enjoying him, but at the same time he also proceeds eternally as 'giveable' and, in this sense, as Gift, so that this can be regarded as one of his attributes and one of his proper names. When the Spirit is given to us, he unites us to God and each other by the same principle that seals the unity of Love and Peace in God himself. It is not enough to speak here of the created gift of grace, even though it is in effect through that gift that the Spirit is given to us.[40] The Spirit, however, is given as the principle of the Church's unity:

> In our way of speaking, the Holy Spirit is not only the Spirit of the Father and the Son who have given him to us, but also ours, given to us who have received him. It is as in the words 'the deliverance of the Lord' (Ps 3:8), which is the salvation given and our salvation given to us who receive it. The Holy Spirit is therefore the one of God who gives him to us, and ours for us who receive him.[41]
>
> It is because he is common both to the Father and to the Son that they wanted us to have communion with each other and with them, that is to say, through the Holy Spirit, who is God and gift of God.
>
> It is in the Holy Spirit that we are reconciled with God and that we have our delight. . . . It is through the Holy Spirit that the people of God (the Church) are gathered together in unity. . . . Since the remission of sins can only be given in the Holy Spirit, it can only be given in that Church which has the Holy Spirit. . . . The society of unity of the Church of God, outside which there is no remission of sins, is the work of the Holy Spirit, although the Father and the Son clearly collaborate in this, because the Holy Spirit himself is in a sense the society of the Father and the Son. . . . The Spirit is possessed in common by the Father and the Son, because he is the only Spirit of both.[42]

This brings us to the very heart of Augustine's ecclesiology. As I have pointed out elsewhere,[43] Augustine saw the Church as existing at two levels or in two orbs or circles. The first of these is the *communio sacramentorum*, which is the work of Christ, and the second is the *societas sanctorum*, which is the work of the Holy Spirit. Augustine calls this heart of his teaching about the Church *ecclesia in sanctis, unitas, caritas, Pax*. He also calls it *Columba*, since its principle is the Holy Spirit, who performs in the Church that function that is carried out in the body by the soul.[44] This idea can be expressed in contemporary language by saying that there is the *institution* of the Church which comes from Christ, the Word, the sacraments and the ministry, but that, if this institution is to bear the Christian fruit of salvation and communion with God, there must also be the *event* of the Holy Spirit. The word 'event' expresses in this case the values of not being given in advance, of contemporaneity and penetration. If, however, the Church is seen as a whole, the Spirit always dwells in it. Augustine often refers to the Church as the Temple of the Holy Spirit.[45] His view of the Church is also very profound in a truly theo-logical sense; he wants us to believe that God aims to bring us together and unite us to himself by the same Spirit, who is the bond between the Father and the Son, that is, *in Spiritu Sancto, quo in unum Dei populus congregatur*.[46]

80

The part played by the Holy Spirit in the Church and in our personal lives of grace is of the very greatest importance. Augustine became acquainted with the work of the 'Platonists' through Marius Victorinus. It was to them that he owed the idea of *regressus*, that is, the return of the soul to its source. (Centuries later, Thomas Aquinas was to build up his synthesis on the basis of the idea of *egressus* and *reditus*.) The Spirit was seen by Augustine as the end and the seal of intra-divine fertility, who communicates that fertility to us and is also the principle of our return to the Father through the Son. He is also at the deepest level the longing that impels us towards God and causes us to end in him: *donec requiescat in Te*!

NOTES

1. Apart from articles in dictionaries, see J. Lebreton, *Les origines du dogme de la Trinité*, I (Paris, 1919); II: *Histoire du dogme de la Trinité* (Paris, 1928), II. B. Swete, *The Holy Spirit in the Ancient Church* (London, 1912); T. Ruesch, *Die Entstehung der Lehre vom Heiligen Geist* (Zürich, 1953); G. L. Prestige, *God in Patristic Thought* (London and Toronto, 1936; repub. London, 1952); G. Kretschmar, *Studien zur frühchristlichen Trinitätstheologie* (Tübingen, 1956); *idem*, 'Le développement de la doctrine du Saint-Esprit du Nouveau Testament à Nicée', *Verbum Caro*, 88 (1962), 5–55; H. Opitz, *Ursprünge frühchristlicher Pneumatologie* (Berlin, 1960). For the Stoic context, see G. Verbeke, *L'evolution de la doctrine du Pneuma du stoïcisme à S. Augustin* (Paris, 1945); M. Spanneut, *Le Stoïcisme des Pères de l'Eglise de Clément de Rome à Clément d'Alexandrie* (Paris, 1957). For the Gnostic context, see A. Orbe, *La teología del Espíritu Santo (Estudios Valentinianos, IV)* (Rome, 1960).
2. *PG* 36, 161; cf. Anselm of Havelberg, *Dialogi* I, 6 (*PL* 188, 1147D; *SC* 118, p. 62).
3. See the *Shepherd of Hermas*, cc. 41; 58; 59, 5–6; 78, 1 (numbering of chapters according to R. Joly, *SC* 53 [1958]); see also Justin, *1 Apol*. 39.
4. See P. Smulders, 'Esprit Saint', *Dictionnaire de Spiritualité*, IV/2, col. 1274.
5. See E. Schweizer, '*pneuma*', *TDNT*, VI, pp. 401, esp. note 440, 451, note 842.
6. Justin, *1 Apol*. 61, 3, not quoting Mt 28:19; nor do the texts of Irenaeus' *Demonstration* quoted below, whereas, fifteen years before this, Irenaeus referred explicitly to Mt 28:19 as the Lord's words: see *Adv. haer*. III, 17, 1 (*PG* 7, 929; ed. W. W. Harvey, II, p. 92). See also *1 Apol* 67 for the Eucharist.
7. *Dem*. 3 (Fr. tr. L.-M. Froidevaux, *SC* 62, p. 32 [Paris, 1959]). See also *Adv. haer*. III, 17, 1 (*SC* 211, pp. 328ff.).
8. *Dem*. 7 (*SC* 62, p. 41). The text continues: 'Those who have the Spirit of God are led to the Word, that is, to the Son, but the Son presents (them) to the Father and the Father obtains incorruptibility (for them). Without the Spirit, then, it is not (possible) to see the Son of God and, without the Son, no one can approach the Father, since knowledge of the Father (is through) the Son and knowledge of the Son (is) through the Holy Spirit. As for the Spirit, it is according to whether it pleases the Father that the Son dispenses (him) as a minister to whom the Father wishes and as he wishes': see also chapter 99. For Irenaeus' pneumatology, see A. d'Alès, 'La doctrine de l'Esprit Saint chez S. Irénée', *RSR*, 14 (1924), 496–538; H.-J. Jaschke, *Der Heilige Geist im Bekenntnis der Kirche. Eine Studie zur Pneumatologie bei Irenäus von Lyon im Ausgang vom altchristlichem Glaubensbekenntnis* (Münster, 1977).
9. P. Meinhold, 'Pneumatomachoi', Pauly-Wissowa, *Real-Encyclopädie der classischen*

Altertumswissenschaft, XXI/1 (1951), cols 1066–1101; W. D. Hauschild, *Die Pneumatomachen* (Hamburg, 1967). The error of the Pneumatomachi was attributed to Macedonius, who was Bishop of Constantinople from 342 to 360. According to the Pneumatomachi, the being and the activity of the Holy Spirit were not those of a divine Person.

10. Athanasius, *Ad Ser. Ep*. I, 28 (*PG* 26, 593 and 596); *Ep*. III, 6 (*PG* 26, 633; the Spirit is not a different substance, *allotrioousion*); IV, 7 (*PG* 26, 648; Fr. tr. J. Lebon, *SC* 15 (1947)). The same argument is also found about 380 in Italy, in Faustinus, *De Trin*. VII, 3 (*PL* 13, 78). Hilary of Poitiers made a connection, in 355–356, between his confession of the three Persons and the text of Mt 28:19; see *De Trin*. II, 1 (*PL* 10, 50–51).

11. Basil of Caesarea, *De spir. sanct.* (Fr. tr. B. Pruche, *SC* 17bis (1968)). To the bibliography given in this translation, pp. 243ff., should be added the following contributions to *Verbum Caro*, 89 (1968): B. Bobrinskoy, 'Liturgie et ecclésiologie trinitaire de S. Basile', 1–32; J.-M. Hornus, 'La divinité du Saint-Esprit comme condition de salut personnel selon Basile', 33–62; T.-F. Torrance, 'Spiritus creator', 63–85; P. C. Christou, 'L'enseignement de S. Basile sur le Saint-Esprit', 86–99.

12. *Ep*. 125, 3 (*PG* 32, 549; in 373); 159, 2 (*PG* 32, 620–621; in 373); 226, 3 (*PG* 32, 849; in 375).

13. The text will be found in *DS*, 150 and in *Conciliorum Œcumenicorum Decreta* (= *COD*), J. Alberigo *et al.*, 3rd ed. (Bologna, 1973), p. 24 with a short history and bibliography, pp. 21–23. This creed was only presented as such and as having come from the 150 Fathers of the Council in 381 by the Council of Chalcedon (451): see the bibliography in *COD, op. cit*.

14. *COD*, pp. 25–30.

15. For the letter *Ea gratia*, see *DS*, 145; Synod, *DS*, 152–177. I am following dates given in *DS*, although C. Pietri, *Roma Christiana* (Rome, 1976), pp. 828ff., dates these texts to 377.

16. Athanasius, *Ad Ser. Ep*. I, 22ff. (*PG* 26, 584ff.; *SC* 15, pp. 127ff.).

17. Gregory Nazianzen, *Orat. theol*. V, 28 (*PG* 36, 165). W. Jaeger, who specialized in the study of Gregory of Nyssa, showed that, in Christian teaching, humanity is completed in the holiness of which the Spirit is the principle. See *Gregor von Nyssa's Lehre vom Heiligen Geist, aus dem Nachlass* (ed. H. Dörries, Leiden, 1966).

18. See Gregory Nazianzen, *Orat. theol*. V, 28 (*PG* 36, 165); Didymus, *De Trin*. II, 7 (*PG* 39, 560–600); Cyril of Alexandria in N. Charlier, 'La doctrine sur le Saint-Esprit dans le "Thesaurus" de S. Cyrille d'Alexandrie', *Studia Patristica*, II, pp. 187ff.; G. M. de Durand has edited and Fr. tr. Cyril's *Dialogues on the Trinity*, Vol. I, *SC* 231; Theodore of Mopsuestia, *Hom. cat.* 9, 15; Augustine, *Ep*. 238, 21 (*PL* 33, 1046).

19. R. Piault, 'Tertullien a-t-il été subordinatien?' *RSPT*, 47 (1963), 181–204; J. Moingt, 'Théologie trinitaire de Tertullien', *RSR*, 54 (1966), 337–369; *idem*, *Théologie trinitaire de Tertullien*, 3 vols and one volume of tables (*Théologie*, 68, 69, 70) (Paris, 1966)—a total of 1,094 pages!

20. Tertullian, *Adv. Prax*. 8–9 (*PL* 2, 163–164; *CC* 2, 1168–1169).

21. Piault, *op. cit.*, 204.

22. *DS*, 126.

23. *Ep*. 15 to Pope Damasus (*PL* 22, 356–357): 'Speaking of three hypostases. . . . The entire school of profane literature recognizes only ousia as hypostasis. Who, I ask you, would speak of three substances?' An echo of this can be found in Thomas Aquinas, *ST* Ia, q. 29, a. 3, ad 3; q. 30, a. 1, ad 1. Augustine was more serene and also went deeper: 'To speak of what cannot be expressed, we have to express as we can what cannot be explained. The Greeks among us (*a nostris Graecis*) used the terms "one essence, three substances", whereas the Latins spoke of "one essence or substance, three persons" ' (*De Trin*. VII, 4, 7; cf. 6, 11; *Bibl. August.*, XV, pp. 527, 541; cf. p. 584).

24. *DS*, 421.

25. Hilary, *De Trin.* II, 2 (*PL* 10, 51), in 355.
26. See O. Casel, 'Art und Sinn des ältesten christlichen Osterfeier', *Jahrbuch für Liturgiewis-senschaft*, 14 (1938), 1, 78; J. Daniélou, *Bible et Liturgie (Lex Orandi*, 11) (Paris, 1951), pp. 429–448; G. Kretschmar, 'Himmelfahrt und Pfingsten', *Zeitschrift für Kirchen-geschichte*, 66 (1954–1955), 209–253; see especially R. Cabié, *La Pentecôte. L'évolution de la cinquantaine pascale au cours des cinq premiers siècles* (Tournai and Paris, 1965), with a bibliography, pp. 11–14. See also 'Esprit Saint', *Dictionnaire de Spiritualité*, IV/2, col. 1285.
27. See Emmanuel-Pataq Siman, *L'expérience de l'Esprit par l'Eglise d'après la tradition syrienne d'Antioche (Théologie historique*, 15) (Paris, 1971); cf. P. Rancillac, *L'Eglise, manifestation de l'Esprit chez S. Jean Chrysostome* (Dar Al-Kalima, Lebanon, 1970).
28. Augustine, *De fid. et symb.* IX, the beginning of 18 and 19 (*PL* 40, 190 and 191).
29. *De Trin.*; *PL* 42; Latin text, with Fr. tr. and explanatory notes by M. Mellet and T. Camelot in *Bibl. August.*, Vol. 15 (1955). by P. Agaësse and J. Moingt, Vol. 16 (1955). For the Trinitarian theology of Augustine, see the classic studies by M. Schmaus (1927), I. Chevalier (1940) and O. du Roy (1956). For his pneumatology, see F. Cavallera, 'La doctrine de saint Augustin sur l'Esprit Saint à propos du "De Trinitate"', *RTAM*, 2 (1930), 365–387; 3 (1931), 5–19; I. Chevalier, *S. Augustin et la pensée grecque. Les relations trinitaires* (Fribourg, 1940); 'La théorie augustinienne des relations trinitaires. Analyse explicative des textes', *Divus Thomas*, 18 (1940), 317–384; M. Nédoncelle, 'L'intersubjectivité humaine est-elle pour S. Augustin une image de la Trinité?' *Augus-tinus Magister* (Paris, 1954), I, pp. 595–602; O. du Roy, 'L'expérience de l'amour et l'intelligence de la foi trinitaire selon S. Augustin', *Recherches augustiniennes*, 2 (1962), 415–445; P. Smulders, 'L'Esprit Saint chez les Pères', *Dictionnaire de Spiritualité*, IV/2, cols 1279–1283; F. Bourassa, *Questions de théologie trinitaire* (Rome, 1970); B. de Margerie, *La Trinité chrétienne dans l'histoire (Théologie historique*, 31) (Paris, 1975), pp. 159–172; E. Bailleux, 'L'Esprit du Père et du Fils selon saint Augustin', *RThom*, 77 (1977), 5–29.
30. *De fid. et symb.* IX, 19 (*PL* 40, 191): 'Some have dared to believe that the communion between the Father and the Son, that is, if I may say it, the deity that the Greeks call *theoteta*, may be the Holy Spirit. . . . This deity that they also want to understand of the mutual love of the two and of the charity that they (the Father and the Son) have for each other is, according to them, called the Holy Spirit.' Later, in his treatise *De haeresibus*, Augustine was to say that these 'some' were Semi-Arians and Macedonians who denied the personality of the Holy Spirit: see B. de Margerie, *op. cit.*, p. 161, note 180.
31. First hymn, lines 3–5 (Fr. tr. P. Hadot, *SC* 68 (Paris, 1960), pp. 620–621); cf. the Third Hymn, lines 245–246 (*ibid.*, pp. 650–651). Victorinus, however, has his own theology of the Trinity, which does not contain any idea of a procession on the part of the Holy Spirit.
32. *De Civ. Dei*, XI, 24 (*PL* 41, 337ff.).
33. *In Ioan. ev.* XCIX, 6–9 (*PL* 35, 1888–1890); *De Trin.* XV. 27, 48.
34. *De Trin.* VI, 5, 7; this translation is slightly changed, but is based on the Fr. tr. of Mellet and Camelot (see above, note 29). The text can be compared with the following, among others: 'Ecce tria sunt ergo, amans, et quod amatur, et amor' (*De Trin.* VIII, 14; *PL* 42, 960); 'Spiritus est Patris et Filii, tamquam charitas substantialis et consubstantialis amborum' (*In Ioan. ev.* CV, 3; *PL* 35, 1904).
35. 'I say "in the first place" (*principaliter*) because it is established that the Holy Spirit also proceeds from the Son. But the Father gives this privilege to the Son. It is not that the Son ever existed without having it, but everything that the Father has ever given to his only Word has been given to him by begetting him. He has therefore begotten him in such a way that their shared Gift proceeded also from the Son and that the Holy Spirit is spirit of the other two Persons' (*De Trin.* XV, 17, 29; cf. 26, 45–47).
36. *De Trin.* XV, 17, 27 (*Bibl. August.*, Vol. 16, p. 501).
37. Table in *Bibl. August.*, Vol. 16, pp. 586ff.; cf. pp. 593ff.

38 *De Trin*. XV, 27, 50: '(What is) suggested is the outline of a distinction between birth and procession, since to understand by thinking is not the same as desiring or even enjoying by the will' (*Bibl. August.*, Vol. 16, p. 563).

39. *De Trin*. V, 11, 12; 12, 13; 15, 16; VII, 4, 7; XV, 17, 29; 18, 32; 19, 33; 27, 50. F. Cavallera, *op. cit.* (note 29), pp. 368–370, has given a full account of this.

40. 'It is, I think, for a good reason that the Lord speaks in the gospel of John so many times and in such a striking way of unity—his unity with the Father or our unity among ourselves—without ever saying that we and they are one, but always saying (Jn 17:20) "that they may all be one *even as* we are one" ' (*De Trin*. VI, 3, 4; *Bibl. August*. Vol. 16, p. 479); 'It is what we are commanded to imitate in the order of grace' (*De Trin*. VI, 5, 7; Vol. 16, p. 485). J. Moingt has rightly insisted on this aspect of Augustine's teaching, but, in my opinion, has not gone far enough in exploring his thought in *Bibl. August.*, Vol. 16, pp. 655–656.

41. *De Trin*. V, 14, 15 (*Bibl. August.*, Vol. 16, p. 459).

42. *Sermo* 71, 12, 18; 12, 19 and 17, 28; 20, 33 (*PL* 38, 454; 455 and 459; 463–464). This sermon has been dated to about 419.

43. See my general introduction to *Traités antidonatistes*, *Bibl. August.*, Vol. 28 (Paris, 1963), pp. 100–124.

44. *In Ioan. ev*. XXVI, 6, 13 (*PL* 35, 1612–1613); XXVII, 6, 6 (*PL* 35, 1618); *Sermo* 267, 4 (*PL* 38, 1231); 268, 2 (*PL* 38, 1232–1233). The last text is quoted, together with those of John Chrysostom, Didymus, Thomas Aquinas, Leo XIII and Pius XII, to illustrate this theme in the Dogmatic Constitution *Lumen Gentium*, 7, 7, on the Church.

45. See D. Sanchis, 'Le symbolisme communautaire du Temple chez S. Augustin', *RAM*, 37 (1961), 3–30, 137–147.

46. *Sermo* 71, 12, 18–20, 33 (*PL* 38, 454–464); *De Trin*. XV, 21, 41 (*PL* 42, 1087).

THE THEME OF THE
HOLY SPIRIT AS THE MUTUAL LOVE
OF THE FATHER AND THE SON[1]

The story of this theme is studded with the reflections of various great Christian thinkers who have followed one another and have been acquainted with the work of their predecessors, which they may have accepted or corrected. These great thinkers were all members of the Western Church, since there is hardly any evidence of this theme in the Eastern Church.[2] In this chapter, we shall consider above all Anselm, Achard and Richard of Saint-Victor, Bonaventure and Thomas Aquinas.

Anselm (1033–1109) wrote his *Monologion* about 1070, when he was the ✓ Abbot of Bec, and his *De Processione Spiritus Sancti* after the Council of Bari, in which he took part in 1098 with the Greeks, as Archbishop of Canterbury, during one of his periods of exile. Just as it would be controversial to call Augustine an 'essentialist', so too would it be restricting the theological legacy of Augustine to only one aspect of his teaching if Anselm were to be called an Augustinian. Anselm does not treat of the Holy Spirit as the mutual Love of the Father and the Son. What he does is to extend the anthropological analogy, but he does this not in the psychological, but in the metaphysical sense that came naturally to him.[3] In the *Monologion*, he deduces the existence of a Word and a Love from the perfection that it is necessary to attribute to the *Summus Spiritus*. It is, according to Anselm, not possible to deny that this Supreme Spirit is capable of an act of understanding and therefore of saying; the Word thus expressed is perfect similarity and therefore also consubstantial and the Son. But the one who remembers himself and knows himself necessarily also loves himself, and this forms the basis for the existence of the third Person (*Mon.* 49). In this Supreme Spirit, however, Memory is the Father and Understanding is the Son. It is therefore evident that Love proceeds from both (*Mon.* 51) and does so as from a single principle (*Mon.* 53). H. F. Dondaine observed correctly that 'there is a difference of perspective between Augustine and Anselm. In the case of the latter, the friendship of the Father and the Son is no longer the principle by which the second divine procession is explained. This friendship is only a secondary consideration and is seen as an aspect assumed by divine Love, when this is considered in the Father and the Son. Anselm introduces the third Person first and foremost as the Love of the Supreme Spirit proceeding from his memory and his thought (*Mon*. 50).'

In *De Processione*, Anselm develops the argument outlined by Augustine—an argument which Thomas Aquinas was later to recognize as having an absolute value in favour of the *Filioque* that could not be refuted. This is that, in God, everything is one at the point where there is no opposition in relationship.

It would be impossible to overestimate the genius of Anselm, but it has to be said that his deduction is too closely related to that of faculties or properties from an essence. How is it that he, as a man of prayer, was not able to express more clearly the demands made by the personalization of the three Persons, whom he calls the *tres nescio quid* (*Mon*. 78)?

One of the greatest mystics and theologians of the Middle Ages, William (†1148), who left Liège to become Abbot of Saint-Thierry near Rheims, wrote, in 1119–1120, a treatise *De contemplando Deo* (*SC* 61, Paris, 1959). In it, he comments on these words in Jesus' high priestly prayer (Jn 17:22–23, 26): 'The glory which thou hast given me I have given to them, that they may be one even as we are one, I in them and thou in me, . . . that the love with which thou hast loved me may be in them and I in them'. In this meditation, which is written in the form of a prayer, William reaches the greatest depths of knowledge of our communion with the mystery of God. Here is this prayer, based on F. Bourdeau's French translation in *Les quatre saisons, Automne* (Paris, 1977):

> You love yourself, O most lovable Lord, in yourself, when, from the Father and the Son, the Holy Spirit proceeds—the Holy Spirit who is the love of the Father for the Son and the love of the Son for the Father, such a sublime love that it is the unity of both, such a deep unity that, of the Father and the Son, the substance is one.
>
> And you love yourself in us, when, having sent the Spirit of your Son into our hearts, by the sweetness of the love and the warmth of the good will that you inspire in us, crying 'Abba, Father', you cause us to love you with a great love. You also love yourself in us so much that we, who hope in you and cherish your name of Lord, . . . who dare to believe by the grace of your Spirit of adoption that everything that belongs to the Father is also ours and who are your adopted sons, call you by the same name that your only natural son used for you!
>
> In this way, such a firm bond, such a clinging and such a strong taste of your sweetness comes about that our Lord, your Son, called it 'unity', when he said: 'that they may be one in us'. And this unity has such dignity and glory that he added: 'As I and you are one'. O joy, O glory, O wealth, O pride—for wisdom also has its pride! . . .
>
> We therefore love you, or rather you love yourself in us, we loving with affection, you loving with effectiveness, making us one in you by your own unity, or rather by your own Holy Spirit, whom you have given to us. . . .

> Adorable, terrible and blessed one, give him to us! Send your Spirit and
> everything will be created and you will renew the face of the earth. . . . May the
> dove bearing the olive branch come! . . . Sanctify us with your holiness! Unite us
> with your unity!

Richard, Prior of Saint-Victor in Paris, who died in 1175, wrote a treatise *De
Trinitate* (*SC* 63, Paris, 1959; Fr. tr. G. Salet), although it has been established that his teaching follows that of Achard of Saint-Victor.[4] His
approach is also very similar to that of Anselm, in that he introduces reasons
that are not only probable, but also necessary,[5] but he ends by building up a
very different structure, which is much more directly linked to prayer and
personal experience. He also claims that we must attribute to God what we
regard as supreme in our scale of values (*De Trin*. 1, 20). That supreme value
is love, *caritas*. This idea makes it possible for the two affirmations that faith
and prayer make us confess to be combined: *tres*, three, and yet *unus*, one
(see the Creed *Quicumque*). For *caritas* calls for a multiplicity of subjects—
there is a transition here from essentialism to personalism, and Richard
works out a new definition of the person. But even this is not saying enough,
for we have to go further and speak of a charity that is perfect, since that is
what we have to attribute to God (3, 2 and 5). This perfect charity requires a
consortium amoris (3, 11), that is, a loving together of a third and an
enabling together of that third to share in the happiness of the first two. The
Spirit is therefore postulated as the *condilectus* of the Father and the Son (3,
11 and 19; 6, 6; Salet translates this word as 'a common friend': see p. 192,
note 2; he also calls it 'a third equally loved'). It is clear, then, that Richard of
Saint-Victor follows Augustine (whom he quotes 87 times[6]) and Anselm
(whom he quotes 44 times), but, instead of speaking of understanding and
will, he deduces everything from love. The prayerful confession of faith—
tres who are *unus*—is translated into 'one Love and three lovers'.

As it is not my aim to outline a history of the theology of the Trinity here, I
shall not discuss the teachings of Alexander of Hales, although I would not
want to overlook the importance of his *Summa*. It would not, however, be
possible to leave out Alexander's disciple Bonaventure, who combined in
his work the precise formulations of his master and an inheritance from
Augustine and Richard of Saint-Victor.[7] He was undoubtedly in sympathy
with Richard's theology of unselfish and communicative love. This is clear
from his statement: 'Mutual love is more perfect than love of oneself.
Mutual love that communicates itself is even more perfect, since the one who
is not inclined to communicate has a flavour of desire' (*In I Sent*. d. 10, a. 1, q.
1). J.-G. Bougerol has defined Bonaventure's understanding of this love in
the following way: 'Essential love or the love with which each person loves
himself and with which each person loves the other two is *complacentia*.
Notional love or the love in which the Father and the Son are united in

spirating the Holy Spirit is the love of *concordia* or *dilectio*. Personal love is produced by the Holy Spirit, by means of liberality, of the *concordia* of the Father and the Son.'[8] The Spirit is the *nexus* or bond between the two. For us, he is Gift. As Bonaventure himself says: 'Spirit, Love and Gift all refer to the same reality, but to different aspects of it. They are different names for the same emanation. "Spirit" expresses that emanation mainly by reference to the power that produces it. "Love" expresses it mainly with regard to its mode of emanation, that is, as a *nexus*. "Gift" expresses it with regard to the relationship which is the consequence of it, . . . (because) it is made to unite us (*connectare*)' (*In I Sent*. d. 18, a. 1, q. 3, ad 4). The Spirit is the principle of our return to God.

Throughout the whole of his career as a theologian, Thomas Aquinas was open to the idea, which had come down to him from a long and deeply rooted tradition, of the Holy Spirit as the bond of love between the Father and the Son.[9] What part did Thomas make the Spirit play in his attempt to account intellectually for the mystery of the Trinity, which was not accessible to natural reason and transcended all human explanation, even within the framework of faith? It was, in his opinion, only possible to look for an *intellectus* of what faith enables us to hold by using the resources available to human reason. The theme of mutual love meant a great deal to the religious and poetical aspects of man and there is undoubtedly a deep relationship between prayer and poetry, but Thomas did not believe that this theme had sufficient intellectual force to provide a basis for organizing the treatise on the Trinity. He did not employ it in his *Contra Gentiles*, his *Compendium Theologiae* or the very important articles at the beginning of the *Summa*: Ia, q. 27, a. 3 ('Is there in God another procession other than the begetting of the Word?') and a. 4 ('Is the procession of love in God a begetting?'). This theme can, however, be found in the *Summa* in Thomas' statements concerning the procession from the Father *and* the Son (q. 36, a. 4, ad 1), his attempts to explain that, as the bond between the two, the Spirit was not a term, but a *medius* (q. 37, a. 1, ad 3) and finally his attempts to elucidate certain traditional expressions (q. 37, a. 2; q. 39, a. 8). He preserved Augustine's analogy derived from the structure of the spirit[10] and given special emphasis by Anselm, whose train of thought Thomas followed. There is a clear expression of the Augustinian image of the Trinity in his *Compendium Theologiae*:

> Three aspects of man can be considered here: man existing in his nature, man existing in his intellect and man existing in his love. These three aspects are, however, not one, since thinking here is not being, nor is loving; and only one of the three is a subsisting reality, that is, man existing in his own nature. In God, however, being, knowing and loving are one, with the result that God existing in his own natural being, God existing in his intellect and God existing in his love are only one, each of the three being one subsisting reality.[11]

Presented in this way, this view has rather too philosophical a character, however valuable it may otherwise be, and shows the spirit as three times in itself. If this statement had been made by Hegel, it would have aroused great interest! It might also lead us to believe that Thomas thought of the Persons on the basis of essence, as modes or faculties. This, however, is not the case, as A. Malet, E. Bailleux and others have shown. Everything active in God was, for Thomas, done by Persons (*actiones sunt suppositorum*). The essential knowledge and love of self exist only as hypostasized in personal subjects, which can be distinguished only by the opposition in the relationships which constitute them. These relationships are established in the divine substance, which is absolute existence, and are therefore themselves subsisting, in other words, they make the Persons exist according to the divine substance, the first *sub ratione intellectus*, under the aspect of knowledge (although the Word is *spirans amorem*: see *Comm. in ev. Ioan.* c. 6, lect. 5, no. 5) and the second *sub ratione voluntatis*, under the aspect of will or love. 'The Person in God signifies the relationship in the mode of substance.'[12] In these conditions, as Thomas explained in his *Summa*:

> It is necessary to state that the Holy Spirit proceeds from the Son. If he did not proceed from him, it would not be possible to distinguish the one from the other. This goes back to our previous arguments. In fact, it is not possible to say that the divine Persons can be distinguished one from the other by any absolute thing. If this were so, it would follow that the three were not a single essence, since every absolute attribute in God belongs to the unity of essence. It is clear, then, that the divine Persons can only be distinguished from each other by their relationships. These relationships, however, can be used to distinguish the Persons only insofar as they are opposed. The evidence of this is that the Father has two relationships; he is related by the one to the Son and by the other to the Spirit. As these relationships are not opposed to each other, however, they do not constitute two Persons, but only belong to one Person, that of the Father. If, then, it is only possible to find in the Son and the Holy Spirit these two relationships, each of which refers to the Father, these relationships will not be mutually opposed, just as the two relationships between the Father and each of them are not opposed. Just as the Father is only one Person, then, it would follow that the Son and the Holy Spirit would only be one Person possessing two relationships opposed to the two relationships of the Father. This, however, is a heresy, since it destroys faith in the Trinity. It is therefore necessary for the Son and the Holy Spirit to refer to each other by opposed relationships. In God, however, the only opposed relationships there can be are relationships of origin, and these opposed relationships of origin are, on the one hand, relationships of principle and, on the other, of term resulting from that principle. It is therefore necessary to say either that the Son proceeds from the Holy Spirit—but no one says this—or that the Holy Spirit proceeds from the Son—which is what we confess.
>
> The explanation that we have given above of their respective procession is in accordance with this teaching. It has been said that the Son proceeds according to the mode that is peculiar to the intellect, as Word, and that the Holy Spirit proceeds according to the mode that is peculiar to the will, as Love. Love,

however, has of necessity to proceed from the word, since we can love nothing but what we can apprehend in a conception of the mind. On this basis, then, it should be clear that the Holy Spirit proceeds from the Son (*ST* Ia, q. 36, a. 2).[13]

I have carefully re-read, in chronological order, the various accounts of Thomas Aquinas of the Trinity and the studies that have been devoted to this subject (see below, note 9) and the most acceptable explanations and conclusions have, in my opinion, been provided by H. F. Dondaine. I give a few extracts from his study:[14]

To defend the territory acquired by Anselm in his synthesis, Thomas relegates mutual love to the second level. It is not invoked to introduce the second procession in q. 27, it is recalled as a traditional datum which has to be taken into account in theory in q. 37 and it is taken into account exactly as it is by Anselm in ad 3. . . .

Thomas often has recourse to this aspect of the Holy Spirit as the *nexus duorum*. His aim is to safeguard Augustine's datum (whatever may be the case with Richard of Saint-Victor) and he does not forget that the Holy Spirit is the bond of love uniting the Father and the Son. *It is clear, however, that he does not regard this as a suitable context in which to introduce the mystery of the third Person*; to do this would expose him to the danger of anthropomorphism and those inequalities and oppositions which caused Richard's disciples to stumble.[15]

In fact, the metaphor of love as the 'bond between lovers' cannot be raised above the image. What two friends have in common to unite them is not the reality experienced in their act of love. Each experiences his own act, which makes two loves, two acts of loving. What they have in common is the object and their common good. . . . But it is to this one object, their community in good, that they adapt their two hearts and their two wills by two loves. It is useless to change the image by speaking, for example, about a single breath, one kiss,[16] one balm or one single liquor distilled from the two. These images are not capable of grasping the mystery of the origin of the Holy Spirit in an intelligible way. It is clear that this mystery contains only one act, only one spiration and only one 'loving' that is common to both loving Persons, but this is so *because of the unity of essence*, not because of friendship as such. . . .

It is therefore illuminating and very interesting to present the Holy Spirit as the friendship of the Father and the Son or the mutual Love of the Father and the Son. This view can, however, not be used metaphysically, since it does not provide a consistent analogy for our understanding of the Person of the Holy Spirit. The other way of presenting the Holy Spirit, that is, as the Love which God bears for his Goodness or the Love that proceeds from the divine Knower and Lover, and from his Word, is much plainer, but it is more certain, and Thomas preferred it to introduce in a rational way the procession of the third Person.

NOTES

1. In addition to F. Bourassa, *Questions de théologie trinitaire* (Rome, 1970) and B. de Margerie, *La Trinité chrétienne dans l'histoire* (*Théologie historique*, 31) (Paris, 1975), see H. F. Dondaine, 'Saint Thomas et la Procession du Saint-Esprit', *S. Thomas d'Aquin, Somme Théologique. La Trinité*, II (Paris, 1946), pp. 387–409; A. Malet, *Personne et*

amour dans la théologie trinitaire de saint Thomas d'Aquin (Bibl. Thom., XXXII) (Paris, 1956).

2. Almost the only Greek author who can be quoted here is Epiphanius of Salamis, *Ancoratus*, VII, 'Sundesmos tēs Triados' (*PG* 43, 28B).

3. R. Perrino, *La dottrina trinitaria di S. Anselmo nel quadro del suo metodo teologico e del suo concetto di Dio* (*Studia Anselmiana*, 29) (Rome, 1952); A. Malet, *op. cit.*, pp. 55–59.

4. A. M. Ethier, *Le De Trinitate de Richard de Saint-Victor* (Paris and Ottawa, 1939); G. Dumeige, *Richard de Saint-Victor et l'idée chrétienne de l'amour* (Paris, 1952); A. Malet, *op. cit.*, pp. 37–42; O. González, *Misterio Trinitario y existencia humana. Estudio histórico teológico en torno a San Buenaventura* (Madrid, 1966), pp. 295–363. For Achard of Saint-Victor, see J. Ribaillier's edition of Richard's *De Trinitate* (1958); J. Chatillon, *Théologie et spiritualité dans l'œuvre oratoire d'A. de St-Victor* (Paris, 1969).

5. Richard of Saint-Victor, *De Trin.* 1, 4. M.-D. Chenu has observed, correctly, that 'the *necessariae rationes*, following St Anselm, continued to influence the school': see his *Introduction à l'étude de S. Thomas* (Paris, 1950), p. 158.

6. Richard also resumes and defines more precisely Augustine's argument about the Holy Spirit as the Love of the Father and the Son: *Quomodo Spiritus Sanctus est Amor Patris et Filii* (*PL* 196, 1011–1012).

7. J.-F. Bonnefoy, *Le Saint-Esprit et ses dons selon S. Bonaventure* (Paris, 1929); A. Malet, *op. cit.* (note 1), pp. 42–48 (Alexander), 48–53 (Bonaventure); O. González, *op. cit.* (note 4). To these works can also be added monographs by J. Kaup (1927), Z. Alszeghy (1946) and P. Prentice (1951) on Bonaventure's theology of love. Our knowledge of the Franciscan school is continuously being increased by historical research. The following recent works are worth consulting: W. H. Principe, 'St. Bonaventure's Theology of the Holy Spirit with Reference to the Expression "Pater et Filius diligunt se Spiritu Sancto" ', *S. Bonaventura: 1274–1974*, IV (Grottaferrata, 1974), pp. 243–269; idem, 'Odo Rigaldus, a Precursor of St Bonaventure on the Holy Spirit as Effectus formalis in the Mutual Love of the Father and Son', *Mediaeval Studies*, XXXIX (1977), 498–505.

8. J. F. Bougerol (ed.), *Lexique Saint Bonaventure* (Paris, 1969), pp. 16ff., 'Amor', with references.

9. See the following texts, among others: *In I Sent.* d. 10, q. 1, a. 3; d. 32, q. 1, a. 1, ad 4 (in 1254); *De Pot.* q. 9, a. 9, ad 2; q. 10, a. 2, ad 15 ('cum enim Spiritus Sanctus sit amor mutuus et nexus duorum, oportet quod a duobus spiretur') and a. 4, ad 10; a. 5, ad 11 (in 1256?); *Resp. ad 108 art.* a. 25 ('procedit ut nexus duorum'; in 1265–1266); *ST* Ia, q. 36, a. 4, ad 1 ('Si considerentur supposita spirationis, sic Spiritus Sanctus procedit a Patre et Filio un sunt plures. Procedit enim ab eis ut amor unitivus duorum'); q. 37, a. 1, ad 3 (the whole); q. 39, a. 8, where Thomas considers the opinions of several of the doctors of the Church (in 1267). See also J. Slipyi, *De Principio Spirationis in SS. Trinitate* (Lwow, 1926); M.-T. L. Penido, ' "Cur non Spiritus Sanctus a Patre Deo Genitus". S. Augustin et S. Thomas', *RThom*, 13 (1930), 508–527; idem, *Le rôle de l'analogie en théologie dogmatique* (*Bibl. Thom.*, XV) (Paris, 1931), pp. 295–311, also published in *ETL*, 8 (1931), 5–16 under the title 'La valeur de la théorie psychologique de la Trinité'; idem, 'Gloses sur la procession d'amour dans la Trinité', *ETL*, 14 (1937), 33–68; H. F. Dondaine, *op. cit.* (note 1); A. Malet, *op. cit.* (*ibid.*); C. Vagaggini, 'La hantise des *rationes necessariae* de S. Anselme dans la théologie des processions trinitaires de S. Thomas', *Spicilegium Beccense*, I (*Congrès internationale du IXᵉ centenaire de l'arrivée d'Anselme au Bec*) (Paris, 1959), pp. 103–139; E. Bailleux, 'Le personnalisme de S. Thomas en théologie trinitaire', *RThom*, 61 (1961), 35–38; F. Bourassa and B. de Margerie, *op. cit.* (note 1).

10. *De Pot.* q. 9, a. 5: 'Ad manifestationem aliqualem hujus quaestionis, et praecipue secundum quod Augustinus eam manifestat'.

11. Chapter 50, translated by Dondaine, *op. cit.*, II, p. 406, note 1; cf. *C. Gent.* IV, 26.

12. *In I Sent.* d. 23, a. 3, sol.; or 'the relationship as it subsists in the divine nature': *ST* Ia, q. 29, a. 4; q. 39, a. 1.

13. Cf. *C. Gent*. IV, 24; *De Pot*. q. 10, a. 5; *Comm. in ev. Ioan*. c. 15, lect. 6.

14. H. F. Dondaine, *op. cit*. (note 1), II, pp. 397–401.

15. The danger, to which Dondaine pointed, of anthropormophism in the theme of the Spirit as the mutual love of the Father and the Son can be illustrated by several of the formulae found in the otherwise deep and edifying books of Yves Raguin: see especially *La Profondeur de Dieu* (Collection *Christus*, 33) (1973) and *L'Esprit sur le Monde* (Collection *Christus*, 40) (1975). Some of these formulae, seen from the point of view of the strict theology of the Trinity, are not exact and to some extent ambiguous; see, for example, 'life of relationships in God' (*La Profondeur*, p. 137); 'the persons are centres of action and consciousness; this consciousness is a consciousness that is totally mutual' (p. 138); 'the Father is Father in the depths of the Son; the Son is Son in the depths of the Father; this relationship is the Love of both, which is called the Spirit' (p. 159); 'in the Trinity, it is the relationship which we call the Holy Spirit that is the ultimate depth of God; that Spirit is both the relationship that unites the Father to his Son and the ultimate intimacy of that relationship' (*L'Esprit*, p. 16); 'the relationship of the Father and the Son is united in the Spirit' (p. 7); 'between these three, if it is possible to speak of "three", what matters is not the number, but the fact that there is, in their total identity, a constant relationship of knowledge and love' (p. 27). In all these texts, the word 'relationship' is used in the sense in which it occurs in human psychology, whereas, in the doctrine of the Trinity, it has a technical and metaphysical meaning. Human interpersonal experience is transferred to God without being subjected to a necessary and purifying process of criticism. What Raguin says, however, in *La Profondeur*, p. 148, is quite correct: 'I do not claim that we project our mode of being on to that of the ultimate reality; all that I am claiming is that our mode of being provides us with a vocabulary by which we can express what is inexpressible'. There is, however, an obvious danger of anthropomorphism if our mode of being is projected as it is.

16. See Bernard, *Sermo 8 on the Canticle*, 2 (*PL* 183, 810ff.); *Sermo 89 de diversis* (*PL* 183, 707).

4

ST SIMEON THE NEW THEOLOGIAN
AN EXPERIENCE OF THE SPIRIT

[*Note:* For convenience, this not being a scholarly study, I give in this chapter two-figure references in parentheses: the volume number in the series *Sources chrétiennes* and the page number of the translation; a third figure, appearing occasionally, is the line number.]

St Simeon was one of the greatest Christian mystics. He was born in 949. He became a monk, first at Studion and then at St Mamas, where he became hegumenos in 982. He often refers to Simeon the Pious (†987) as the one who revealed the way of the spirit to him. He experienced great difficulties and strong opposition because of this reference, his exacting enthusiasm and his determination to tell others about his spiritual experiences. He gave up the hegumenate and was sent in 1009 to the opposite bank of the Bosporus, where he died on 12 March 1022. He left behind a considerable body of writings.[1]

The title 'New Theologian' refers to his having had and having communicated a (new) experience of God. In accordance with the categories that we use, we would say that Simeon was essentially a spiritual writer. His teaching is the result of his spiritual experience, which was extremely intense. He gives several accounts of it, using quite staggering language.[2] He describes, for example, how, as something of an elegant man of the world, he met his spiritual father and followed him with docility. In the following passage, he is addressing Christ:

> You did not leave me lying, defiling myself in the mud, but by the bowels of mercy you sent for me and made me rise up out of this swamp. . . . You seized hold of me and dragged me out of it. . . . You entrusted me to your servant and disciple; I was covered in dirt and my eyes, ears and mouth were blocked with mud. . . . While he washed and purified himself again and again at every spring and every fountain, I saw nothing and went past them almost every time. If he had not taken me by the hand and left me near the spring, I would never have been able to find the source of the water. But as he showed it to me and often let me cleanse myself in it I would take not only the pure water into my hands but also the mud and slime and make my face dirty. . . .
>
> One day, I was on the way and running towards the spring when once again you, who had only recently taken me out of the mud, came to meet me on the path. For

the first time, you dazzled my weak sight with the immaculate splendour of your face. . . . From that time onwards, more and more frequently, when I was beside the spring, you, who are without pride, did not scorn to come down (to me), but came close to me and took hold of my head, bathed it in the waters and enabled me to see more and more clearly the light of your face. . . . You came in this way and left again and gradually you appeared more and more clearly. You flooded me with those waters and gave me the grace better to see a purer light.

You were close to me, you washed me, so it seemed to me, in the waters, you flooded me with them and plunged me into them again and again. I saw the lightning shining around me and the rays of your face mixed with the waters and I was stupefied, finding myself sprinkled with luminous water. . . . You took me and, going up to heaven again, you raised me up with you, either in my body or out of my body, I do not know. . . . Then, after a little time, when I was here below, on high the heavens opened and you deigned to show me your face, like a sun without a shape. . . .

After having shown yourself in this way again and again and concealed yourself again and again. . . . I saw the lightning flashes of your face and its brilliance. . . . You showed yourself to me in this way after you had entirely purified my understanding in clarity by the light of the Holy Spirit (*Cat.* XXXVI, Thanksgiving 2 (113, 335–349)).

One day he (= Simeon) stood up and said: 'O God, show me, a sinner, your favour'. He said this in his spirit rather than with his lips, when suddenly a divine light shone down from on high on him in great profusion and completely filled the place where he was standing. The young man could not understand what was happening. He did not know whether he was in a house or whether he was beneath a roof. All that he could see everywhere was light. . . . He was entirely present to this immaterial light and it seemed to him that he had himself become light. Forgetting the whole world, he was overwhelmed with tears and with inexpressible joy and happiness. His understanding rose up to heaven and discovered another light there, even brighter than the one that was close to him (*Cat*. XXII (104, 273)).

In this account of his spiritual experience, Simeon moves from water to light, that is, from the act of washing, which represents the ascetic effort, to the breaking-in of light, which he calls the 'light of the Holy Spirit'. Light plays a very important part in his mystical experience.[3] This mysticism is entirely pneumatic and entirely Christological. Prayers to the Holy Spirit are rare in the Eastern Church.[4] Simeon introduces his hymns with such a prayer: 'Come, true light! Come, eternal life!. . . Come, light that never sets! . . . Come, you whom my wretched soul has desired and still desires! Come, only one, to one who is alone, since you can see that I am alone! . . . Come, you who have yourself become desire in me and have made me long for you—you who are absolutely inaccessible! Come, my breath and my life! . . .' (156, 151ff.).

For Simeon, the Holy Spirit is the principle of all spiritual life. Need we quote references? All Simeon's writings proclaim it: 'It is by the Holy Spirit that everyone experiences the resurrection, by which I do not mean the ultimate resurrection of the body. . . . I am speaking about the resurrection that takes place every day of dead souls, a spiritual regeneration and resurrection, occurring in a spiritual fashion.'[5] He believed that the end and the goal of the Incarnation was the communication of the Holy Spirit (*Cat.* VI (104, 45ff.); *Hymn* XV (156, 287, 121ff.); XLIV (196, 81, 145 and 95, 342); LI (p. 193); *Cent.* 3, 88 (51, 108–109)). This is in accordance with both the economy and the sequence of processions in God and it also explains a number of elements in the patristic and liturgical tradition. The end of the economy corresponds to the fullness of intra-Trinitarian life and is nothing less than our own deification: 'Who, if he has the grace of the Spirit in his heart, does not possess, dwelling in him, the revered Trinity which enlightens him and makes him god?' (*Hymn* XIX, 53–55 (174, 99); XLIV, 266–271 (196, 89ff.); L, 153ff. (p. 169); LI, 95ff. (p. 193)).

This life of the spirit, which is entirely pneumatological, is also entirely Christological. Again, what need of quoting references when everything proclaims it? The appearances are Christological and the face is the face of Christ. 'Christ is the principle, the means and the end. He is in all' (*Cent.* 3, 1 (51, 80); cf. *Cat.* XX (104, 333)). The spiritual life comes about by Christ's invitation (*Cat.* VI (104, 41); XX (pp. 331ff.)). Here too, the economy determines the order of Christian progress—it is necessary to go through the Passion in order to reach the resurrection of which the Spirit is the agent, and to follow the way of asceticism in order to achieve union.[6]

It is at this point that Simeon's own distinctive positions become clear. His pneumatology is to some extent autonomous, not with regard to Christ but with regard to the hierarchy and the sacraments. Simeon writes: 'In holy baptism, we receive the remission of our faults, we are delivered from the old curse and we are made holy by the presence of the Holy Spirit, but we do not yet have perfect grace according to the promise "I will dwell in them and I will go there", because that is the privilege of those believers who are confirmed in faith and who have proved this by their works'.[7] Again: 'By baptism and in divine communion with my fearful mysteries, I give life to all. And when I say "life" I mean my divine Spirit' (*Hymn* LV, 145–147 (196, 265)). The sacrament as such, however, is only a symbol, a statement, a beginning or an initiation. It must be followed by a baptism of the Spirit before it can be made effective, fruitful and true. 'If one is not baptized in the Holy Spirit, one cannot become a son of God or a co-heir of Christ' (*Cat.* XXXIII (112, 259)). It is worth quoting here a number of very clear statements made by Simeon in *Ethical Treatise* X and *Hymn* LV:

> Our salvation is not to be found only in the baptism of water. It is also to be found in the Spirit; just as it is not exclusively in the bread and wine of communion that we are given remission of our sins and enabled to share in life. . . . May no one venture to say: 'Since holy baptism, I have received Christ and I possess him'. Let him, on the contrary, learn that not all those who are baptized receive Christ through baptism, but only those who are strengthened in faith and (who reach)

perfect knowledge, or those who have been prepared by purification and are therefore well disposed to come to baptism (*Ethical Treatise* X (129, 273, 283)).

Those who received your baptism in early infancy and who have throughout their lives lived unworthily of you will be more severely condemned than those who have not been baptized. . . . O Saviour, you gave repentance for a second purification and you established as its end the grace of the Spirit that we first received at baptism, since it is not only 'by water' that grace comes, according to your words, but rather 'by the Spirit', in the invocation of the Trinity. Since we were baptized as unknowing children and as beings who were still imperfect, we receive grace also very imperfectly (*Hymn* LV, 28–39 (129, 255ff.); cf. 61ff. (p. 259)).

Just as the sacrament alone is insufficient in itself, so too is faith which is mere belief, faith based on catechetical formulae. Faith calls for works[8], and these are above all works of 'repentance' (the baptism of tears, which plays such an important part in Simeon's teaching[9]) and works of effective charity. It is then that the fruits of the Spirit follow, as the signs of his indwelling (*Ethical Treatise* IX (129, 241)). For Simeon, then, possession of the Spirit and animation by the Spirit were normally the object of experience. This is an essential aspect of his spiritual teaching.

Once again I find myself grappling with those who say that they have the Spirit of God in an unconscious manner and who imagine that they have possessed him since their baptism. They may be convinced that they have this treasure, but they do not recognize its importance. I have to deal with those who confess that they felt nothing at their baptism and who believe that the gift of God has dwelt in them in an unconscious and intangible manner and that it is still subsisting even now in that way in their souls.[10]

If someone were to say that each one of us believers receives and possesses the Spirit without knowing it or being conscious of it, he would be blaspheming by making Christ lie when he said: 'In him there will be a spring of water welling up to eternal life' (Jn 4:14) and: 'He who believes in me, out of his heart shall flow rivers of living water' (7:38) (*Ethical Treatise* X (129, 297)).

The Lord who has favoured us with good things that transcend our senses will also give us a new sensitivity that transcends our senses through his Spirit, so that his gifts and his favours, which transcend our senses, will be supernaturally perceived in a clear and pure way by our very senses, and through them all.[11]

The Spirit is light. Simeon's mystical experience was above all an experience of light and an experience of the Spirit. 'As for the power and effectiveness of his most holy Spirit, otherwise known as his light, no one can speak about it if he has not first seen the light with the eyes of his soul and has not become aware in himself of its illuminations and its effective powers.'[12] Simeon makes use of a comparison which is very striking and which also throws light on the part played by the Spirit in his relationship with Christ as the Son of God. The following text contains this image and also a very important problem that we shall consider without delay:

What can I say to those who like to hear themselves praised, who want to be appointed as prelates and superiors (*hēgoumenoi*) and who want to be given (the confidence) of others' thoughts (*logismoi*) and to be considered worthy to be entrusted with the task of binding and loosing? When I see them and know that they have no understanding of the divine and necessary things and that they neither instruct others nor lead them to the light of knowledge, I recognize that this is just what Christ himself said to the scribes and Pharisees: 'Woe to you lawyers, for you have taken away the key of knowledge; you did not enter yourselves and hindered those who were entering' (Lk 11:52). What is this 'key of knowledge' if it is not the grace of the Holy Spirit given by faith, which, by illumination, really brings about a state of knowledge and indeed of full knowledge? . . .

And I would also say that the door is the Son: 'I am the door' (Jn 10:7, 9) and that the key of the door is the Holy Spirit: 'Receive the Holy Spirit. If you forgive the sins of any, they are forgiven; if you retain the sins of any, they are retained' (Jn 20:22–23). What is more, the house is the Father: 'In my Father's house are many rooms' (Jn 14:2). Pay great attention, then, to the spiritual meaning of the word. If the key does not open—for 'to him the gatekeeper opens' (Jn 10:3)— then the door will not be open; but if the door is not open, no one will enter the Father's house. Christ himself said: 'No one comes to the Father, but by me' (Jn 14:6).

Now that it is the Holy Spirit who first opens our spirit (see Lk 24:45) and teaches us about the Father and the Son, is what he himself has said (*Cat*. XXXIII (113, 255ff.)).

This very important text, which I have had to quote at some length, continues with scriptural citations from Jn 16:13 and 15:26; 16:13 and 14:26; 16:7; 14:15–17 and 20; and finally concludes with the promise: 'John baptized with water, but . . . you shall be baptized with the Holy Spirit' (Acts 1:5; 11:16). Simeon's comment on this text is: 'This is normal, since, if one is not baptized in the Holy Spirit, one cannot become a son of God or a co-heir of Christ' (*Cat*. XXXIII (p. 259)). He then continues by developing the idea of the activity of the Spirit as the key that opens for us our life as children of God:

If the Holy Spirit is called the key, then it is above all through and in him that our spirit is enlightened and that we are purified, illuminated by the light of knowledge, baptized from on high, born anew (see Jn 3:3, 5) and made children of God. Paul himself said: 'The Spirit himself intercedes for us with sighs too deep for words' (Rom 8:26) and 'God has sent the Spirit of his Son into our hearts, crying Abba! Father!' (Gal 4:6). It is therefore he who shows us the door and that door is light (*Cat*. XXXIII (p. 261)).

These texts are very clear, but they also raise important questions. The relationship between the Spirit, Christ the Son and the Father is defined biblically and traditionally as a return to a principle. The comparison with the key and the door brings together, in a very remarkable way, pneumatology and Christology and shows them to be inseparable and as together forming access to the Father. The problem raised by the beginning of this series of texts is this: If it is the Spirit that opens, who in fact has the 'power of the keys'? Is it the monk or spiritual man, or is it the priest or ordained hierarchical minister?

This question is similar to that raised by the sacraments. We have already considered Simeon's idea of baptism as an introduction to the state of being a member of Christ and a child of God, but as a dead reality if it is not given life in the Spirit. The same applies to his conception of the Eucharist. He believed in what we would call the Real Presence, but he also insisted that communion should be what Thomas Aquinas called a *manducatio spiritualis*, that is, a partaking with an understanding that was full of the Spirit (*Ethical Treatise* X (129, 293); XIV (339); *Hymn* XXVI, 151ff. (174, 269)). If it were only a question of receiving a confession of thoughts (*logismoi*), there would be no problem—it would be the task of the spiritual father. The practice of confessing and entrusting oneself to a spiritual father was an essential aspect of the search for God in monasticism.[13] Simeon lived this out heroically and speaks about it frequently and forcefully in several of his writings.[14] What we have here, however, is the forgiveness of sins and the exercise of the power of the keys and that is an episcopal or presbyteral function. It is not that Simeon is denying the sacrament of order. He had himself been ordained and he took the charism of his ordination into account.[15] He was anxious, however, to castigate those who wanted to appoint themselves to such a sublime responsibility (*Ethical Treatise* VI (129, 149ff.); III (122, 433ff.)) and those who were not possessed and even crushed by it: 'Is there not and does it not seem to you that there is something fearful in this encroachment upon the apostolic dignity, brother? Can you really regard it as unimportant when you come close to the inaccessible light and become a mediator between God and men?' (*Cat.* XVIII (104, 287); XXXIII (113, 255)).

Without the Spirit, the sacrament is empty, and the same applies to the office of hegumenos and that of the priest: 'As for guiding others or teaching them the will of God, he would not be capable of doing this any more than he would be worthy to receive (the confidence of) others' thoughts—even if he were chosen by men to be a patriarch—until he possessed the light shining in him' (*Cat.* XXXIII (113, 251)). Simeon believed that it was not possible to communicate the Spirit by means of an external, visible and social process as such, even though it might be canonical, and therefore to open the door, bind or loose, in this human way with the key of the Spirit. This can only be given by the Spirit himself to the one who has opened himself or has responded to his coming by doing penance or practising ascesis. The same applies to the celebration of the holy mysteries:

> Those who have not preferred him (Christ) to the whole world and who have not regarded it as a glory, an honour and great wealth simply to adore him, to officiate and merely to be in his presence are also unworthy of the spotless vision, the joy, the happiness and all the good things in which they will never share unless they are

repentant and . . . do everything zealously what my God has said. Only then, and even so with great fear and respect, if God commanded it, could they be in touch with the sacred realities! Not all those people have the right to officiate after all. Even if (someone) had received the whole grace of the Spirit, . . . so long as God did not give him a guarantee by his choice and his command by illuminating him with his divine light and embracing him with the desire of his divine love, it would not seem to me to be reasonable for him to offer the divine (sacrifice) and to be in touch with such untouchable and fearful mysteries.[16]

In the treatise *Peri exomologeseos*, which was until recently attributed to John Damascene, but which K. Holl has, in his new edition, restored to Simeon,[17] the latter says that he 'does not deny that the power to bind and loose was handed on from Christ to the apostles and from the apostles to the bishops and priests of the Church, but affirms that the latter are unable to exercise it because of their fallen moral state. In order to be reconciled to God's holiness, it is necessary to be holy. In order to give the Holy Spirit, it is necessary to have the Spirit because of the purity of one's own life. At the present time, those who satisfy these conditions are the monks and even then only those who live in accordance with their profession, not those who *gegonasi monachoi pampan amonachoi* (monks who have become totally non-monks).'[18]

Simeon's decisive scriptural text here is Jn 20:22–23; 'Receive the Holy Spirit. If you forgive the sins of any, they are forgiven; if you retain the sins of any, they are retained.' Only those who have the Spirit and manifest him in their lives, he insists, can bind and loose. Only holy monks, even if they have not been ordained, are therefore able to exercise this ministry. Simeon's own spiritual father received ordination, not from men, but from God!

There were many antecedents pointing in this direction—if not Origen,[19] then certainly Anastasius of Sinai (†after 700), who taught that it was right to confess one's sins to spiritual men.[20] Pseudo-Dionysius, despite his letter to Demophilus, also inclined towards a spiritual interpretation that was outside, if not opposed to, the hierarchy, in the sacramental and juridical sense of the term, since, for him the hierarchy was one of purification and mystical illumination.[21]

Simeon's position was also certainly followed. His disciple and biographer (or hagiographer), Nicetas Stethatos, did not deny that the words of the gospel 'you are the salt of the earth. . . . You are the light of the world' (Mt 5:13–14) referred to priests, but summarized Simeon's teaching in the following way:

Am I perhaps insisting too much? Is it possible for someone without the rank of bishop to go beyond the bishops of knowledge of God and wisdom? In this case, I would repeat what I have just said: the brilliance of episcopal dignity also shines on the man who has been given the power to manifest the Spirit by the word. In fact, if someone, even though he may not have been ordained a bishop by men, has received, whether he is a priest, a deacon or a monk, the grace from on high of the apostolic dignity . . . he is in effect the bishop with God and the Church of Christ who has been manifested in that Church under the influence of the Holy Spirit as God's spokesman, rather than the man who has received episcopal ordination from men and has still to be initiated into the mysteries of the kingdom of God. . . . I believe, then, that the man who has been purified as a result of sharing abundantly in the Holy Spirit . . . is the bishop. . . . In these conditions, he possesses the knowledge of these mysteries, he is the one who is the hierarch and the bishop, even if he has not received from men the ordination making him a hierarch and a bishop.[22]

It is hardly surprising that Nicetas, who had, it seems, just completed his *Life of Simeon*, came into conflict with Cardinal Humbert of Silva Candida, whom he met during the latter's dramatic mission to Constantinople in 1054 to talk with the Patriarch Michael Cerularius. Humbert may have adopted a rigid attitude, but he can hardly be blamed for saying to Nicetas: 'Every state or profession must remain within the limits of its investiture and its degree, so that it does not overturn the whole order of dignity in the Church'.[23]

What were the results, and the success, of Simeon's position, as taken up by Nicetas Stethatos, in the Eastern Church? In the *Admonitio* at the head of his edition of the treatise *De confessione*, which had until then been attributed to John Damascene (*PG* 95, 279–282), Lequien quoted texts for and against, and K. Holl has also produced testimony, such as that of John of Antioch in the twelfth century, that confession of sins, *epitimiai* and absolution to a great extent became the prerogative of monks until the middle of the thirteenth century.[24] Holl's thesis encountered a great deal of criticism and was even rejected. His leading critics were M. Jugie,[25] I. Hausherr[26] and H. von Campenhausen.[27] The texts should be re-examined now and the whole question reconsidered.

I would now like to look at a rather different question, although I do not claim that I can elucidate it satisfactorily. Augustine also attributed the remission of sins to the Holy Spirit, to the dove, the Church united by charity and the Spirit.[28] He frequently pointed out that, in these conditions, it is the Christian community, the *ecclesia*, that binds and looses.[29] One text which synthesizes this idea is: 'Has enim claves non unus homo, sed unitas accepit ecclesiae. . . . Columba ligat, columba solvit; aedificium supra petram ligat et solvit.'[30] In this context of unity and charity, Augustine goes so far as to tell believers: 'Audeo dicere, claves ista habemus et nos. Et quid dicam? Quia nos ligamus, nos solvimus? Ligatis et vos, solvitis et vos.'[31]

Augustine's theology in this case is different from that of Simeon, which can be compared with certain statements made by Tertullian as a Montanist.[32] For Augustine, binding and loosing was the task, not of spiritual men, but of the *ecclesia* as *caritas*, *pax* and *unitas* through the Holy Spirit: 'Pax ecclesiae dimittit peccata . . . columba tenet, columba dimittit; unitas tenet, unitas dimittit'.[33] In addition, the united activity of the saints who together form the *columba* is closely connected with the sacraments celebrated by the ordained ministers of the Church. The bond between what proceeds from Christ (the sacrament and the ordained minister) and what proceeds from the Holy Spirit (the spiritual fruit of salvation), is, moreover, expressed in this close connection.[34] Augustine would not have separated the two orders of reality as much as Simeon did and he would not have given such autonomy to the spiritual reality (or to spiritual men). Some of Simeon's arguments are reminiscent of those of the Donatists and even of a statement by Cyprian, who said: 'Quomodo autem mundare et sanctificare aquam potest qui ipse immundus est et apud quem Sanctus Spiritus non est?'[35] We may therefore conclude that Simeon did not sufficiently emphasize the importance of the sacrament of ordination, which is derived from the saving activity of the incarnate Word. On the other hand, he overemphasized a certain autonomy of the Spirit and of experience of the Spirit with regard to this sacrament of order, which forms part of the structure of the Church.

NOTES

1. The works of Simeon the New Theologian include *PG* 120; the treatise *Peri exomolog-ēseōs*, ed. K. Holl, *Enthusiasmus und Bussgewalt beim griechischen Mönchtum. Eine Studie zu Symeon dem Neuen Theologen* (Leipzig, 1898), pp. 110–127. Several of his works have appeared in a critical edition and translated into French in *Sources chrétiennes*. These include his *Catéchèses*, with an introduction, text and notes by Basile Krivochéine and tr. J. Paramelle: *SC* 96, 104, 113 (Paris, 1963, 1964, 1965); *Chapitres théologiques, gnostiques et pratiques*, tr. J. Darrouzès: *SC* 51 (Paris, 1957) (the 'Centuries'); *Traités théologiques et éthiques*, ed. and tr. J. Darrouzès: *SC* 122 and 129 (Paris, 1966 and 1967), with a valuable introduction; *Hymns*, crit. ed. by J. Koder, tr. J. Paramelle and L. Neyrand: *SC* 156, 174, 196 (Paris, 1969, 1971, 1973). There have been several important studies of Simeon. These include I. Hausherr and G. Horn, *Un grand mystique byzantin: Vie de Syméon le Nouveau Théologien par Nicétas Stéthatos (Orient. Chr., XII)* (Rome, 1928); S. Gouillard, 'Syméon', *DTC*, XIV/2, cols 2941-2959; B. Krivochéine, 'The Writings of St Symeon the New Theologian', *Or. Chr. Period.*, 2 (1954), 298–328; L. Bouyer in *Histoire de la Spiritualité chrétienne, 2: La spiritualité du Moyen Age* (Paris, 1961), pp. 662–675. There are quotations and comments in M.-J. Le Guillou, *Les témoins sont parmi nous. L'expérience de Dieu dans l'Esprit-Saint* (Paris, 1976), but they do not appear in any systematic form. An article by A. L. van der Aalst which I know only by name is 'Ambten, Charisma bij Simeon de nieuwe theoloog', in *Het Christelijk Oosten*, 22 (1970), 153–172.
2. Especially in the 'Catecheses' or instructions given to his monks: see, for example, *Cat.* XXII (104, 367ff.); XXXV and XXXVI (the two Thanksgivings: 113, 305ff., 331ff.); *Hymn* XVIII (174, 77ff.).
3. See *Cat.* XXXV (Thanksgiving 1: 113, 313ff.). Simeon's experiences of light are reported in Nicetas' *Life of Simeon*, Nos. 5, 26 and 69; see I. Hausherr and G. Horn, *op. cit.* (note 1).
4. A. Renoux noted this in 'L'office de la génuflexion dans la tradition arménienne', *Le Saint-Esprit dans la liturgie (XVIᵉ Semaine de Saint-Serge)* (Rome, 1977), pp. 149–163.

The Armenian liturgy includes a prayer to each of the three Persons at Pentecost; the text of the prayer to the Holy Spirit can be found on pp. 161ff.

5. *Cat.* VI (104, 45ff.; cf. p. 23: 'The kingdom of heaven consists of sharing in the Holy Spirit'); *Cat.* XXXIII (113, 249ff.); XXXV (307 and 325).

6. *Cat.* VI (104, 45); XIII (pp. 191ff.); *Hymn* LI, 89ff. (196, 593). It is worth noting how far removed Simeon's teaching here is from quietism. The coming of God, of his Spirit is as much an act of pure grace as it demands from us the keeping of the commandments, the effort and the striving of asceticism: see *Hymn* XIII (156, 257ff.); *Cat.* XII, XXII and XXVI and B. Krivochéine's Introduction (96, 35–40).

7. *Cent.* 3, 45 (51, 93); cf. 1, 36 (p. 50): 'In the first baptism, the water is the symbol of tears and the oil of anointing prefigures the inner anointing of the Spirit; in the second baptism, however, there is no symbol of truth—it is the truth itself'.

8. See *Hymn* XVII, 558–560; L, 172–176; LII, 69–77; *Cat.* VII and XIII (104, 61 and 201); *Ethical Treatise* X (129, 295): 'You see that those who do not possess the Spirit acting and speaking in them are unfaithful'.

9. This theme appears again and again in Nicetas' *Life* and very often in Simeon's own work; see *Cat.* IV (96, 48ff.); *Cent.* 1, 64, 67, 69–71; 2, 45, 46, 49, 50; 3, 34. See also I. Hausherr, *Penthos. La doctrine de la componction dans l'Orient chrétien (Or. Chr. Anal.,* 132) (Rome, 1944); M. Lot-Borodine, 'Le mystère du don des larmes dans l'Orient chrétien', *Suppl. de la Vie Spirituelle* (September, 1936).

10. *Ethical Treatise* V (129, 79ff.); *ibid.* (p. 105): ' "How do you know, much loved friend of Christ, that you will resemble him? Tell us how you know!"—"By the Spirit that he has given us!" he said (1 Jn 3:24). "It is through him that we know that we are children of God and that God himself is in us" '.

11. *Cent.* 2, 3 (51, 72). Following J. Darrouzès (p. 34) it is worth noting these brief texts: 'The indwelling of divinity in three Persons in those who are perfect, which comes about in a way that can be perceived by the mind' (*Cent.* 1, 7 (p. 42)); 'The soul no longer has the firm assurance that it will be united for ever to its God . . . if it does not have the pledge of his grace and does not possess this consciously' (3, 47 (p. 94)); 'The Son of God, God himself, came to earth so that he might unite us consciously to himself through his holy and consubstantial Spirit' (3, 58 (p. 97)); 'The man who has consciously received in himself the God who gives knowledge to men (3, 100 (p. 112)). J. Darrouzès, however, notes that the word *agnōstōs* occurs twice: 'Simeon therefore must have believed that God could act and even teach without our being conscious of it' (p. 104, note 1).

12. *Ethical Treatise* V (129, 99); cf., for the Spirit as light, IX (p. 225); XI (p. 381); *Cat.* XXXIV (113, 301). For antecedents in the writings of the Greek Fathers, see S. Gribomont, 'Esprit', *Dictionnaire de Spiritualité*, IV/2, cols 1269ff.

13. I. Hausherr, *Direction spirituelle en Orient autrefois (Or. Chr. Anal.,* 144) (Rome, 1955). For Russian Orthodoxy, see K. Holl, *op. cit.* (note 1), p. 154; I. Smolitsch, *Leben und Lehre der Starzen* (Vienna, 1936); *idem, Das altrussische Mönchtum (11.-16. Jahrhundert). Gestalter und Gestalten* (Würzburg, 1940).

14. See, for example, *Hymn* IV, 25ff. (156, 193); V, 11 (p. 201); Simeon's personal case, *Cat.* XXXVI (Thanksgiving 2: 113, 337).

15. *Cat.* XXXIV (113, 283); see also no. 16 of his treatise on Confession (*PG* 95, 304): he desired to be ordained.

16. *Hymn* XIX, 147–165 (174, 107ff.); *Ethical Treatise* XV: 'Is it necessary to speak, in the case of men of this kind (the false hesychasts), of the power to bind and loose, while those who have in them the Paraclete, who remits sins, are afraid to do the slightest thing that might be contrary to the judgement of the one who is in them and who speaks through them? But who would be so foolish . . . as to speak and do the works of the Spirit without having received the Paraclete and to deal with the affairs of God without the judgement of God?' (129, 459).

17. K. Holl, *op. cit.* (see note 1), edition of the text, pp. 110–127. This treatise was also edited

by M. Lequien; his edition appears in *PG* 95, 283–304, together with a Latin translation by Thomas Gale, the Dean of York. This is the version that I have read. I. Hausherr's summary (*op. cit.*, note 13) is not full, but it is exact.

18. I. Hausherr, *op. cit.* (note 13), p. 107, provides a summary of the argument of the treatise.

19. This is so, whatever may be said by W. Völker, *Der Wahre Gnostiker nach Clemens Alexandrinus* (1952), p. 172. See also K. Rahner, 'La doctrine d'Origène sur la pénitence', *RSR*, 37 (1950), 47–97, 252–286, 422–456; B. Poschmann, *Poenitentia secunda* (Bonn, 1949), pp. 462ff.

20. Anastasius of Sinai, *Quaestiones et Responsiones*, q. VI, 1; *PG* 89, 369ff.

21. See J. Stiglmayr, 'Die Lehre von den Sakramenten und der Kirche nach dem Ps.-Dionysios', *ZKT*, 22 (1898), 246–303.

22. Nicetas Stethatos, 'De la Hiérarchie', chapter V, nos. 32–40: *Opuscules et Lettres*, Fr. tr. J. Darrouzès, *SC* 81 (Paris, 1961), pp. 335–345.

23. Quoted by I. Hausherr, *op. cit.* (note 1), p. lxxix, in accordance with C. Will, *Acta et Scripta quae de Controversiis Ecclesiae Graecae et Latinae saeculo XI° composita exstant* (1861), p. 137. *PL* 143, 973–984 contains a treatise written by Nicetas criticizing the Latins for their use of unleavened bread (indicating an absence of life and of the Spirit), fasting on Saturday and insistance on priestly celibacy. *PL* 143, 983–1000 contains Cardinal Humbert's violent reply to this, which begins by insulting Nicetas and calling him *stultior asino* and also includes him among various heretics. In his account of his mission of 1054, however, he says that Nicetas had retracted, had been restored to communion and had even become a *familiaris amicus*.

24. K. Holl, *op. cit.* (note 1). See also H. Koch, 'Zur Geschichte der Bussdisziplin und Bussgewalt in der orientalischen Kirche', *Historisches Jahrbuch*, 21 (1900), pp. 58–78; J. Hörmann, *Untersuchungen zur griechischen Laienbeicht* (Donauwörth, 1913); J. T. McNeill, *A History of the Cure of Souls* (London, 1952), pp. 370ff.

25. M. Jugie, *Theologia dogm. Christian. Oriental.*, III (Paris, 1930), p. 365.

26. I. Hausherr, *op. cit.* (note 13), pp. 106–107.

27. H. von Campenhausen, *Kirchliches Amt und geistliche Vollmacht in den ersten drei Jahrhunderten* (Tübingen, 1953), p. 287, note 1.

28. With reference to Jn 20:22, *Sermo* 99, 9 (*PL* 38, 600); *Sermo* 71, 13, 23: 'Spiritu Sancto in ecclesia peccata solvuntur' (*PL* 38, 457). The *columba* is the *ecclesia sancta: De bapt.* III, 17, 22; VII, 51, 99 (*PL* 43, 149 and 241). 'Columba tenet, columba dimittit': *De bapt.* III, 18, 23 (*PL* 43, 150), taken up again in *In Ioan. ev.* CXXI, 4 (*PL* 35, 1958).

29. Augustine never tired of commenting in this way on the gift of the keys and the power to bind and loose in Mt 16:19ff.; see especially *In Ioan. ev.* CXXIV, 7 (*PL* 35, 1976). See also A.-M. La Bonnardière, 'Tu es Petrus. La péricope Mt 16, 12–23 dans l'œuvre de S. Augustin', *Irénikon*, 34 (1961), 451–499.

30. *Sermo* 295, 2 (*PL* 38, 1349).

31. *Sermo Guelf.* 16, 2; ed. G. Morin, *Anal. Agostin.*, I (Munich, 1917), p. 62.

32. There is the well-known text in *De jud.* 21: 'Ecclesia quidem delicta donabit; sed ecclesia spiritus per spiritalem hominem, non ecclesia numerus episcoporum'.

33. *De bapt.* III, 18, 23 (*PL* 43, 150). It is within this context that Augustine explains the logion on blasphemy against the Spirit; see his *Sermo* 71 (*PL* 38, 445ff.). It would be interesting to compare this with Simeon's explanation: see his *Cat.* XXXII (113, 238ff.); *Ethical Treatise* V (129, 111).

34. See my 'Introduction générale aux Traités antidonatistes' in the *Œuvres de Saint Augustin*, 28 (Paris, 1963), pp. 97–115.

35. Cyprian, *Ep.* LXX, 1 (ed. W. von Hartel, p. 767).

5

THE HOLY SPIRIT IN THE PRAYER OF THE WESTERN CHURCH DURING THE MIDDLE AGES

There was a kind of 'classical' period in the history of the Church during the centuries between the First Council of Nicaea (325) and the deaths of Gregory the Great (†604) and St Isidore (†636). It was during this period that the brilliant and holy Fathers of the Church were teaching and writing, and the great Councils defined the Church's faith in the Trinity and its Christology and promulgated the canons which provided the basis for the Church's discipline. It was also the time of the first appearance of several of the liturgical texts that were later collected and published in the classical sacramentaries of the Church.

THE LITURGY

Although there were great differences between the liturgy of the East and that of the West both in form and in expression, the reality and genius underlying them were, at the deepest level, the same. In both, the liturgy was a celebration of the 'mystery'. In other words, it was in the liturgy that believing Christians professed their faith as a community in words and gestures and the grace that God had given to men in the economy of revelation and above all in Jesus Christ and his Passover was made present in the lives of men. This act of making present was and is the work of the Lord, who is Spirit in the sense described by Paul (2 Cor 3:17). It takes place, in other words, through the inseparable action of the incarnate Son in glory as the supreme celebrant of the liturgical celebration and of his Holy Spirit, communicated as the fruit of his baptism and his Passover. The whole of the liturgy expresses and brings about a movement of God towards us and of us towards God. This movement passes from the Father through the Son in the Spirit and returns in the Spirit through the Son to the glory of the Father, who takes us, as his children, into communion with him. The Spirit is therefore invoked in every liturgical action, to be active and present in the liturgy.

I do not intend to examine this process in the missals, sacramentaries and euchologia of the various rites,[1] not only because the results would fill a large volume, but also because this approach would only bear fruit if it were followed by each individual in his living experience. I would like to begin by saying a few words about the three sacraments of initiation: baptism, confirmation and the Eucharist.

The Holy Spirit is certainly given at baptism. He raised Jesus from the dead (Rom 1:4; 8:11), he makes it possible for the believer to enter the Lord's Passover and it is in him that believers are baptized into one body, the body of Christ (1 Cor 12:13). I shall speak later about 'baptism in the Spirit'. An important place is accorded to the Holy Spirit in the solemn celebration of baptism provided in the Gelasian Sacramentary (c. 750) for the Easter vigil. The first reference to the Holy Spirit in this liturgy is in the blessing of the water. In heavily charged Latin, the bond established between the Spirit and the water of baptism is first called to mind in a great prayer of consecration:[2]

> God, whose Spirit hovered over the waters at the origin of the world, in order to confer on them the power to sanctify. . . . Look, Lord, on the face of your Church and increase in it the number of your children, you who delight your City by the waves of your grace. . . . May it receive, by your sovereign will and from the Holy Spirit, the grace of your only Son. . . .
>
> May it be a living spring, a water that regenerates and purifies, so that all who receive this saving bath will be totally purified by the action of the Holy Spirit. . . .
>
> So I bless you (water) through Jesus Christ the only Son, our Lord, who . . . was baptized in you by John in the Jordan and who made you flow from his side with the blood. . . . May the virtue of your Spirit descend into the depths of these fonts. . . .

After the triple immersion in the triple confession of faith, the priest anoints those who have just been baptized with chrism and the bishop lays on his hand and pronounces this prayer, which is the prayer of 'confirmation':

> All-powerful and eternal God, who have deigned to regenerate by water and the Holy Spirit your servants here and who have granted them the remission of all their faults, send down on them from highest heaven your Holy Spirit the Paraclete with his gifts of wisdom and understanding, counsel and strength, knowledge and piety, fill them with the spirit of your fear in the name of our Lord Jesus Christ with whom you live and reign, one God, for ever, with the Holy Spirit.

Here, clearly, we pass from baptism to confirmation. In fact, baptism and the 'seal of the Spirit' are really two aspects and two actions in the same sacramental process.[3] In the early Church, both took place in the same celebration. Dozens of studies have been written about the bond uniting them and about the differences between them.[4] There are also very many articles and longer works on the history of the rite[5] and on the dogmatic and pastoral theology of the sacrament of confirmation.[6] There can be no doubt that this sacrament is in an unstable state at present. How can the one who celebrates it claim to be able to 'give the Holy Spirit'?

I have written several times about this question, which, in my opinion, has both a doctrinal and a pastoral aspect. At the doctrinal level, confirmation is the liturgical expression firstly of a 'theo-logical' reality and secondly of an 'economic' reality. What it signifies is firstly that the Spirit exists beyond the Word and 'after' the Word (in the sense of being the third Person). Secondly, it points to the fact that Jesus received two anointings of the Spirit, the first constituting his human and divine holy being and the second constituting, or at least declaring, his quality of Messiah or minister of salvation.[7] Following this, the apostles were also constituted as the 'Twelve' by their call and their life with Jesus.[8] This, in their case, took the place of baptism. After this first constitution, they were constituted as those who were sent or 'apostles', witnesses and founders of Churches; this second constitution was brought about by Pentecost.[9] The Spirit brings about God's communication of himself by animating the body or the structure thus constituted. He is the fulfilment of the promise.

At the pastoral level, two different situations can be distinguished. In both of these situations, sacramental confirmation should, in accordance with its nature, be connected with baptism, of which it is the liturgical fulfilment. Since baptism is above all the sacrament of faith, infant baptism is problematical. There is no doubt, of course, that babies are baptized in the faith of the Church, their parents and their godparents. They are baptized with the prospect that they will be instructed in a catechetical process that ought normally to precede baptism. They ought also to be sacramentally 'confirmed' at the same time as they are baptized, but there is a need for a celebration of personal commitment in the Christian community, the people of God and the body of Christ. This commitment can best be made after puberty, between the age of about fifteen and thirty. The preparation for this celebration should occupy several weekends and take place with already committed Christians, so that it is possible for those preparing for this confirmation to see what it means to be a Christian in the Church today.[10] In the case of adults, this preparation, baptism and confirmation ought to take place within the same movement. The fundamental problem that arises here is not so much that of confirmation as that of the baptism of babies within a few days of their arrival in the world. Pascal wrote a little treatise on this subject which is worth reading.[11]

I do not wish to speak here about the third 'sacrament of initiation', the Eucharist, but would like to observe that the Greek word *teleiōsis*, 'perfection', would be more suitable in this context than the Latin word *initiare*, 'to begin'. I shall deal with the part played by the Holy Spirit in the Eucharist and the changing of the holy gifts into the body and blood of Christ as well as our communion in the Lord's body and blood in Volume III of this whole work. Those final chapters are, I believe, extremely important. We have already seen above how a spiritual space or framework for celebration is created by the Spirit by means of an exchange of a promise and a bearing witness to his presence: 'The Lord be with you'—'And with your spirit'.[12] This is a sign of the reciprocity that constitutes the full truth of the relationships between the Christian community and the minister who is the president and the pastor of that community.

This mutual relationship, which expresses the constant aspect of the activity of the Spirit, can also be found in the process of the ordination of ministers. It may even be because of this that it takes place in the celebration. There was also a theological meaning in the early tradition and practice of the Church that we need to recover. The most important moment in the process of ordination was the liturgical act, but, in the early Church, the process in fact began before the celebration.[13] The community took part in an election which, like all the acts that regulated the life of the Church, had to be 'inspired'.[14] In this election, the talents or charisms of the one elected were recognized. The consecrating bishop took up this intervention on the part of the community. In the consecration of another bishop, all the bishops present were ministers of the Spirit within the epiclesis of the entire assembly. In Hippolytus' prayer of consecration, the gift of the sovereign Spirit, *Pneuma hēgemonikon*, was besought. All the prayers of ordination ask for the Spirit to be communicated to the new minister as he was in the beginning to the apostles who were sent to the people of God as their teachers and pastors. The fine rite of placing the book of the gospels on the head of the one elected symbolizes the tongues of fire which, at the first Pentecost, inaugurated Christian preaching.[15]

> The Christian priesthood . . . is charismatic and spiritual. It is clear that it also has juridical and liturgical powers, . . . but it would impoverish the Christian priesthood if only this aspect were taken into consideration. The episcopate, the priesthood and the diaconate appear, in the early Church, as charisms for the building-up of the Church rather than as ritual functions.[16]

I have already said a few words about four of the sacraments, but it is the idea of sacrament as such, or rather the way in which it is understood that has to be considered carefully in this context. It is an idea that is applied in a flexible and analogous way to the different sacraments, but analogy is not ambiguity. It is therefore legitimate to speak in general terms of an idea of those realities that we call sacraments.

It is a fact, however, that several different values were attributed to the word *sacramentum* and that it was applied in various ways. Augustine defined the word and his definition was taken up later by Isidore of Seville (†636). The liturgy celebrated by Isidore was Hispano-Visigothic. In the *Post pridie* of the eucharistic prayer of this liturgy, the Holy Spirit was invoked over the sacrament.[17] Isidore believed that the offerings were consecrated by what he called the *oratio sexta*, which included all the prayers

107

contained between the *Sanctus* and the *Pater noster*. He distinguished two aspects in the *oratio sexta*: the *sacrifice* or consecration of the gifts by the *prex mystica* in memory of the Passion—this is the Christological aspect—and the sanctification, which makes a *sacrament* of the action by the invisible operation of the Holy Spirit. There is, Isidore claims, a 'sacrament'—and it is at this point that he cites the text of Augustine—when 'in a celebration an act of the history (of salvation) is commemorated in such a way as to be able to perceive in it the meaning of something that is to be received holily'.[18] There is, then, in the celebration of the Eucharist—and, with the necessary modifications, also in the other 'sacraments'—a commemorative aspect, recalling a Christological act, and a sanctifying aspect, in which the commemoration receives its fruit, this aspect being the work of the Holy Spirit.[19] Christ himself only offered, in his flesh, a sacrifice that was acceptable to God thanks to the Spirit associated with the flesh that was offered.[20] For us, there is only a 'sacrament' when the liturgically celebrated commemoration is animated by the activity of the Spirit. In this systematization, which has become classical, however, it has become customary to speak of a visible sign of grace within the framework of a theology of created grace which may well presuppose uncreated grace, that of the Holy Spirit, but does not make this explicit in the definition.[21] It is important to make the present intervention of the Spirit that is implored in the epiclesis explicit in every act of salvation.

If we follow the liturgy now in the way in which it unfolds in its annual cycle, we encounter the feast of Pentecost. This is not a feast of the Person of the Holy Spirit—there is no separate feast of the Persons of the Holy Trinity—but a feast of the event of Pentecost as the conclusion of the paschal mystery. We have already seen above (p. 76) that it was constituted as a feast at the end of the fourth century. There are several fine Latin prayers still used today which go back to the Middle Ages. Among these are the hymn *Veni Creator*, composed by an unknown author in the ninth century, the twelfth-century antiphon *Veni, Sancte Spiritus*, and the sequence *Veni, Sancte Spiritus*, which was probably written by Stephen Langton and dates back to the beginning of the thirteenth century. The following translation of the hymn *Veni Creator* is as close as possible to the original Latin and is also largely based on Dom Wilmart's verse translation into French. The reader may like to join me in praying it:[22]

THE HYMN

I. Come, Creator, Spirit,
   visit the souls of your own;
   fill with heavenly grace
   the breasts that you have created.

II. You who are called Paraclete,
gift of the most high God,
living water, flame, charity
and spiritual anointing;

III. You who are sevenfold in your gift,
finger of God's right hand,
you who were rightly promised by the Father,
enrich our throats with speech.

IV. Inflame the light of our senses,
pour love into our hearts,
the weakness of our bodies
strengthen with lasting power.

V. Drive the enemy far back,
and at once grant us peace;
with you going ahead of us,
may we avoid all harm.

VI. Through you may we know the Father
and recognize the Son;
and may we always believe
in you, Spirit of both.

THE SEQUENCE

I. Come, Holy Spirit,
and send out a ray
of your heavenly light.

II. Come, father of the poor,
come, giver of gifts,
come, light of our hearts.

III. Come, kindly comforter,
sweet guest of our soul
and sweet freshness.

IV. Rest in hardship,
moderation in the heat,
relief in pain!

V. O most blessed light,
fill the innermost hearts
of those who believe in you.

VI. Without your divine power
there is nothing in man,
nothing that is harmless.

VII. Wash what is unclean,
water what is arid,
heal what is wounded.

VIII. Bend what is stiff,
warm what is cold,
guide what has gone astray.

IX. Give to those who believe in you
and who trust in you
your seven sacred gifts.

X. Give the reward of virtue,
give the end of salvation,
give lasting happiness!

The antiphon *Veni, Sancte Spiritus* appears in an antiphonary of Bamberg in the eleventh century in the first Vespers of Pentecost: 'Come, Holy Spirit, fill the hearts of your faithful and light in them the fire of your love; you who, by the diversity of all tongues, have brought the peoples together in the unity of faith'.[23]

In the tenth and eleventh centuries, the feast of Pentecost was chosen as the day for the anointing of the kings of France when there was no reason to anoint the king at some other time.[24] There seems also to have been a renewal of interest at the end of the eleventh century and during the twelfth in the Holy Spirit and the meaning of Pentecost. It was at this time that the *vita apostolica* flourished, that is, the common life led together without private property, and many institutions and churches placed themselves under the protection of the Holy Spirit.[25]

In this context, Pope Urban II, who left Champagne and became a monk at Cluny, deserves special mention. He actively promoted the way of life of the canons regular and regarded the revival of interest in them as taking place *instinctu Spiritus Sancti*.[26] To enable a secular priest to enter the religious life, Urban wrote the famous text on the two laws, *Duae leges sunt*, which is reproduced in the canonical collections and especially in the *Decretum Gratiani*. It was frequently quoted in the Middle Ages. Thomas Aquinas, for example, cited it in several of his works. The text is as follows:

There are two laws; one is public, the other private. The public law is the one that was written and made by the holy Fathers and includes the law of the canons. . . . The canons, for example, stipulate that a priest must not move from one diocese to another without a written recommendation from his bishop. . . . The private law, on the other hand, is the one that is written in the heart by the instinct of the Holy Spirit. The Apostle, for example, speaks of those who have the law of God written on the tablets of their hearts and elsewhere . . . that they are a law to themselves.

If one of these lives in his church and under his bishop in a secular manner, keeping his own goods, and if, driven by the Spirit, he wants to seek his salvation in a monastery or as a canon regular, as he is guided by the private law, there is no reason why he should be bound by the public law. The private law is, after all, superior to the public law. It is the Spirit of God who makes the law and those who are guided by the Spirit of God are guided by the law of God. And who can resist the Holy Spirit? If a man is guided by that Spirit, then, he should go freely, by virtue of our authority, and even defy the opposition of his bishop. In fact, there is no law for the righteous man—where the Spirit of the Lord is, there is freedom. And if you are guided by the Spirit, you are no longer subject to the law.[27]

I do not propose to trace the history of this text or the effects of the general principle to which it appeals. It would be possible, if one did so, to quote Bernard, Innocent III, Ignatius Loyola and a whole series of texts.[28] Research into this question would have to be undertaken systematically, and would go far beyond my ability and my present intention. The same would apply to any attempt to examine, even only cursorily, the prayers addressed to the Holy Spirit.

EVIDENCE OF FOUNDATIONS

Since the end of the eleventh century, the church of Saint-Sernin in Toulouse has been dedicated to the Holy Spirit. A village on the Rhône, originally called Saint-Saturnin and, in 1045, the site of a Cluniac priory, changed its name to Pont-Saint-Esprit. These data together with several others were provided by Etienne Delaruelle and were also confirmed by G. Schreiber. Delaruelle said: 'One has the impression that there was a great spiritual movement at that time, in which the idea of the Holy Spirit was associated with that of pilgrimage and its routes as well as with the notion of the *vita apostolica*'.[29] It is a fact that hospitals and communities of the Holy Spirit were founded above all along the routes of the great pilgrimages and especially in the south of France. Another factor, however, also played a part.

The twelfth century is notable for its renewed interest in the idea of human society and of the brotherhood of man. This renewal was often linked with a strong devotion to the Holy Spirit. Stephen of Muret founded the Order of Grandmont in 1076 and the lay brothers of this Order asked their priests to celebrate the votive Mass of the Holy Spirit for them; this information is reported by Jacques de Vitry. In 1129, Peter Abelard placed the abbey to which Héloise had retired under the patronage of the Paraclete. In 1113, confraternities of the Holy Spirit appeared in the Auvergne and cared for the poor and for foundlings. In 1170–1185, a Heiliggeisthaus was founded in Cologne; similar houses were also founded in Lüneberg, Marseilles and Rostock, and provided for the poor.[30] In 1177, Abdenago of Pantasi founded a brotherhood of the Holy Spirit at Benevento. In 1195, Guy of Montpellier (†1208) opened a hospital of the Holy Spirit in his own town and founded a congregation of the same name in the region. Innocent III raised it to the status of an Order in 1204 and called Guy to Rome, where he founded a hospice under the patronage of the Holy Spirit.[31]

111

NOTES

1. For the Latin rite, see B. Neunheuser, 'Der Heilige Geist in der Liturgie', *Theologie und Glaube*, 35 (1943), 11–24, repr. in *Liturgie und Mönchtum*, 20 (1957), 11–33; F. Vanderbrouke, 'Esprit Saint et structures ecclésiales', *Questions liturgiques et paroissiales*, 39 (1958/3), 115–131; *idem*, 'L'Esprit Saint dans la liturgie', *Dictionnaire de Spiritualité*, IV (1961), cols 1283–1296; C. Vagaggini, *Theological Dimensions of the Liturgy* (Eng. tr.; Collegeville, Minn., 1976), chapter 7.

2. Gelasian Sacramentary, ed. H. A. Wilson (Oxford, 1894), pp. 85–87. Studies of this prayer of consecration over the water have been made by J. Lécuyer, 'La prière consécratoire des eaux', *M-D*, 49 (1957), 8–29; E. Stommel, *Studien zur Epiklese der römischen Taufwasserweihe* (Bonn, 1950); J. de Jong, 'Benedictio fontis', *Archiv für Liturgiewissenschaft*, 8 (1963), 21–46; E. Lengeling, 'Blessing of Baptismal Water in the Roman Rite', *Concilium*, 2, no. 3 (1967), 35–37, in which the author suggests a number of simplifications.

3. This is fundamentally what emerges from the works of L. Bouyer (see note 6 below), L. S. Thornton (*ibid.*) and B. Neunheuser (note 4) on the subject, and H. Küng, 'La confirmation comme parachèvement du baptême', *L'expérience de l'Esprit. Mélanges Schillebeeckx (Le Point théologique*, 18) (Paris, 1976), pp. 115–151. The basic work in this context is J. Amougou-Atangana, *Ein Sakrament des Geistesempfangs? Zum Verhältnis von Taufe und Firmung* (Freiburg, Basle and Vienna, 1974).

4. J. B. Umberg, 'Confirmatione Baptismus "perficitur" ', *ETL*, 1 (1924), 505–517; P. T. Camelot, 'Sur la théologie de la confirmation', *RSPT*, 38 (1954), 637–657; B. Neunheuser, *Baptism and Confirmation* (Eng. tr.; Freiburg and London, 1964); A. Hamman, *Je crois en un seul baptême. Essai sur 'Baptême et Confirmation'* (Paris, 1970); H. Auf der Maur and B. Kleinheyer, eds, *Zeichen des Glaubens. Studien zur Taufe und Firmung. Festgabe B. Fischer* (Zürich, 1972).

5. E. Llopart, *Las formulas de la confirmación en el Pontifical romè (Liturgica*, 2) (Montserrat, 1958), 121–180, presented by P. M. Gy, 'Histoire liturgique du sacrement de confirmation', *M-D*, 58 (1959), 135ff.; see also B. Neunheuser and J. Amougou-Atangana, *op. cit.*

6. Apart from P. T. Camelot, *op. cit.* (note 4), and the instalments of *M-D*, see A. G. Martimort, 'La confirmation', *Communion solennelle et Profession de foi (Lex Orandi*, 14) (Paris, 1952), pp. 159–201; L. Bouyer, 'Que signifie la confirmation?' *Parole et Liturgie*, 34 (1952), 3–12; *idem*, 'La signification de la confirmation', *VS (Suppl.)* (15 May 1954), 162–179; L. S. Thornton, *Confirmation. Its Place in the Baptismal Mystery* (Westminster, 1954); A. Adam, *Firmung und Seelsorge* (Düsseldorf, 1959); H. Mühlen, 'Die Firmung als sakramentales Zeichen der heilsgeschichtlichen Selbstüberlieferung des Geistes Christi', *Theologie und Glaube*, 57 (1967), 263–286; W. Breuning, 'When to Confirm in the Case of Adult Baptism', *Concilium*, 2, no. 3 (1967), 48–54; J.-P. Bouhot, *La confirmation, sacrement de la communion ecclésiale* (Paris, 1968); H. Bourgeois, *L'avenir de la confirmation* (Paris, 1972); L. Ligier, *La confirmation. Sens et conjoncture œcuménique hier et aujourd'hui (Théologie historique*, 23) (Paris, 1973), in which the author criticizes the present rite for the emphasis that it places on the anointing, whereas the essential aspect, in the author's opinion, is the laying-on of hands.

7. Hence the parallel $\dfrac{\text{incarnation}}{\text{baptism of Jesus}} = \dfrac{\text{baptism}}{\text{seal of the Spirit}}$;

   See J. Lécuyer, 'Le sacerdoce royal des chrétiens selon S. Hilaire de Poitiers', *Année Théologique*, 10 (1949), 302–325; *idem*, *M-D*, 27 (1951), 40ff.; *idem. Le sacerdoce dans le mystère du Christ (Lex Orandi*, 24) (Paris, 1957), chapters VIII and IX.

8. See Mk 3:14, literally translated: 'And he made twelve so that they might be with him and that he might send them to proclaim'.

9. J. Lécuyer, *Le sacerdoce, op. cit.*, chapters XI and XII, who makes use of the aspects of Easter and Pentecost. This is the line followed by Cyril of Jerusalem, *Cat. Myst.* III, 1–2

(*PG* 33, 1088ff.). See also W. Breuning, 'Apostolizität als sakramentale Struktur der Kirche. Heilsökonomische Überlegungen über das Sakrament der Firmung', *Volk Gottes. Festgabe J. Höfer* (Freiburg, 1967), pp. 132–163. See also E. Schillebeeckx, *Christ the Sacrament of Encounter with God* (London and New York, 1963), especially pp. 197ff.

10. With the help of modern psychological insights, this might best be done by presenting in a contemporary form the Thomist idea that the sacraments correspond to certain decisive aspects and moments in life. Confirmation, according to Thomas, corresponds to the time of transition from a life led for oneself to a life with and for others, in other words, a truly social life: 'antea quasi singulariter sibi ipsi vivit' (*ST* IIIa, q. 72, a. 2). See P. Ranwez, 'La confirmation constitutive d'une personnalité au service du Corps mystique du Christ', *Lumen Vitae*, 9 (1954), 17–36; J. Latreille, 'L'adulte chrétien ou l'effet du sacrement de confirmation chez S. Thomas d'Aquin', *RThom*, 57 (1957), 5–28; 58 (1958), 214–243; A. Auer, *Weltoffener Christ*, 2nd ed. (Düsseldorf, 1962), pp. 146ff.

11. Pascal, 'Comparaison des Chrétiens des premiers temps avec ceux d'aujourd' hui', *Pensées et Opuscules*, ed. L. Brunschvicg, pp. 201–205.

12. See above, pp. 36–37.

13. See B. Botte, 'L'Ordre d'après les prières d'ordination', *Etudes sur le sacrement de l'Ordre (Lex Orandi*, 22) (Paris, 1957), pp. 13, 35, 41; the Canons of Mondaye under the direction of Y. Congar and B.-D. Dupuy, *L'évêque d'après les prières d'ordination (Unam Sanctam*, 39) (Paris, 1962), pp. 739–780; L. Mortari, *Consecrazione episcopale e collegialità* (Florence, 1969); H. Legrand, 'Theology and the Election of Bishops in the Early Church', *Concilium*, 77 (1972), 31–42.

14. Election: the original text of the Roman formula of the pontiff addressing the faithful is: 'Et ideo electionem vestram debetis voce publica profiteri'; see B. Botte , *op. cit*., p. 19, note 1. Inspired: see the texts and references in my *Tradition and Traditions* (Eng. tr.; London and New York, 1966), Part One, Excursus B, pp. 119–137, esp. pp. 125ff.

15. This is the explanation given by Severian of Gabala, *c*. 400; see J. Lécuyer, 'La grâce de la consécration épiscopale', *RSPT*, 36 (1952), 389–417, especially 402.

16. B. Botte, *op. cit*. (note 13), p. 34.

17. For the history of these *Post pridie* prayers, see W. S. Porter, 'The Mozarabic Postpridie', *JTS*, 44 (1943), 182–194. For the sacramental and eucharistic theology of Isidore of Seville, see J. B. Geiselmann, *Die Abendmahlslehre an der Wende der christlichen Spätantike zum Frühmittelalter. Isidor von Sevilla und das Sakrament der Eucharistie* (Munich, 1933); J. Havet, 'Les sacrements et le rôle du Saint-Esprit d'après Isidore de Séville', *ETL*, 16 (1939), 32–93.

18. Augustine's Latin text is unfortunately almost untranslatable: 'Sacramentum est autem in aliqua celebratione cum rei gestae commemoratio ita fit, ut aliquid etiam significare intellegatur, quod sancte accipiendum est': *Ep*. 55, 2 (*PL* 33, 205).

19. Isidore, *Etym*. VI, 19, 38–42: 'Sacrificium dictum, quasi sacrum factum, quia prece mystica consecratur in memoriam pro nobis Dominicae passionis; unde hoc eo iubente corpus Christi et sanguinem dicimus. Quod, dum sit ex fructibus terrae, sanctificatur, et fit sacramentum, operante invisibiliter (Migne (*PL* 82, 255) has *visibiliter* here!) Spiritu Dei. . . . Sacramentum est in aliqua celebratione, cum res gesta ita fit ut aliquid significare intellegatur, quod sancte accipiendum est. . . . Quae ob id sacramenta dicuntur, quia sub tegumento corporalium rerum virtus divina secretius salutem eorumdem sacramentum operatur. . . . Quae ideo fructuose penes Ecclesiam fiunt, quia sanctus in ea manens Spiritus eundem sacramentorum latenter operatur effectum'; ed. W. M. Lindsay (1911); cf. *De officiis eccl*. I, 18, 4 (*PL* 83, 755).

20. After quoting Jn 1:33, Isidore says: 'carnem Christi Spiritui Sancto sociatam per mysterium passionis sacrificium Deo in odorem suavitatis accipimus': *In Lev*. c. 6, 4 (*PL* 83, 523).

21. In the Augustinian tradition, 'visibile signum invisibilis gratiae'. Via Peter Lombard and Thomas Aquinas, this definition in the Roman Catechism was reached: 'rem esse, sensibus

113

subiectam, quae ex Dei institutione sanctitatis et iustitiae tum significandae tum efficiendae vim habet': Pars II, c. i. q. 11.

22. A. Wilmart, 'L'hymne et la séquence du Saint-Esprit', *La vie et les arts liturgiques*, 10 (1924), 395–401; repr. in *Auteurs spirituels et Textes dévots du Moyen Age latin* (1932; reissued Paris, 1971), pp. 37–45.

23. R. J. Hesbert, *Corpus Antiphonalium Officii*, III (Rome, 1968), p. 528, antiphon no. 5327. The Dominicans preserved the words 'qui per diversitatem linguarum multarum gentes in unitate fidei congregasti'.

24. In the debate which followed a lecture given by E. Delaruelle, M. F. Lemarignier commented: 'Louis V was associated on the throne with Lothair and anointed on the day of Pentecost, 979 A.D. In the same way, during the reign of Robert II the Pious, Robert's sons Hugh and Henry were anointed at Pentecost in 1017 and 1027 respectively. Finally, during the reign of Henry I, the future King Philip I was consecrated at Pentecost in 1059': *La vita commune del clero nei secoli XI e XII* (Milan, 1962), p. 180.

25. See the lecture given by E. Delaruelle on 'La vie commune des clercs et la spiritualité populaire au XIᵉ siècle' in *La vita commune*, *op. cit.*, pp. 152ff., repr. in *La piété populaire au Moyen Age* (Turin, 1975), pp. 81–112; especially pp. 91–95.

26. See C. Dereine, 'L'élaboration du statut canonique des Chanoines réguliers spécialement sous Urbain II', *RHE*, 46 (1951), 534–565, especially 546–547.

27. Jaffé Loewenfeld, 5760; Mansi 20, 714; *PL* 151, 535. Quoted by Gratian, c. 2, C. XIX, q. 2 (ed. E. Friedberg, 829–840). Migne's text is defective. Quoted by Thomas Aquinas, *De perf. vitae spir.* c. 25; *Quodl.* III, 17; *ST* IIa IIae, q. 184, a. 6 and 8; q. 189, a. 7. See also M. Duquesne, 'S. Thomas et le canon attribué à Urbain II (c. 2, C. XIX, q. 2)', *Studia Gratiana*, I (Bologna, 1955), pp. 415–434.

28. See Bernard, *De praecepto et dispens.* 16 (*PL* 182, 885ff.); Innocent III, *Reg.* VIII, 195 and IX, 182 (*PL* 215, 774 and 1495). See also H. Tillmann, *Papst Innozenz III* (Bonn, 1954), pp. 28–31; W. A. van Roo, 'Law of the Spirit and Written Law in the Spirituality of St Ignatius', *Greg*, 37 (1956), 417–443.

29. E. Delaruelle, *op. cit.* (note 25), p. 154. See also G. Schreiber, *Gemeinschaften des Mittelalters. Recht und Verfassung. Kult and Frömmigkeit* (Münster, 1948), especially the tables.

30. For the great increase in the number of these Hospitals of the Holy Spirit towards the end of the twelfth century, see G. Schreiber in *Historische Vierteljahrschrift*, 15 (1912), 136ff.; W. Liese, *Geschichte der Caritas*, II (Freiburg, 1922), pp. 15ff.; M. Mollat, *Les pauvres au Moyen Age. Etude sociale* (Paris, 1978), p. 174; for the fourteenth century, *ibid.*, pp. 323 and 346 (Paris in 1360 and 1363), p. 333 (Brussels), p. 341 (Danzig) and p. 345 (Oporto).

31. A. Castan, 'Notice sur l'Ordre du Saint-Esprit', *Annuaire du Doubs* (1864), p. 152; M. Poête, *Etude sur les origines et la règle de l'Ordre hospitalier du Saint-Esprit* (Paris, 1890); P. Brune, *Histoire de l'Ordre hospitalier du Saint-Esprit* (Paris, 1892).

6

THE HOLY SPIRIT IN THE
WRITINGS OF THE THEOLOGIANS

I do not intend to provide, in this part of my work, a history of the theology of the Holy Spirit in the twelfth and thirteenth centuries, that is, during the first and greatest period of Scholasticism. I would, however, be giving a very incomplete picture of the experience of the Spirit in Christianity if I were not to examine, however briefly, the teachers of that period, who were so often spiritual men.

The Holy Spirit is active in history and causes new and sometimes very confusing things to taken place in it. This was certainly the case during the first half of the twelfth century, when so many new religious orders came into being.[1] This was a cause of scandal to Rupert of Deutz, for example, who did not like new questions. The Premonstratensian canon Anselm of Havelberg, on the other hand, was aware that many of his contemporaries were disconcerted and asking the question: 'quare tot novitates in Ecclesia Dei fiunt?'— 'Why are there so many new things in the Church?' and answered it, in 1149, in the following way:

> There is only one body of the Church. The Holy Spirit gives life to that body, rules it and governs it. The Holy Spirit to which that body is joined is manifold, subtle, moving, fine, pure, strong, sweet, loving what is good, penetrating, doing good without hindrance, a friend of men, benevolent, stable, certain, seeing everything, capable of everything, containing all spirits, understandable and spotless. According to the Apostle, 'there are varieties of gifts, but the same Spirit' (1 Cor 12:4). He also said: 'To each is given the manifestation of the Spirit for the common good. To one is given through the Spirit the utterance of wisdom and to another the utterance of knowledge according to the same Spirit, to another faith by the same Spirit, to another gifts of healing by the one Spirit, to another the working of miracles, to another prophecy, to another the ability to distinguish between spirits, to another various kinds of tongues, to another the interpretation of tongues. All these are inspired by one and the same Spirit, who apportions to each individually as he wills' (1 Cor 12:7–11).
>
> It would seem, then, that the body of the Church, which is one, is given life by the Holy Spirit, who is one, single in himself and yet manifold (1 Pet 4:10) in the distribution of his many different gifts. This true body of the Church, which is given life by the Holy Spirit and differentiated into diverse members at different ages and periods, began with the first righteous man Abel and will end with the last of the elect. It is always one in a single faith, but it is differentiated into diverse forms by the manifold variety of its way of life.[2]

We have already seen that Urban II ascribed the new way of life of the canons regular to the Holy Spirit. It should be added here that Anselm of Havelberg had been to Constantinople, where he had been in contact with Greek thought. Towards the middle of the twelfth century, Burgundio of Pisa translated into Latin the fifth *Theological Oration* of Gregory Nazianzen on the Holy Spirit. Greek influence was particularly strong in the sphere of anthropology and especially epistemology; but the controversy concerning the *Filioque* may have stood in the way of the diffusion of the Eastern Church's pneumatology.

Following the teaching of Augustine, the Church as the body of Christ was almost universally regarded in the West as animated by the Holy Spirit and the distribution of different gifts in the Church to different members for the common good was also attributed to the Holy Spirit.[3] The most classical author at this time was Hugh of Saint-Victor. He inspired others and was himself inspired by Augustine. He wrote his treatise *De sacramentis christianae fidei* in 1137 or a little earlier. The following extract is relevant to our theme:

> Just as the spirit of man descends from his head to give life to his members, so too does the Holy Spirit come, through Christ, to Christians. Christ is the head and the Christian is the member. The head is one and the members are many, but there is only one body consisting of the head and the members and in that one body there is only one Spirit. The fullness of that Spirit is in the head and the participation is in the members. If, then, the body is one, and the Spirit is one, the man who is not in the body cannot be given life by the Spirit. . . . The Church is the body of Christ. It is given life by one Spirit and united and sanctified by one faith. The believers are each one members of that one body and all believers are one body because of the one Spirit and the one faith. Just as, in the human body, each one of the members has its own distinct function and yet what it does for itself alone is not simply for itself alone, so too, in the body of the Church, the gifts of grace are distributed to individuals and yet what each one has for himself alone is not for himself alone.[4]

At this period of Christian history, a treatise on Christ as the Head—*De Christo capite*—and a theology of created grace had not yet been properly worked out. The idea of what was later (from about 1160 onwards) to be known as the 'mystical Body' (which would become equivalent to and synonymous with 'Church') was at this time strongly pneumatological. It was, in other words, not the *gratia Capitis*, but the Holy Spirit who made the body of which Christ was the Head. That Head had the Spirit first and he had that Spirit in its fullness. That Spirit then descended to the members. This pneumatology can also be found in the traditional connection between the three realities that testify to the truth of the title 'body of Christ': his natural, personal body, born of Mary, his sacramental body, and his body as the Church or a communion.[5] This connection can be seen as marked by the Holy Spirit who is one and the same and at work in each of these three 'bodies': as the principle of sanctification of Jesus (see Lk 1:35), of the gifts of the bread and wine, and of the believers who form the Church. This is precisely what the mysterious author known by the name of Honorius Augustodunesis taught, that is, that the third body—the ecclesial body—is connected to the first by the second, eucharistic body, which is so, *Spiritu sancto consecrante*. It is therefore possible to speak of the three 'bodies' as a single body of which the Holy Spirit is the principle of unity: 'Unde non tria sed unum corpus Spiritu Sancto coadunante recte affirmatur'.[6]

It is certain that the absence of a real epiclesis to the Holy Spirit in the Roman Canon deprived any corresponding theology of a chance of developing. It is therefore all the more remarkable that the affirmation is so often found that the bread and wine are consecrated by the Holy Spirit.[7] In 1208, Innocent III required Waldensians rejoining the Church to make a profession of faith which extended to all the sacraments the affirmation that the Holy Spirit operated in them: *inestimabili atque invisibili virtute Spiritus Sancti cooperante*.[8] This was a common conviction. There is concrete evidence of it, based on living experience, in the lives of the saints and the visions that they are reported to have had.[9]

At the period which we are considering, a special place must be given to the gifts of the Holy Spirit.[10] For a long time and even when the text of Isaiah (11:2–3) was taken into account, it was believed that these gifts were discrete gifts of grace, distinguished in accordance with the subject-matter denoted by their name, and in virtue of which Christians were able to do what God expected of them. In the West especially, the number 'seven' was regarded as very important. It was understood not as indicating completeness, but rather as referring to a number of specific operations. The Vulgate translation was followed and this itself followed the Septuagint: 'Et requiescet super eum spiritus Domini: spiritus sapientiae et intellectus, spiritus consilii et fortitudinis, spiritus scientiae et pietatis; et replebit eum spiritus timoris Domini'—'And the spirit of the Lord shall rest upon him, the spirit of wisdom and understanding, the spirit of counsel and might, the spirit of knowledge and piety and a spirit of fear of the Lord shall fill him'. From the twelfth century onwards, often in the context of more active reading of the works of Augustine, the Christians of the Western Church frequently asked for the seven gifts of the Spirit, celebrated them and tried to understand them. These, like the virtues, were the principles of action according to God. They were often related to other septenaria, such as the seven women who were in disgrace and looked for a man who would take it from them (Origen had already made this comparison), the seven capital sins, the seven requests of the Our Father, the seven beatitudes and other more artificial groups of seven.

A little before 1135, Rupert of Deutz placed the different aspects of

117

history, which formed the theme of the 42 books of his *De Trinitate*, under the headings of the seven gifts of the Holy Spirit and linked these with the seven days of creation and the seven ages of the world. The third part of his work consists of the nine books *De operibus Spiritus Sancti*. In this part, the various aspects of the history of the Church are placed under the headings of particular gifts.[11]

Gerhoh of Reichersberg copied whole pages from Rupert's work. He also quoted two hymns with quatrains of the same plan as Rupert's.[12] His *De ordine donorum Spiritus Sancti* also has the same source and the same view.[13]

Jacques de Vitry (†1240) placed the life of St Mary of Oignies under the sign of the seven gifts of the Holy Spirit. In the iconography of the end of the twelfth century and almost the whole of the thirteenth century, Christ is frequently shown as giving the seven gifts of the Spirit. The gifts with which the Messiah was filled (Is 11:2–3) are presented as being communicated to the Christian.[14] The part played by these gifts in the practice of the spiritual life was very present in men's minds at this period. A treatise consisting of 23 chapters, probably originating in England and dating from the second half of the thirteenth century, was edited some years ago by A. Wilmart. Each chapter of this treatise, from chapters XIII to XIX, deals wth one of the gifts.[15] God the Father is described in it as loving justice, the Son judges severely(!) and the Spirit is the mercy which gives confidence to the sinner, who would not be able to stand before a Father and a Son who would condemn him, if it were not for the Spirit. The same scholar also edited and published a 'Prayer to the Holy Spirit according to the Seven Gifts',[16] in which each of the gifts is related to one of the capital sins, from which it sets man free, to the opposite virtue, to the corresponding beatitude and to the fruit that it brings. This is a monastic text dating from the middle of the fourteenth century. It presupposes a theological elaboration similar to the one provided by Thomas Aquinas.

The gifts of the Holy Spirit were not distinguished from the virtues until about 1235. The first to make this distinction was Philip the Chancellor. Thomas Aquinas reduced it to a remarkably coherent system that was closely in accordance with a very real aspect of the life of the children of God. I therefore now briefly outline this theology as presented in the *Summa* in 1269–1270.

Thomas situates the Christian within the framework of the movement by which creatures move and are moved towards their end. He understands 'movement' in this context in the widest sense of the word, that is, as every kind of movement from one state to another. In this case, however, it is a *motus hominis ad Deum*, the journey or the ascent of man to God and nothing less than God. God alone is the beginning and the end. God's life is divine and can be and is communicated by grace, which is characteristic of the Holy Spirit.[17] As creator, God originally gave to each nature the principles of a behaviour which is truly its own. In the case of man, God made him free. This means not only that man determines and realizes himself and his own existence, that he is *causa sui* and that he builds himself up and fulfils himself by his actions and his *habitus* or 'haviours', but also that, if God moves him, he moves him through his own freedom and so that he may act freely.[18] In God's name, then, man has in himself the principle of his own movement and this includes his abilities, actions, 'haviours' and virtues (or vices). There are, however, also motivating forces of moral action that are external to man, and Thomas distinguishes these according to whether their influence is exercised by information or suggestion or by efficiency.[19] The demon acts on our freedom by means of suggestion and this is the basis of temptation. God, on the other hand, acts in the case of our coming or returning to him *per instructionem et per operationem*, that is, by teaching and by action.[20] This accounts for the following statement, which introduces us directly to the question that we are considering here: 'Principium exterius movens ad bonum est Deus, qui et nos instruit per legem et iuvat per gratiam'—'The principle outside us that moves us towards the good is God, who teaches us by the law and helps us by grace'.[21]

'By grace': this does not mean simply by means of the help received from actual graces, but by means of deep and lasting gifts: 'grace', the virtues and the 'gifts'. The distinction between the virtues and the gifts had been made comparatively recently in theology. In his *Sentences* (III d. 34, q. 1, a. 1; cf. *In Isaiam*, c. XI), Thomas Aquinas simply said that, with the help of the gifts, the believer was able to act *ultra modum humanum*, 'beyond the means of man'. In the *Summa*, however, he added that this was possible because he was moved by a superior principle (Ia IIae, q. 68, a. 2).

Thomas kept to the Isaian text, which does not refer vaguely to 'gifts', but speaks quite precisely about 'spirits'—*spiritus sapientiae* and so on. This, he claims, points to a movement by inspiration (q. 68, a. 1) and we are clearly in touch here with the biblical value of 'breath' which we discussed earlier in this book. Thomas had, from 1259 or 1260 onwards, an unexpected *confirmatur* at his disposal (he says at least twice: '*et etiam Philosophus*'— 'even Aristotle') in *De bona fortuna*, a short treatise consisting of two chapters taken from Aristotle's works, the first from the *Eudemian Ethics* and the second from the second book of the *Magna Moralia*. Aristotle spoke of the *hormē* or the inclination or impulse of the superior appetite, and Thomas applied this idea to the divine impulse which goes beyond the use of reason.[22] This understanding of the term was, of course, clearly remote from that of the Greek philosopher himself.

As lasting realities that are distinct from the virtues, then, the gifts are these dispositions which make the Christian ready to grasp and follow the inspirations of the Spirit.[23] They are in themselves only a permanent disposition, but one which makes the disciple of Jesus permanently open to have his activity guided, beyond the power of the virtues, beyond his reason as

119

animated by faith, beyond his supernatural prudence, by another who is infinitely superior and has sovereign freedom, in other words, the Holy Spirit.

This is a position far removed from a purely rational moral attitude, or from an attitude often imputed to Thomas, that is, a morality based on models derived from a nature of things that is established outside time. Thomas allows for the *event* of the Spirit; for him, morality is based on the saving and sanctifying will of God, according to norms which go beyond human and even supernatural reason. We are led by another, who does not act without us or violently (see above, p. 119, and below, note 18), but who goes beyond our own vision and the behaviour for which we have made provision, not only beyond the perspective of our human reason, but also beyond that revealed by our faith. These gifts are not superior to the theologal virtues. The latter unite us to God himself and can therefore have nothing above them. The gifts are at the service of those virtues, enabling them to be practised perfectly. Only God can, however, by intervening personally, give his fullness to the practice of these virtues and only he can complete the activity of one of his children. Thomas quotes Paul's words: 'Qui Spiritu Dei aguntur, hi sunt filii Dei'—'All who are led by the Spirit are sons of God' (Rom 8:14).

Thomas' aim, then, is to determine the part played by the gifts in the practice of the theologal and moral virtues. As he saw the perfect exercise of the virtues and especially of the gifts reflected in the beatitudes, he tried to make one gift of the Spirit and one of the beatitudes correspond to each of these virtues. He even attempted to attribute to each virtue, with its gift and its beatitude or beatitudes, one or other of the 'fruits' of the Spirit of which Paul spoke. He devoted one question to these 'fruits', in which he stresses the struggle of the spirit against the 'flesh', with a clear reference to Gal 5:22–23 (see *ST* Ia IIae, q. 70).

There is, of course, something a little forced and artificial in these parallels and I do not intend to discuss them in detail. They do not have an absolute value, but neither should their value be ignored, since they frequently reveal very deep insights. Thomas' understanding that the appeals and interventions of the living God go beyond all our human expectations enables us to recognize that the holiness of the Christian saints is the most perfect form of Christian life. It consists of continually going beyond supernatural, but still human, boundaries through generous responses to 'inspirations'. Consider Teresa of Lisieux.

It is the Holy Spirit who makes man holy. He is also the principle of the 'revelation' to the people of God of the thought, the plan and the will of God. I shall return later to the use that the Church Fathers and the theologians of the Middle Ages made of the categories of 'inspiration' and 'revelation'. In the past, I found that these categories were, in my opinion, used excessively,[24] but I am now able to understand better what they mean, by considering them in the light of pneumatology. I can also understand more fully the interest taken by the Scholastic theologians in the study of prophecy.[25] It is, of course, true that they studied the question of prophecy analytically and with a confidence, which we would regard as questionable, in the instruments, in other words, the concepts, that they used for that analysis. They were at least interested in ways of knowing that were not rational but linked to the activity of the Spirit. Following his fellow-Dominican Hugh of Saint-Cher, Thomas called prophecy an event: *non est habitus, sed actus*; 'prophetic enlightenment only exists in the spirit of the prophet at the moment of inspiration'. It is, in other words, a charism that is given for the benefit of others and for the community.[26]

The charism of prophecy has continued to be manifested in the Church, no longer in the form of the inspiration of the canonical books of Scripture, but in the form of God's action on souls and on the Church. Scholars have pointed to the existence of this charism in the Middle Ages[27] and have outlined the part played by it and the conditions under which it flourishes in the present life of the Church.[28] The term is understood here in the extended sense in which Thomas Aquinas used it: 'All the gifts that are related to knowledge can be included under the heading of prophecy'.[29] There are, however, many different forms of prophecy.

The first is that of *counsel, advice and warnings* of the kind given, for example, by Hildegard of Bingen (†1179), formally accepted by Pope Eugenius III and his successors.[30]

The second form of prophecy is *spontaneous preaching*. At certain periods in the history of the Church, hermits began to wander, abandoning hearth and home, giving themselves to a life of *peregrinatio* and preaching on their way. This happened particularly in the sixth and seventh centuries and again in the eleventh and twelfth centuries. It is possible to include within this category of great charismatic missionaires such people as Boniface (675–755), Bruno of Querfurt (†1009), Francis Xavier (†1552) and many other more recent figures. P. Boglioni has pointed to the important part played by hermits and monks who preached the Crusades, in this way affirming a kind of autonomy of the inspired word: 'per virtutem mortificationis pervenitur ad licentiam praedicationis'. It is well known that the Crusades took place in a climate of signs, visions and apocalyptic prophecies.[31] In the twelfth century, wandering preachers committed to poverty in accordance with the ideal of the *vita apostolica* were found all over Western Europe, calling on men to repent and to be converted to the gospel.[32]

The third form consists of *interventions in the life of the Church* in a spirit of prophecy. Women have played a remarkable part in this movement. They included, for example, Hildegard of Bingen, already mentioned above, Elizabeth of Schönau (†1164), Rose of Viterbo (1233–1251), Margaret of

Cortona (1247–1297), Bridget of Sweden (1303–1373), Catherine of Siena (1347–1380) and, of course, Joan of Arc (1412–1431). What a succession of saints! Each one had an exceptional mission, thanks to her astonishing charisms.

It has always been in troubled and controversial times that visions and prophecies have abounded, such as those of Robert of Uzès (†1296) during the pontificates of Celestine V and Boniface VIII[33], of the Franciscan John of Roquetaillade (†c. 1365),[34] of Vincent Ferrer[35] and of Savonarola. The great Western schism was a particularly favourable time for visions and prophecies of doom. This provoked a great deal of critical reaction on the part of theologians and the Fathers of the Council of Constance.[36]

The fourth form of prophecy is a *deep understanding of the saving truth* and a correspondingly truthful form of *teaching*. In the patristic and Scholastic tradition of the Church, prophecy is placed firmly within the framework of this activity of the word of God, the sacred texts and the doctrine of salvation.[37] Newman also believed in the prophetic tradition and even in the 'prophetical office', which he distinguished from the episcopal tradition.[38] Theologians who really deserve the name should surely be honoured!

*   *   *

It is the Holy Spirit who sanctifies, but it would clearly be impossible to follow him in his sanctifying process. It is his secret and it is as spacious as the love and mercy of the Father. In the West, theologians and spiritual writers have often described the sanctifying activity of the Spirit under the rather artificial heading of the seven gifts. It would also be impossible to retrace this history.[39] I will do no more than mention one chapter of it, because of the intensity and the insistence of the details of the activity of the Holy Spirit. This is the life of St Dorothy of Montau (1347–1394).

Her life was described by the man who was her spiritual director in her last years, John of Marienwerden.[40] The 'missions' or visits of the Holy Spirit to Dorothy are reduced to an excessively systematic account by this author, who, for example, counts the number of times when Dorothy received ten, nine, eight, seven, six, five, four or three visits! He also reduces these 'missions' to seven modes of manifestation or presence, according to different categories, which he illustrates by means of biblical texts. Despite the form of this treatise, however, the freedom of the Spirit and the generosity of grace break through, and one is conscious of a soul experiencing the fullness of that grace at a time when the Church was experiencing the drama of the Great Schism. Dorothy, a married woman who had had nine children, had been seized hold of by God. Words, a song, cries of joy and supplication and many tears figure in this account of her life, but above all one is aware of a great sweetness.

NOTES

1. See my *L'Eglise de S. Augustin à l'époque moderne* (*Histoire des dogmes*, III/3) (Paris, 1970), pp. 131–132.
2. Anselm of Havelberg, *Dialogi* I (*PL* 188, 1144; Fr. tr. G. Salet, *SC*, 118, pp. 43 and 45); see also M. van Lee, 'Les idées d'Anselme de Havelberg sur le développement des dogmes', *Anal. Praemonstr.*, 14 (1938), 5–35; G. Schreiber, 'Studien über Anselm von Havelberg. Zur Geistesgeschichte des Hochmittelalters', *ibid.*, 18 (1942), 5–90; M.-D. Chenu, *La théologie au douzième siècle* (Paris, 1957), pp. 235ff.; G. Severino, 'La discussione degli "Ordines" di Anselmo di Havelberg', *Bullettino dell' Istituto Storico Italiano per il Medio Evo*, 78 (1967), 75–122. H. Grundmann, *Studien über Joachim von Fiore* (Leipzig, 1927; new ed., Darmstadt, 1966), pp. 92–95, suggests that Anselm may have influenced Joachim.
3. See A. M. Landgraf, 'Die Lehre vom geheimnisvollen Leib Christi in den frühen Paulinen-kommentaren und in der Frühscholastik', *Divus Thomas* (1946), 407–419; see also my book, *op. cit.* (note 1), p. 161. I am also bound to mention Peter Damian, *Liber gratissimus*, c. 15 (*PL* 145, 119; *Lib. de Lite*, p. 37) and *Opusc.* 11, '*Dominus vobiscum*', c. 5–7 (*PL* 145, 235–237).
4. Hugh of Saint-Victor, *De sacramentis*, II, pars 2, c. 1 (*PL* 176, 415); quotation based on Fr. tr. by E. Mersch.
5. See H. de Lubac, *Corpus mysticum. L'Eucharistie et l'Eglise au Moyen Age* (Paris, 1944; 2nd ed., 1949); F. Holböck, *Der eucharistische und der mystische Leib Christi in ihren Beziehungen nach der Lehre der Frühscholastik* (Rome, 1941); my own work, *op. cit.* (note 1), pp. 165ff.
6. Honorius Augustodunensis, *Eucharistion seu de Corpore et Sanguine Domini*, c. 1 (*PL* 172, 1250); see also H. de Lubac, *op. cit.*, p. 186.
7. See, for example, Paschasius Radbert (*c.* 830), *De Corp. et Sang. Domini*, c. 7, n. 1 (*PL* 120, 1284); Alger of Liège, *De sacr.* I, 17 (*PL* 180, 790D); Honorius Augustodunensis, *op. cit.* and *Gemma animae*, I, c. 105 (*PL* 172, 578); Rupert of Deutz (*c.* 1115), *De Trin. et operibus eis. In Exod. lib.* II, c. 10 (*PL* 167, 617); Gerhoh of Reichersberg, *Expos. Psalm. Ps. XXXIII*: see *Gerhohi Opera inedita*, II: *Expositio Psalmorum pars tertia et pars nona*, ed. D. and O. van den Eynde and A. Rijmersdael, II/1 (Rome, 1956), p. 168; Hildegard of Bingen, *Scivias*, lib. II, vis. 6 (*PL* 197, 526 and 528); Peter Celestine, *Sermo* 39, *De Coena Domini* 6 (*PL* 202, 761), who compared the consecration of the Eucharist with the incarnation.
8. Denz. 424; *DS* 793.
9. See K. Goldammer, *Die eucharistische Epiklese in der mittelalterlichen abendländischen Frömmigkeit* (Bottrop, 1941).
10. Full documentation, a bibliography and theological explanations will be found in the articles on 'gifts' ('Dons') in *DTC*, IV (1911), cols 1728–1781 (A. Gardeil) and the *Dictionnaire de Spiritualité*, III, cols 1574–1641 (G. Bardy, F. Vandenbroucke, A. Rayez, M. Labourdette and C. Bernard).
11. Rupert of Deutz, *PL* 167; *SC* 131 and 165. Books I to III: Incarnation, redemption and Sacrament of the Passion = wisdom; Book IV: Apostles = understanding (of Scripture); Book V: Rejection of the Jews in favour of the gentiles = counsel; Books VI to VIII: Martyrs, teachers and penitential monks = power against sin; Book IX: Eschatology = fear of God.
12. *Gerhohi Opera inedita*, *op. cit.* (note 7), II. pp. 448–450.
13. *Ibid.*, I (Rome, 1955), pp. 65–165.
14. I had intended to try, later in this study, to provide some information on the iconography of the Holy Spirit, in which Christian experience and understanding of the Spirit are also expressed. Let me here simply reproduce the following comment that appeared at the end of an article by T. Spasskij on 'L'Office liturgique slave de la "Sagesse de Dieu" ', *Irénikon*,

30 (1957), 188, note 1: 'In a stained-glass window in the cathedral at Chartres (west front, right-hand window, upper panel in the tree of Jesse), Christ is represented as surrounded by seven doves, the upper ones personifying Wisdom (*Sapientia*) and forming an integral part of him (see J. Verrier, *Vitraux de France aux XII*e *et XIII*e *siècles*, Paris, *Histoire des Arts plastiques*, n.d., Plate II). Another stained-glass window, in the Abbey of Saint-Denis, shows Christ between the Church and the synagogue. On his breast is a dove, connected by rays to six other doves (the seven gifts). With his left hand, he is unveiling the synagogue and with his right he is crowning the Church (see E. Male, *L'art religieux au XII*e *siècle en France*, Paris, 1947, p. 166). Finally, in one of the stained-glass rose-windows of Chartres cathedral above the windows in the great nave, there is a representation of the Virgin seated, with a medallion on her knees of Christ as Wisdom. This medallion is attached by rays to six doves surrounding the main figure, as in the window of Saint-Denis.'

15. A. Wilmart, 'Les méditations sur le Saint-Esprit attribuées à S. Augustin', *RAM*, 7 (1926), 17–63, reprinted in *Auteurs spirituels et Textes dévots du Moyen Age latin* (Paris, 1932; repub. 1971), pp. 415–456. Long sections of text are provided by the author.

16. A. Wilmart, 'Prière au Saint-Esprit suivant les sept dons', *VS (Suppl)*, 16 (1927), 323–344, repr. *op. cit.* (note 15), pp. 457–473.

17. For this view of things, see *C. Gent.* IV, 21 and 22; *Comp.* I, 147. It is this idea that governs Thomas' theology of merit.

18. *ST* Ia IIae, q. 9, a. 4 and 6; q. 68, a. 3, ad 2; IIa IIae, q. 23, a. 2, q. 52, a. 1, ad 3. To translate *habitus* as 'habit' would be misleading [the author therefore prefers the old French word *ayance*, which this translation renders by the cognate old English word 'haviour' (see *OED*)].

19. For this distinction, so often stressed by Thomas, see my 'Tradition et sacra doctrina chez S. Thomas d'Aquin', *Eglise et Tradition* (Le Puy and Lyons, 1963), pp. 157–194.

20. See *In I Sent.* d. 16, q. 1, a. 3; *ST* Ia IIae, q. 108, a. 1.

21. *ST* Ia IIae, q. 90 prol; q. 109 prol.

22. See T. Deman, 'Le "Liber de Bona Fortuna" ', *RSPT*, 17 (1928), 38–58.

23. 'Prompte mobilis ab inspiratione divina', 'a Spiritu Sancto', *ST* Ia IIae, q. 68, a. 1 and 8; q. 69, a. 1; IIa IIae, q. 52, a. 1; q. 121, a. 1, etc.

24. See my *Tradition and Traditions* (Eng. tr.; London and New York, 1966), Part One, pp. 91–94, 119–137, 174–176, text and notes.

25. B. Decker, *Die Entwicklung der Lehre von der prophetischen Offenbarung von Wilhelm von Auxerre bis zu Thomas von Aquin* (Breslau, 1940); *idem*, art. in *Angelicum*, 16 (1939), 194–244; J.-P. Torrell, 'Hugues de Saint-Cher et Thomas d'Aquin. Contribution à l'histoire du traité de la prophétie', *RThom*, 74 (1974), 5–22; *idem*, *Théorie de la prophétie et Philosophie de la connaissance aux environs de 1230. La contribution d'Hugues de Saint-Cher* (Louvain, 1977).

26. Thomas Aquinas, *De ver.* q. 12, a. 1 and 5; *ST* IIa IIae, q. 171, a. 2; q. 172, a. 4.

27. See I. von Döllinger, *Der Weissagungsglaube und das Prophetentum in der christlichen Zeit* (1871); P. Alphandéry, 'De quelques faits de prophétisme dans les sectes latines antérieures au joachimisme', *Revue de l'Histoire des Religions*, 52 (1905), 177–218; P. Boglioni, 'I carismi nella vita della Chiesa Medievale', *Sacra Doctrina*, 59 (1970), 383–430.

28. R. Grosche, *Das prophetische Element in der Kirche* (1956), reprinted in *Et intra et extra. Theologische Aufsätze* (Düsseldorf, 1958); K. Rahner, *The Dynamic Element in the Church* (Eng. tr.; London, 1964); A. Ulbyn, *Actualité de la fonction prophétique* (1966); *Concilium*, 37 (Sept. 1968); my *Vraie et fausse réforme dans l'Eglise* (Paris, 1950), pp. 196–228, 2nd ed. (1969), pp. 179–207.

29. *ST* IIa IIae, q. 171 prol. See also, for this wider meaning, q. 174, a. 6; *De ver.* q. 12, a. 2; *Comm. in Mat.* c. 7, lect. 2 and c. 11.

30. Hildegard of Bingen, *PL* 197, 95 and 104, 150 and 153.

31. P. Rousset, *Les origines et les caractères de la Première Croisade* (Neuchâtel, 1945); P.

Alphandéry and A. Dupront, *La Chrétienté et l'idée de croisade*, 2 vols (*L'évolution de l'Humanité*, XXXVIII) (Paris, 1959).

32. H. Grundmann, *Religiöse Bewegungen im Mittelalter*, 2nd ed. (Hildesheim, 1961), made a special study of this question.

33. J. Bignami-Odier, 'Les visions de Robert d'Uzès O.P. (†1296)', *Arch. Fr. Praedic.*, 25 (1955), 258–310. Robert is said to have predicted the plague of 1348.

34. J. Bignami-Odier, *Etudes sur Jean de Roquetaillade* (Paris, 1952).

35. E. Delaruelle, 'L'Antéchrist chez S. Vincent Ferrier, S. Bernardin de Sienne et autour de Jeanne d'Arc', *L'Attesa dell'Età nuova nella Spiritualità della fine del Medio Evo (Convegni, VII)* (Todi, 1962), pp. 37–64.

36. P. Boglioni, *op. cit.* (note 27), p. 420, mentions the reaction of Henry of Langenstein to the illuminism of Telesphorus of Cosaga (see Fliche and Martin, XIV, p. 510), the treatises of Bernardino of Siena, Pierre d'Ailly, Gerson and later Dionysius the Carthusian (†1471). Gerson, Henry of Oorcum and Guillaume Bouillé discussed the case of Joan of Arc and believed that the spirit of prophecy has always been present in the Church.

37. See P. Alphandéry, *op. cit* (note 27), 207ff. See also my *Vraie et fausse réforme, op. cit.* (note 28). Rupert of Deutz, for example, saw prophetism in the understanding that God gives us the words we pronounce in liturgical prayer: see *PL* 170, 12.

38. Newman, *The Via Media*, I, Lect X, note 11, pp. 249–251.

39. See the article on 'gifts' ('Dons') in the *Dictionnaire de Spiritualité*, III, cols 1594ff., for information about Henry of Ghent, St Gertrude, Jan Ruysbroeck, Richard Rolle, Dionysius the Carthusian and, from the sixteenth to the eighteenth centuries, cols 1601ff., for Ignatius Loyola, John of Osuna and others. F. Vandenbroucke is responsible for the first part; A. Rayez for the second. See also the publication of John of Avila (1499–1569), *Sermons sur le Saint-Esprit* (Namur, 1961).

40. John of Marienwerden, *Septililium B. Dorotheae*, ed. F. Hipler, the Rector of the Seminary of Braunsberg, in *Analecta Bollandiana*, 2 (1883), 381–472; 3 (1884), 113–140, 408–448; 4 (1885), 207–251. See also H. Westpfahl, *Dictionnaire de Spiritualité*, III, cols 1640 and 1664–1668. Of particular interest is Treatise II, *De Spiritus Sancti Missione: Analecta Bollandiana*, 3, 113–140.

7

JOACHIM OF FIORE
AND THE FATE OF JOACHIMISM[1]

Born about 1135 in Calabria and possibly of Jewish origin, Joachim gave up legal work, travelled in Syria and Palestine and then entered the Cistercian order and set up the Cistercian monastery of Fiore (Flora) in 1189. He later became abbot, reformed the monastery according to much stricter monastic rules, broke with the order and founded half a dozen daughter-houses. He died on 30 March 1202. In addition to a number of minor works, he left behind a *Concordia Novi ac Veteris Testamenti*, an *Expositio in Apocalypsim*, a *Psalterium decem chordarum*, which he edited in 1184 and subsequently, a *Tractatus super quatuor Evangelia*; and a *Liber Figurarum*, which was written down by one of his disciples.

Joachim's thought was based on a vision of the *concordia* or an understanding of the relationships between the different elements of Old Testament history, New Testament history, and the past or future elements in the history of the Church. He believed that the *littera veteris Testamenti* and the subsequent *littera novi Testamenti* would inevitably be succeeded by a *tertius status*, a new era and a new order. He ascribed each of the three states thus distinguished to one of the Persons of the Trinity: 'Tres status mundi propter tres Personas Divinitatis'.[2] Just as the Spirit proceeds from the Father and the Son, he taught, so too does a 'spiritual understanding' proceed from the Old and the New Testaments.[3] The eternal gospel or the *Evangelium Regni* must succeed the gospel of Christ as preached and celebrated until that time. The people and the events featured in the gospel of Christ symbolize future realities in the age of the Spirit and in the spiritual Church. Each of the three ages has its own first inauguration, a kind of epiphany. The first is inaugurated in Adam and is confirmed in the patriarchs: it is the age of the Father and, in history, the age of the laity. The second is inaugurated in Uzziah and bears fruit in Jesus Christ: it is the age of the Son and the clergy. The third age began with St Benedict and was, according to Joachim, still to be fully manifested.

Joachim was in fact proclaiming the beginning of an age of the Spirit, of spiritual understanding and of the eternal gospel. This age was to be the age of monks, contemplatives and *viri spirituales*, all intimately penetrated by the Spirit. The time of the letter, then, was to be followed by the time of the freedom of the Spirit, a sabbath of pure praise. What had, in other words, generally been reserved for the eschatological era at the end of history was, according to Joachim, introduced into history as the object of hope and expectation. The Church's hierarchy and its sacraments would continue in this age of a religion *omnino libera et spiritualis*, but they would be spiritualized and would correspond more to the Johannine than to the Petrine type. The coming of this age was, Joachim believed, imminent: *tempus prefinitum adest* (*Conc*. V, c. 119; fol. 135b).

Joachim's writings were almost unknown during his own lifetime, but from about 1240 onwards they were widely circulated and associated with tendentious pseudepigraphical texts. The Franciscan Gerard of Borgo San Donnino edited an *Introductorius in Evangelium aeternum* in 1247 and distributed it in 1254. This work caused a great stir and was condemned on 23 October 1255 in the bull *Libellum quendam*. The minister general of the Franciscans, who was favourably disposed towards Joachimism, was replaced in 1257 by Bonaventure.

Bonaventure accepted that certain aspects of the Joachimite proclamation of a historical growth towards the eschatological reality should be applied to Francis of Assisi, who had been an eschatological spiritual man. He also attributed to Scripture a prophetic character and a seminal value with regard not only to Christ—this was also emphasized by Thomas Aquinas, who used it as the basis for a radical criticism of Joachimism—but also to the history of the Church and to the theme of man's knowledge of God within the Church. Bonaventure also included within this framework of knowledge the historical messianism or eschatology by which he was able to accept within the history of salvation the fact of Francis of Assisi. In this way, he was able to deal satisfactorily with certain principles in Joachim's theory of history, but at the same time he succeeded in retaining, in the Franciscan tradition, the absolute primacy and the central position of Christ. According to Bonaventure, there could be no relatively autonomous and new time of the Spirit. The time of the Spirit, as experienced by the Church, had to be the time of Christ.[4] This emphasis neutralizes the venom contained in Joachimism and even eliminates it altogether.

Thomas Aquinas was resolutely, severely and radically critical of Joachim's teaching.[5] He regarded Joachim as a lout playing with theology: 'in subtilibus fidei dogmatibus rudis',[6] and his theology of the Trinity in particular as wrong.[7] Thomas dissociated himself from Bonaventure in his recognition of the typological meaning of the facts contained in the canonical texts of the Old Testament, but rejection of the idea that one particular fact in the New Testament could be seen as corresponding to one particular fact in the Old. Such concordances were, in his opinion, matters not of prophecy, but of human ingenuity.[8]

Thomas did not explicitly refer to Joachim, but cited him almost literally and tacitly alluded to the second of the theses that had been criticized by the theologians of Paris. He expressed this fundamental criticism within the framework of a treatise on the 'new law' which appears to have been an original contribution of his own to thirteenth-century theology (Ia IIae, q. 106). This new law consists principally (and this word should be understood in its full sense) of the grace of the Holy Spirit given in it.[9] The sacramental signs and the rules of belief and conduct have a place in this new law, since this is required by the logic of incarnation (q. 108, a. 1), but they are secondary and at the service of the grace of the Spirit. The *status* or the régime of the New Testament is that of Christ and the Spirit together. It is a definitive *status* and no other age can be expected to follow it. It would be mere *vanitas*, lacking any content of truth, to claim anything else.

In his attempt to disclose future perspectives, Joachim in fact turned his back on the real meaning of Scripture so well disclosed by the early tradition of the Church and the liturgy, according to which the Spirit enables us to understand the Word-Son, who reveals the Father and leads men to the Father. The Thomist theme of *exitus* and *reditus*, on the other hand, was fully in accordance with this traditional meaning of Scripture.

Thomas belonged to an order in which the charisms had been present in the founder, Dominic.[10] In addition, the presence of a *gratia praedicationis* was also taken into account in the Dominican order when it was a question of sending out a friar to preach.[11] Thomas himself used the term.[12] This is an admirable apostolic charism the exercise of which in the history of the Church deserves further study. It was clearly a privilege which the Friars Preachers enjoyed, but which does not seem to have placed them at any time in a critical situation. The chapters took care that friars avoided strange readings and disordered enthusiasms.

The same cannot be said of the Franciscans, who did not avoid a grave crisis: that of the Spiritual Franciscans and the Fraticelli.[13] Joachim had proclaimed the imminence of a new age that would be inaugurated by poor and spiritual religious, although he had not himself greatly insisted on poverty, and Francis had appeared on the scene as a miracle of the evangelical ideal and the perfect image of Christ—*Christo totus crucifixus et configuratus*. Joachim had announced a return of Elijah to inaugurate the third age and a more complete revelation of the Spirit. Francis was that new Elijah, the angel of the sixth seal (Rev 7:2), the one who initiated an age of the Spirit and announced an eternal gospel (Rev 14:6). His evangelical rule of total poverty had to be followed, as he himself had said, 'without a gloss and literally'. From about 1240 onwards, the movement of strict observance, in opposition to the 'Conventuals', gathered strength and hardened after the Council of Lyons in 1274. The so-called 'Spirituals' became more numerous and influential, especially in the Marches under the leadership of Angelo Clareno and in Provence with Petrus Joannis Olivi as their leader. On the one hand, there is the striking evangelical spirit of poverty of those who wanted the Church to be poor and without any earthly domain[14] and who were prepared to suffer for their ideal, even to go to the stake. On the other hand, however, there is the disconcerting spectacle of men who fought and were excommunicated because they refused to abandon positions which seem to us now to be exaggerated and even false.

The situation became even worse during the pontificate of John XXII (1316–1334). The name 'Fraticelli' was applied at about this time to those Franciscans who first of all formed an autonomous group which insisted unconditionally on poverty, and later formed various groups of deviants and rebels. They began by insisting on following a purely spiritual rule of Christ, and from there went on to contestation and even rejection of the sacraments of the Church and of the hierarchy as led by the Pope, who came to be regarded by them as the forerunner of the Antichrist. In their preaching, the Fraticelll were passionate and basically irrational, making liberal use of apocalyptic language.

There was no real continuity between the 'spirituals' of the Franciscan or Joachimite traditions and the Brethren of the Free Spirit, but there were points of contact between them and a fundamental kind of community.[15] These Brethren were in no sense homogeneous. They began to appear from the eleventh century onwards and were loosely affiliated in anti-ecclesiastical and anti-sacramental groups and movements. Their ideas differed quite widely. This is clear, for example, from a comparison between the writings of Speroni and those of Amalric of Bène, whose mystical teaching was quite profound, but who advocated a passivity that was almost quietistic and an indifference to external rules that amounted to an almost complete lack of moral reserve, and spoke of a feeling of being in God that was almost pantheistic: 'Spiritus sanctus in nobis quotidie incarnatur'.

Although the ideas of Abbot Joachim and his followers may not have been regarded as theologically important by the theologians of Paris,[16] they certainly gave rise to human hopes and expectations and caused a stir that was to be felt for a very long time.[17] Has Joachimism ever completely died out? Certain religious foundations have seen themselves to some extent as following the tradition of the 'spiritual men' as proclaimed by Joachim.[18] For a very long time renewals in the Church have been linked with the emergence of religious orders, and thus with initiatives taken by the Holy Spirit.[19]

This, however, is not all that has to be said about Joachim and Joachimism. He introduced into the history of this world, which was for him, of course, the history of the Church, an eschatology that was characterized by the great novelty of a rule of the inner life and of freedom. Joachim in this way opened the flood-gates to admit what could well become the torrent of human hopes. This could at any time result in social protest, a polarized attempt to reform the Church, or many different searches for freedom and novelty. It could take the form of philosophies of reason, of progress, of the 'spirit'. This has, in fact, frequently happened, in many cases with an explicit reference to Joachim. Did he not, after all, say that God would do new things on earth—'facere novum super terram et renovare peccatis inveteratam ecclesiam'?[20] There have been, parallel to what Etienne Gilson called 'metamorphoses of the City of God', a series of 'metamorphoses of Joachimism' (K. Löwith, see below, note 17), which have often been forms of secularization of the Spirit. I summarize the most important.

In his *Sacrum Imperium*, Alois Dempf pointed to the connection between a re-emergence of the eschatological spirit expressed in apocalyptic language and a preoccupation with political questions. This combination clearly appeared in the form of Joachimism that flourished in the thirteenth century, with its hope of an emperor who would save the people and a *Papa angelicus*. Such a Pope appeared in the person of Celestine V, the eighty-year-old hermit from the Abruzzi who reigned no more than a few months in 1294. Then came Boniface VIII! Boniface's enemies, the Colonna, formed an alliance with the 'Spirituals'. As a loyal Ghibelline, Dante (1265–1321) remembered that, in their opposition to the temporal claims of the papacy, the emperor's supporters favoured a Church that was spiritual and poor. He therefore thought highly of 'Abbot Joachim of Calabria, who was endowed with prophetic spirit':

> il Calavrese abate Giovacchino
> di spirito profetico dotato.[21]

Joachimist hopes also abounded in the fourteenth century, especially when the Popes were at Avignon. Cola di Rienzo (1313–1354), the leader of the Roman party, was expecting 'an extension of the Holy Spirit, whose pouring out over all flesh had been promised and who was to renew the face of the earth'.[22] He even called himself a soldier and a knight of the Holy Spirit. This was clearly a case of politics animated by mysticism. A renewal of the world could only be expected as the result of a renewal of the Spirit.

The impulse given by Joachimism to the idea of renewal also had an impact on the literary figures and the philosophers of the Renaissance. Many 'prophets' proclaimed that the end of the fifteenth and the beginning of the sixteenth centuries would be a time not only of tribulation, but also of preparation for a *renovatio mundi*. It was in this climate of feeling that an edition of Joachim's works was prepared in Venice, during the second and third decades of the sixteenth century.[23]

Even more interesting in this context are the Joachimist references in the evangelization of Mexico by the Franciscans and Dominicans in the sixteenth century. This process of evangelization was characterized by a combination of an eschatological perspective, the need to convert the last people who had not yet been evangelized, and a clear reference to the early apostolate of the Church in the number of Franciscans sent in 1523 (twelve!), the whole placed within the context of a clearly Joachimist spirit.[24]

The missionaries had the task of trying to build up a millenarian reign. This is obviously another case of reducing eschatology to a historical perspective and of using apocalyptic terminology to express it.

A new time was, however, on the way—the modern era. This is, of course, a very vague term, but it does point to a relatively continuous movement in which man's reason was set free from a dogmatic framework and from dependence on positive and supernatural religion. It was this that made Michelet say: 'The great century, by which I mean the eighteenth'. It was at this time that explanation from on high was replaced by explanation from below, by natural realities and the movement of the human spirit and human society. G. B. Vico based his philosophy of history on divine providence, but he also showed providence as revealed in the development of languages, religions and laws. This movement took place within humanity, which is its own work (*Scienza nuova*, 1725). In 1780, the year before his death, Lessing published his *Erziehung des Menschengeschlechts*, in which he referred explicitly to a 'new eternal gospel'. The mistake made by the enthusiasts who had proclaimed that gospel in the thirteenth and fourteenth centuries had simply been that they had insisted that its coming was imminent, whereas in fact progress towards that new gospel was slow and it would only be gradually achieved in the history of mankind.[25]

Kant also came very close to this idea. He had already published *Was ist Aufklärung?* in 1784 and, in 1793, he published *Religion innerhalb der Grenzen der blossen Vernunft*, in which he interpreted the history of Christianity as a gradual ascent to a religion of reason, through which the kingdom of God would be realized on earth in the form of an ethical community.

Hegel (1770–1831) wanted to dismiss the Enlightenment, which he described as a 'vanity of understanding', and hoped to re-establish the harmony and even the unity that had existed between religion and reason in a philosophy of the absolute spirit. In an early work, *Der Geist des Christentums und sein Schicksal*, he proclaimed his intention to evolve a philosophy based on the Johannine promise and incorporating the idea of reconciliation and reunion between God and man and between the objective and the subjective spirit. Should we think of it as 'spirit' or as 'Spirit'? Hegel moves from one to the other:

> The spirit is the infinite return to oneself and infinite subjectivity that is not represented, but is true divinity, present, not the substantial in-himself of the Father, nor that of the Son and of Christ, who is the true one in that form in that objectivity. It is what is subjectively present and real, which is subjectively present. . . . This is the Spirit of God, God, the present, real spirit, God dwelling in his community.[26]

According to Hegel, then, the Spirit is God in his community and God has to bring about a return to the absolute Spirit. Is that Spirit the third Person—God as spirit? It is the energy of the manifestation in the three aspects of being in oneself, of externalization and of return to oneself. Hegel himself alludes to the Joachimist view in another essay:

> The Middle Ages were the reign of the Son. In the Son, God is not yet complete. He can only be complete in the Spirit. As the Son, he has put himself outside himself and there is therefore a state of being-differently which can only be transcended (*aufgehoben*) in the Spirit, in God's return to himself. Just as the state of the Son comprises exteriority in itself, exteriority was the rule of the Middle Ages. The reign of the Spirit began with the Reformation, when God became known as Spirit.[27]

Hegel's famous principle of *Aufhebung*, which he used in the sense of preserving and raising to a higher level what is suppressed or transcended, appears in the passage quoted above. There is a deep logic of movement in his thought here, and E. Benz, H. Grundmann, and H. Mottu, who quotes them, have compared the Joachimist ideas of *evacuare* and *consummare* with this powerful Hegelian concept.[28] The imperfection of the New Testament will, in other words, disappear (*evacuabitur*; 1 Cor 13:10), but this state will be transcended, recovered and taken up at the same time in the age of the Spirit, when *quod* perfectum est—'what is perfect'—will come.

Hegel's interpretation seems to me to do grave injustice to the witness of the Bible and to traditional Christian conviction. As J. Greisch has observed, it seeks to achieve an 'integration and a rational appropriation of the Spirit as the latter is expressed in the biblical texts (Rom 8, for example) and it claims to disclose the full meaning of those texts'.

The spiritual horizon was definitively widened by the philosophers of the Romantic movement in Germany such as Lessing, Hegel and Fichte. They looked in philosophy for a vision of the whole of reality to express the full depths of the spirit and man's inner experience. The current of Romantic philosophy to a great extent represented a transposition of Christian values. Its philosophy of history is certainly a transposition of Christian eschatology.

Schelling (1775–1854) followed the Romantic tradition and expressed its ideas very clearly. In his 'Essays on the Philosophy of Art', published in 1804, he said, for example: 'Christ has returned to a world above the senses and has stated that the spirit is to replace him. It is as though he has put an end to the past age. He is the last God. After him comes the spirit, the ideal principle, the soul that will rule the new world.'[29]

Schelling became acquainted with Joachim's ideas through the work of Neander, *Geschichte der christlichen Religion und Kirche* (6 vols, 1826–1852), which was also an important source for many other thinkers and theologians, including, for example, Möhler. In a work written in 1841 and published in 1842 with the significant title of *Philosophie der Offenbarung* ('Philosophy of Revelation'), Schelling took as his point of departure the apparent proclamation in the New Testament of a future going beyond itself, that is, Christ's announcement of the Spirit. The seed sowed on earth by Christianity was, in Schelling's opinion, to grow into a universal vision.

This process is outlined by the philosopher in his Lesson 37 in the figures of the three apostles, Peter, Paul and John. Peter is the one who gives the law; he is the principle of stability. Paul is movement, dialectics and knowledge; he was the first Protestant by virtue of his resistance to Peter's unlimited authority (see Gal 2). The true Church is not to be found in either of these two forms as such. From the time when it was founded on Peter, it moves forward through Paul towards its end, which is to become a Church of John.[30] The true Church is therefore still to come.

These ideas had a favourable reception, not only in Germany, but also in Russia, where Schelling had a considerable influence. This influence extended to the Slavophile movement and even later, in the present century, to D. S. Merezhkovski (1865–1941),[31] who inspired A. Moeller van den Bruck to write his book *Das dritte Reich* (1923), a title that inspired Hitler to try to establish a third empire, kingdom or age, whose dramatic fate we have witnessed. Hitler, after all, announced that he was settling the historical future for a thousand years—the millennium!

Modern philosophies of history may or may not refer to Joachimist themes, and may contain a great deal or only a minimum of utopian hope, but they have often been successors, even re-expressions, of Christian eschatology.[32] An 'eschatological' philosophy of the spirit is therefore a laicization of theology.[33] We obviously cannot pursue this theme here. It is however, interesting to note a direct reference to Joachim of Fiore in the theology of the 'death of God' that flourished in the nineteen-sixties. At that time, Thomas Altizer wrote:

> The radical Christian also inherits both the ancient prophetic belief that revelation continues in history and the eschatological belief of the tradition following Joachim of Floris. This tradition maintains that we are now living in the third and final age of the Spirit, that a new revelation is breaking into this age and that this revelation will differ as much from the New Testament as the New Testament itself does from its Old Testament counterpart. . . . We can learn from earlier radical Christians the root radical principle that the movement of the Spirit has passed beyond the revelation of the canonical Bible and is now revealing itself in such a way as to demand a whole new form of faith. To refuse such a new revelation of the Spirit would be to repudiate the activity of the Word which is present and to bind oneself to a now empty and lifeless form of the Word. Nor can we expect the new revelation to be in apparent continuity with the old. . . . Yet this should by no means persuade us that no new revelation has occurred. We can only judge by the fruits of the Spirit and if a new vision has arisen recording a universal and eschatological form of the Word, a form of the Word pointing to a total redemption of history and the cosmos, then we should be prepared to greet it with the full acceptance of faith.[34]

Needless to say, Joachim would have disapproved of such a use of his ideas. He did not suspect that he had opened up an issue and had initiated a movement to which so many would be able to contribute their own dreams!

NOTES

1. Many books and articles have been written about this subject. Among them are: M. Reeves, *The Influence of Prophecy in the Later Middle Ages. A Study in Joachimism* (Oxford, 1969); C. Baraut, 'Joachim de Flore', *Dictionnaire de Spiritualité*, VIII (1974), cols 1179–1201; B.-D. Dupuy, article in *Catholicisme*, VI (1966), cols 878–887 and 887–895; my *L'Eglise de S. Augustin à l'époque moderne* (Paris, 1970), pp. 209ff. My attention was unfortunately not drawn to H. Mottu, *La manifestation de l'Esprit selon Joachim de Fiore* (Neuchâtel and Paris, 1977), with its very full bibliography, until after my work had been completed.

2. Joachim, *Concordia* IV, c. 6, fol. 9a (repr. Frankfurt, 1964).

3. *ibid.*; *Tractatus super quatuor Evangelia*, ed. E. Buonaiuti, pp. 21–22.

4. For Bonaventure and Joachimism, see E. Gilson, *La philosophie de S. Bonaventure*, 2nd ed. (1943), pp. 21–27; J. Ratzinger, *Die Geschichtstheologie des Hl. Bonaventura* (Munich and Zürich, 1959); H. de Lubac, 'Joachim de Flore jugé par S. Bonaventure et S. Thomas', *Pluralisme et Œcuménisme en Recherches théologiques. Mélanges S. Dock* (Gembloux, 1976), pp. 31–49; O. Stephan, 'Bonaventuras christologischer Einwand gegen die Geschichtslehre des Joachim von Fiore', *Miscellanea Mediaevalia*, ed. A. Zimmermann, 11: *Die Mächte des Guten und Bösen* (Berlin, 1977), pp. 113–130.

5. E. Benz, 'Joachim Studien: III: Thomas von Aquin und Joachim von Fiore', *Zeitschrift für Kirchengeschichte*, 53 (1934), 52–116; an incomplete study. Thomas became acquainted with the writings of Joachim of Fiore in a monastery. See Tocco's life, *Acta Sanctorum Martii*, p. 665; *Fontes vitae S. Thomas Aq.*, ed. D. M. Prummer, fasc. 2 (Toulouse, 1913), pp. 93–94; A. Walz, 'Abt Joachim und der "neue Geist der Freiheit" in Toccos Thomasleben c. XX', *Angelicum*, 45 (1968), 303–315. I know no more than the title of B. McGian, 'The Abbot and the Doctors: Scholastic Reactions to the Radical Eschatology of Joachim of Fiore', *Church History*, 40 (1971), 30–47.

6. *In 2ma Decretal.*

7. *ST* Ia, q. 39, a. 5 and the text cited in note 6 above. Joachim's theology of the Trinity was condemned by the Fourth Lateran Council, c. 2 (November 1215; *DS* 803), although the Council stressed that it did not wish to harm the monastery at Fiore (see *DS* 807). This was the 'second decretal' on which Thomas commented. This commentary was intended for the instruction of the clergy, which had to be checked by the archdeacons.

8. 'Quamvis status novi testamenti in generali sit praefiguratus per statum veteris testamenti, non tamen oportet quod singula respondeant singulis, praecipue cum in Christo omnes figurae veteris testamenti fuerint completae; et ideo Augustinus "exquisite et ingeniose illa singula his singulis comparata videantur, non prophetico spiritu, sed coniectura mentis humanae, quae aliquando ad verum pervenit, aliquando fallitur" (*De civ. Dei* XVIII, 32). Et similiter videtur esse de dictis abbatis Ioachim': *In IV Sent.* d. 43, q. 1, a. 3.

9. *ST* Ia IIae, q. 106, a. 1 and 2; q. 107, a. 1; cf. *Comm. in Rom.* c. 8, lect. 1; *Comm. in Hebr.* c. 8, lect. 3, end. A full bibliography is provided in my 'Le Saint-Esprit dans la théologie thomiste de l'agir moral', *Atti del Congresso internazionale 1974*, 5 (Naples, 1976), pp. 9–19. The reference to the second thesis condemned by the theologians of Paris concerns the identification of the *Evangelium Christi* with the *Evangelium Regni*: see *ST* Ia IIae, q. 106, a. 4, ad 4; *Comm. in Rom.* c. 10, lect. 3; *Comm. in Col.* c. 1, lect. 2. Thomas said that it was *stultissimum*—extremely stupid—to deny that they were identical.

10. See M.-H. Vicaire, 'Charisme et hiérarchie dans la fondation de l'Ordre de Prêcheurs', *Vie Dominicaine*, 31 (Fribourg, 1972), 37–60, repr. in *Dominique et ses Prêcheurs* (Fribourg and Paris, 1977), pp. 198–221; see also Bede Jarrett, *The Life of Saint Dominic* (2nd ed., London, 1934).

11. See the *libellus* of Jordan of Saxony, Dominic's successor, 39, 69 and 77: *MOPH*, XVI (Rome, 1935), pp. 45, 57, 62; Process of Dominic's canonization, 24, 26 and 39: *MOPH*,

XVI, pp. 142, 143 and 158; Gérard de Frachet, *Vitae Fratrum*, Part 3, chapter XI: *MOPH*, I (Louvain, 1896), p. 108, see also pp. 138, 150.

12. *ST* IIIa, q. 7, a. 7; cf. the *gratia sermonis*, Ia IIae, q. 111, a. 4; IIa IIae, q. 177, a. 1; *C. Gentes*, III, 154; *Comm. in Rom.* c. 2, lect. 3; *Comm. in 1 Cor.* c. 1, lect. 2.

13. See E. Benz, *Ecclesia spiritualis. Kirchenidee und Geschichtstheologie der franziskanischen Reformation* (Stuttgart, 1934; 2nd ed., 1964). There are excellent articles on the 'Spirituels', *DTC*, XIV (1939), cols 2522–2549, by L. Oliger; 'Fraticelles', *Dictionnaire de Spiritualité*, V (1964), cols 1167–1188, by C. Schmitt. See also G. Leff, *Heresy in the Later Middle Ages: the Relation of Heterodoxy to Dissent, c. 1250–c. 1450* (New York, 2nd ed. 1967); *Franciscains d'Oc. Les Spirituels c. 1280–1324 (Cahiers de Fanjeaux*, X) (Toulouse, 1975). For the condemnation of Olivi by the Council of Vienne, see *DS* 908; of the Fraticelli by John XXII, see *DS* 910–916, 930.

14. W. C. van Dijk, *Le franciscanisme comme contestation permanente dans l'Eglise. Congrès de l'Association internationale des sciences religieuses* (Munich, 1960).

15. R. Manselli, *Spirituali e Beghini in Provenza* (Rome, 1959). Romana Guarnieri has written a remarkable article on the 'Brethren of the Free Spirit': 'Frères du libre esprit', *Dictionnaire de Spiritualité*, V (1964), cols 1241–1268, which is a summary of her study 'Il movimento del libero spirito', *Archivio italiano per la Storia della pietà*, 4 (1965), 351–708. For the condemnation of the Brethren by Boniface VIII, see *DS* 866; for the criticism of the Beghards at the Council of Vienne (1311–1312), see *DS* 891–899.

16. See, for example, Henry of Langenstein, *c.* 1392: 'qualis fuerat abbas Joachim . . . Parisiensis schola non ignorat. Ibi enim nullius est auctoritatis': *Contra vaticinum Telesphori Eremitae*, in B. Pez, *Thesaurus Anecdotorum* (Augsburg, 1721–23), 1/2, col. 521; see also M. Reeves, *op. cit.* (note 1), p. 426.

17. More or less fully documented evidence will be found in J. Taubes, *Abendländische Eschatologie* (Berne, 1947), with a simple table; Joachim von Fiore, *Das Reich des Heiligen Geistes*, ed. A. Rosenberg (Munich, 1955); K. Löwith, *Weltgeschichte und Heilsgeschehen. Die theologischen Voraussetzungen der Geschichtsphilosophie* (Stuttgart, 4th ed., 1961), Appendix I: *Verwandlungen der Lehre Joachims*, pp. 190–195; M. Reeves, *op. cit.* (note 1) and below (note 18); G. Wendelborn, *Gott und Geschichte. Joachim von Fiore und die Hoffnung der Christenheit* (Vienna and Cologne, 1974); G. Bornkamm, *Gesammelte Aufsätze*, III (see below, note 25).

18. This is especially true in the case of the Franciscans, but it also applies to the Dominicans: see Salimbene; Gérard de Frachet, *Vitae Fratrum*, ed. Reichert (*MOPH*, I), p. 13; M. Reeves, *op. cit.* (note 1), pp. 146ff., 161ff. It would be interesting to investigate the anti-intellectual reaction that existed among the Friars Preachers. Was it in some way connected with Joachimism? The Augustinian hermits of the fourteenth century had recourse to the prophetic spirit of Joachimism: see M. Reeves, 'Joachimist Expectations in the Order of Augustinian Hermits', *RTAM*, 25 (1958), 111–141, and again at the beginning of the sixteenth century, exploiting their title of 'hermits'. The Jesuits also appealed to it: see M. Reeves, 'The Abbot Joachim and the Society of Jesus', *Mediaeval and Renaissance Studies*, 5 (1961), 163–181. These two articles by M. Reeves are summarized, *op. cit.* (note 1), pp. 251–273 and 274–290.

19. See, for example, the bull announcing the canonization of St Dominic by Gregory IX, 3 July 1234: *MOPH*, XVI (Rome, 1935), pp. 190–194; Fr. tr. M.-H. Vicaire, *Saint Dominique de Caleruega d'après les documents du XIIIᵉ siècle* (Paris, 1955), pp. 255–259. Written in the florid style of allegory and making use of striking symbolism, the bull refers to four chariots following each other: the martyrs, the monastic Order of Saint Benedict, the Order of Cîteaux *and of Fiore*, and the Order of Preachers and of Friars Minor.

20. Joachim, *Tractatus*, ed. E. Buonaiuti, p. 283.

21. *Paradiso* XII, 140–141. For Dante and Joachim, see L. Tondelli, *Da Gioacchino a Dante* (Turin, 1944); *idem*, *Il libro delle Figure*, I (Turin, 2nd ed., 1953), pp. 183–400. The

possibility that Dante used a Joachimist source for his vision of the Trinity has also been investigated.

22. M. Reeves, *op. cit.* (note 1), pp. 318–319, 420–421, with reference to K. Burdach's great work, *Vom Mittelalter zur Reformation* (Berlin, 1913–1929); P. Piner, *Cola di Rienzo* (Vienna, 1931). This extract from Rienzo's letter No. 58 is worth noting here: 'De vita aeterna disperare posset ecclesia, si de continuo etiam Spiritus Sancti adventu et renovacione humanarum mencium ab eodem eciam assidue desperaret. Tociens enim renovacione Spiritus indigemus quociens inveteramus et senescimus in peccatis' (p. 315).

23. See G. Toffanin, *La religione degli Umanisti* (Bologna, 1950); Gianpaolo Tognetti, 'Note sul Profetismo nel Rinascimento e la letteratura relativa', *Bullettino dell'Istituto Storico Italiano per il Medio Evo e Archivio Muratoriano*, 82 (1970), pp. 129–157. See also the collection *L'Attesa dell'Età nuova . . . (Convegni*, VII) (Todi, 1962). At the time of the Disputation of Lausanne in 1536, it was a physican, Blancherose, who took up the challenge of Viret and Farel, referring to the Joachimist theme: the age of the Father, that of the Empire, had been followed by that of the Son (the Pope), and this would be followed by the age of the Spirit, that is, of goodness and charity. This third period would be that of physicians! See G. Bavaud, *La Dispute de Lausanne (1536). Une étape de l'évolution doctrinale des Réformateurs romands* (Fribourg, 1956), pp. 34–35.

24. See A. López, 'Los doce primeros apóstoles de Méjico', *Semana de Missiología de Barcelona*, II (Barcelona, 1930), pp. 201–226; J. L. Phelan, *The Millennial Kingdom of the Franciscans in the New World* (Los Angeles, 1956); M. Bataillon, 'Evangélisme et Millénarisme au Nouveau Monde', *Courants religieux et Humanisme à la fin du XVᵉ et au début du XVIᵉ siècle* (Paris, 1959), pp. 27ff.; G. Gaudot, *Utopie et Histoire du Mexique. Les premiers chroniqueurs de la civilisation mexicaine (1520–1569)* (Toulouse, 1977).

25. Lessing, *Die Erziehung des Menschengeschlechts*, §86–89, in *Sämtliche Schriften*, ed. K. Lachmann, XIII (1897), pp. 433–434: '§86. The time of a *new eternal gospel* will come, the time that has been promised to us in the elementary books of the new covenant. §87. Some of the enthusiasts (*Schwärmer*) of the thirteenth and fourteenth centuries may have seized hold of a ray of this new eternal gospel. Their only mistake was to have proclaimed that its appearance was imminent. §88. Their idea of the *three ages of the world* may not have been an idle fancy; certainly they had no bad programme when they taught that the new covenant ought to be *declared obsolete* as the old covenant had been. They preserved the same economy of the same God. Expressed in my language, that is the same plan of general education for the human race. §89. But they acted too quickly. They believed that they could, without enlightenment (*Aufklärung*), without preparation, make their contemporaries, who had barely ceased to be children, into men worthy of their *third age*'. See also K. Löwith, *op. cit.* (note 17), pp. 136ff., 190ff.; G. Bornkamm, 'Die Zeit des Geistes', *Geschichte und Glaube*, Part I (*Gesammelte Aufsätze*, III) (Munich, 1968), pp. 90–103.

26. Hegel, *Vorlesungen über die Philosophie der Religion*, posthumous publication (1832); Fr. tr. J. Gibelin, *Leçons sur la Philosophie de la Religion* (Paris, 1954), Part III, 'La Religion absolue', chapter V, p. 173. See also *Die Phänomenologie des Geistes* (1806); Fr. tr. J. Hippolite, *La Phénoménologie de l'Esprit* (Paris, 1941), Chapter VII, pp. 284–290. See also C. Bruaire, *Logique et religion chrétienne dans la philosophie de Hegel* (1964) and A. Chapelle, *Hegel et la religion* (3 vols, 1966).

27. Hegel, *Vorlesungen über die Philosophie der Weltgeschichte*, posthumous publication (1837), ed. G. Lasson, IV (Leipzig, 1920), p. 881. Hegel believed that the Reformers devalued works and despised the world and in this way enclosed themselves within an abstract form of interiority, with the result that it was not possible for them to realize a society that was reconciled in the unity of the universal and the particular, of the inner and the outward realities. It was therefore not possible for Christianity to accomplish its vocation and the state had to carry out this failed mission!

28. H. Mottu, *op. cit.* (note 1), pp. 109–110 and 132.

29. F. W. J. Schelling, *Werke*, Part 5, Vol. V (Stuttgart, 1859), p. 452.

30. F. W. J. Schelling, *Sämtliche Werke*, II. Abteilung, Vol. IV, 2nd half (1858), pp. 298–344. See also K. Löwith, *op. cit*. (note 17), pp. 191–193. For the theme of the three apostles, see my article 'Eglise de Pierre, Eglise de Paul, Eglise de Jean. Destin d'un thème œcuménique', *The Ecumenical World of Orthodox Civilization. Russian and Orthodoxy*, III: *Essays in Honour of George Florovsky*, ed. A. Blane (The Hague and Paris, 1973), pp. 163–179.

31. Merezhkovski believed that a contrast between the Father and the Son—a theme that recurs in the work of Merleau-Ponty—led to an expectation of the Spirit.

32. See E. Hirsch, *Die Reich-Gottes Begriffe des neueren europäischen Denkens* (Göttingen, 1921); E. Gilson, *Les métamorphoses de la Cité de Dieu* (Louvain, 1952); H. Kesting, 'Utopie und Eschatologie. Zukunfterwartungen in der Geschichtsphilosophie des 19. Jahrhunderts', *Jahrbuch für Rechts- und Sozialphilosophie*, XLI (1954–55), pp. 202–230; see also H. Desroches's studies of utopian socialism and forms of messianism. Ernst Bloch saw Joachim as a forerunner of socialism; see his *Erbschaft dieser Zeit* (Frankfurt, 1962), pp. 133ff.; *Atheismus im Christentum* (Frankfurt, 1968), pp. 217, 292. Joachim was also the prophet of openness to the future: see K. Löwith, *op. cit*. (note 17), pp. 136ff

33. E. von Hartmann (1842–1906) followed a pantheistic course in his *Philosophie des Geistes* (1882).

34. Thomas Altizer, *The Gospel of Christian Atheism* (Philadelphia, 1966), p. 27, with reference to William Blake, Hegel und Nietzsche.

8

PNEUMATOLOGY IN THE HISTORY OF PROTESTANTISM

THE REFORMERS

In this section, we shall consider Luther and Calvin.[1] Both kept to the classical teaching of Nicaea and Constantinople (381) and even to the Creed *Quicumque* with regard to the Trinity. Both had to fight on two fronts. On the one hand, they had to combat entrenched 'Catholic' positions which were rightly or wrongly identified with a need to regard the 'Church', or rather the 'hierarchy', as absolute. On the other hand, they had to fight against 'enthusiasts' who appealed to the Spirit in their claim that they were furthering the reforming movement. The enthusiasts whom Luther had to resist were the *Schwärmer* Storch, Müntzer and Karlstadt, and those whom Calvin opposed were the Anabaptists. Both Reformers kept to a middle road, or rather a synthesis, and each in his own way insisted on a close relationship between an external 'instrument' of grace—Scripture—and the activity of the Spirit.

Andreas Karlstadt (originally Bodenstein) had been Luther's friend and had even awarded him his doctor's degree in 1512.[2] He held the same doctrine as Luther on justification by faith alone, but he was much more radical and, while Luther was absent in hiding in the Wartburg, he conducted a fanatical campaign at Wittenberg against images, the Real Presence in the Eucharist, and infant baptism (1524). The break with Luther became wider when Karlstadt wrote and published in March 1525 his *Anzeig etlicher Hauptartikel christlicher Lehre* in reply to the treatise that Luther had just published in the same year: *Wider die himmlichen Propheten, von den Bildern und Sakrament*. The false 'heavenly prophets' mentioned in the title by Luther were Storch and Müntzer. The latter had been active at Zwickau and then at Allstedt.

Not only historians of the left wing of the Reformation, but also Marxist historians and theoreticians have been interested in Müntzer.[3] He was not a 'spiritual' who could be compared with what might have survived from the mysticism of the Brethren of the Free Spirit. As against the theological reformation that took place at Wittenberg, he strove to achieve a popular reformation. He proclaimed the end of the last empire of this world and the disappearance of priests, monks and irreligious lords. He claimed to be the Daniel of the new rule. Since the princes of the world would not follow him, the poor would be chosen. Müntzer claimed that he had assimilated the ideas of Joachim of Fiore—in fact he had read the pseudo-Joachimist commentary on Jeremiah[4]—but, whereas Joachim had proclaimed an age of contemplatives, Müntzer joined the peasants in revolt. When they were defeated at Frankenhausen, he was taken prisoner and hanged on 27 May 1525. His ideas persisted in the Anabaptist movement which was inaugurated at Zwickau in 1521, but that movement became so diversified that it would be impossible to examine it here.

Luther called the Zwickau prophets, the Anabaptists and the sacramentarians *Schwärmer*, fanatical enthusiasts.[5] He described them thus in 1537:

In these things that refer to the external word of the mouth, it is important to insist firmly on this: that God only gives his Spirit or grace through or with the previously existing external word. This is our safeguard against the enthusiasts, in other words, those spirits who flatter themselves that they have the Spirit independently of the word or before it and who consequently judge, interpret and extend Scripture or the word of the mouth according to their will. This is what Müntzer did and what is done today by very many people who want to be judges discerning between the spirit and the letter, and who do not know what they are saying or teaching. Papism is also pure enthusiasm, since the Pope claims to 'keep all laws in the casket of his heart' and since everything that he decides and commands with his Church is spirit and must be regarded as just, even if it goes beyond Scripture or the spoken word and is contrary to them. . . . That is why we have the right and we are obliged to insist that God is only able to enter into a relationship with us men through the external word and the sacraments. Everything that is said of the Spirit independently of this word and the sacraments is the devil![6]

The same idea occurs in Luther's writing two years later:

When we were taught by the gospel that some external thing could not save us because it was a question of simple creatures which the devil had often used for sorcery, even great and learned men (Karlstadt) concluded from this that baptism, as external water, the word, as external and human speaking, Scripture, as external letters made in ink, and the wine and the bread, as baked by the baker, were only external, perishable things. And they began to shout: Spirit! Spirit! It is the Spirit who must act—the letter kills! It was in this way that Müntzer called us, the theologians of Wittenberg, learned in Scripture (*Schriftgelehrte*; scribes), while he himself claimed to be learned in the Spirit (*Geistgelehrter*).[7]

Luther defined quite clearly the rôle that he attributed to the Spirit, as closely related to the gospel and to faith in Jesus Christ as saviour through listening to and clinging to that Word that is preached according to Scripture. It was, according to Luther, through the Word that men were introduced into the Church as the community of those who were sanctified by the Spirit on the basis of faith.[8] In Luther's opinion, the purest example of this process by which the Christian was made was to be found in Mary. He outlined this idea in his commentary on the Magnificat:

In order to understand this holy canticle, it is necessary to note that the Virgin Mary speaks after having had a personal experience through which the Holy Spirit enlightened and taught her. No one can understand either God or his word if he has not been directly enlightened by the Holy Spirit. The activity of the Holy Spirit has to be experienced and felt, and it is by having these experiences that one is taught by the Holy Spirit. If one has not been through that school, words remain no more than words. The holy Virgin, who was so small, so poor and so despised, by having the experience—which God created in her—of such great things, learned from the Holy Spirit that great knowledge that God only wanted to manifest his power by raising up what was lowly and debasing what was exalted.[9]

For Luther, Scripture was self-explanatory and made Christ the saviour recognized; but in order to do this, it required the activity or the witness of the Spirit in men's hearts.[10] It was, however, Calvin who elaborated this theme and he did so with a special emphasis of his own.

It was not, according to Calvin, simply a question of being enlightened by the Holy Spirit in order to understand Scripture. This undoubtedly played a part,[11] but that was also a classical datum in the writings of the Fathers and throughout the Middle Ages. Like Luther, Calvin believed that it was the condition of faith in the Word that constituted the Church, but, whereas Luther maintained that the principle enabling us to discern an apostolic and inspired Scripture is whether it speaks of Jesus Christ, Calvin taught that it was the inner witness of the Holy Spirit that made it possible for us to discern what was the word of God, and therefore inspired, and what was not.

Like Luther, Calvin also had to fight on two fronts. On the one hand, he defended the baptism of infants, the holiness of the Church, the relationship between the Old and the New Testaments and the importance of Scripture against the Anabaptists (those 'furious beasts who are driven by a frenzied lack of restraint to ramble on about spiritual regeneration'). On the other hand, he also had to oppose what he believed to be the Roman position (which was not and still is not that position, even though certain statements made by the Church give the impression that it is), namely that the authority of Scripture is granted by the Church. He was concerned—and rightly concerned—to attribute the authority of Scripture not to the Church, but exclusively to God and therefore to attribute (re)cognition of Scripture to God's activity in us. This was, in his opinion, necessary so that certainty of faith should be totally based in God. The following statement appears in Calvin's *Institutes* of 1539:[12]

We must regard the authority of Scripture as higher than human reasons, factors or conjectures. This is because we base that authority on the inner witness borne by the Holy Spirit. For I know that, in its own majesty, Scripture has sufficient to make it revered, but it only really begins to touch us intimately when it is sealed in our hearts by the Holy Spirit. Because we are enlightened in this way by the virtue of Scripture, we no longer believe either in our own judgement or in that of others that Scripture is from God. Beyond all human judgement, we have no doubt at all

140

that it was given to us from God's own mouth by the ministry of men. It is as if we have sight of the very essence of God in it.[13]

Article IV of the La Rochelle Confession of Faith of 1571, which is that of the French Reformed Church, is in accordance with this fundamental argument.[14] I have criticized this argument elsewhere because it contains the risk of attributing to a feeling or instinct experienced by the subject an ability to discern which Calvin himself attributed firmly to the Holy Spirit. It is, after all, possible to identify the inner witness borne by the Spirit with the voice of man's conscience and ultimately even with his reason. This has in fact happened in history.[15]

The doubtful way in which Calvin applies the inner witness of the Holy Spirit to the discernment of the canonical Scriptures as distinct from those which are not authentic, in the way we discern 'light from darkness, white from black and sharp from sweet', is not of particular interest to us in our present context. What is, however, interesting is the general principle which forms the basis of his ecclesiology (see B. C. Milner) and according to which 'God works doubly in us: within us through his Spirit and outside us through his word' and by the sacraments. The terms that Calvin liked to use in this connection were 'joined by a mutual bond', 'united with' and 'the instrument of'. Such terms are the hallmarks of a sound pneumatology and ecclesiology, even if they are not enough to define all the realism of the presence of Jesus in the Eucharist. This is because for Calvin, that presence was brought about by the Holy Spirit in the recipient, through bread being united with him as a sign and a pledge from God, whilst remaining ordinary bread. As we shall see later, the soundness of a pneumatology can be judged by a Christological reference to the Word, the sacraments, the ecclesial institution, provided always that such a reference fully recognizes and respects the place and rôle of the Spirit.

Has this balance always been preserved in the many different movements that have resulted from and have been more or less directly and legitimately associated with the Reformation of the sixteenth century? It would, of course, be quite impossible to discuss all of these Protestant movements. A selection has to be made and in this chapter I shall confine myself to George Fox and the Quakers, Pietism, the Camisards, and Edward Irving and his followers. Pentecostalism, as a phenomenon that resulted from the holiness movements, which in turn were a product of Methodism, will be mentioned in Volume II.

GEORGE FOX AND THE SOCIETY OF FRIENDS (QUAKERS)[16]

The events and ideas preceding the emergence of Quakerism have been studied in detail by a number of scholars.[17] We can briefly outline them here.

There were in the first place still strong influences from Eckhartian mysticism, the Free Spirit movement, the writings of Nicholas of Cusa and Jacob Boehme (via John Everard; see Sippell, note 16 below). Anabaptists and Schwenckfeldians were still spreading their ideas, which included a criticism of the sacrament and an emphasis on the primacy of the spirit rather than the letter. There was also a prevalent conviction that inner, personal inspiration took precedence over the teaching authority of doctors. Finally, in England especially, religion was seen to be based on a personal inner light, at least according to such groups as the Familists, the Ranters[18] and the Seekers. However, predecessors and influences do not explain a man like George Fox.

He was born in July 1624 and, even as a child, was struck by the seriousness of things and of the inner life. He left his family on 9 September 1643 and, convinced by his own experience that God loved him and illuminated him inwardly, he began to lead a wandering life dedicated to listening to God and to communicating to men, in season and out of season, a message that was full of a powerful inner flame, namely that there is a divine light and that every man is able to experience it. This experience was true Christianity. There was no need for external worship. Fox rejected the sacraments and the established ministry. True worship did not take place in temples or churches, which Fox called 'steeple-houses'. Not even Scripture could, in Fox's opinion, be regarded as the Christian norm. There was no other principle of worship and no other rule than the Holy Spirit, who revealed himself in the inner light and who baptized with the true baptism. The only cult which Fox practised or believed to be acceptable was listening to God in silence. The believer's inner prayer was formed, according to Fox, in that silent listening and only a word of revelation, which one or other of those present at the meeting might be inspired to communicate, would break the silence.

The Friends believe, then, that there are no sacraments and no ministry and that God speaks through and in all men. Even the history of the Bible as a sequence of events is of less value than the experience of the inner presence of God. They are convinced of the sacred character of each man, and that each man is capable of a personal, direct and autonomous relationship with God. It is this conviction that provides the basis for their rejection of violence and their active and boundless help of others. They are active in their struggle for the rights of man as established in God (Sippell particularly stresses this aspect of Quakerism). In 1947, the Friends were awarded the Nobel Peace Prize.

The lives of the Quakers as illuminated by the presence of God can only be admired, but certain misgivings are aroused by the absolute assurance with which Fox ceaselessly identified his own person, his activity and his words with God's cause. He also made little distinction between the inner light of the human conscience and the Holy Spirit; there is in fact no Quaker theology of the Holy Spirit as the third Person. He has no sense of the Church[19] and the absolute individualism of his inspiration imposes a terrible limitation on his life, which was in every way quite heroic.

The Quaker position cannot be justified by recourse to the New Testament. The Spirit does not, in Scripture, have that autonomy with regard to the word that is given and received externally. The apostolic mission has certain conditions of truth. Even from the point of view of pure Christian experience, the whole aspect of the sacraments, doctrine and the Church as a community is an inalienable element of the gifts by means of which God establishes communion with us.

PIETISM[20]

Pietism released those subjective and lyrical elements which had inspired early Lutheranism, but which Luther himself had later banished. The Pietist remained obedient to the institutional Church, but regarded it as necessary to give individual life to the faith of all believers, to commit them fundamentally to the everyday Christian struggle, to stimulate their understanding of personal responsibility and to enlighten them so that they would become true sons of God and betrothed to Christ. Those ardent Christians who were visited in this way by the Spirit would meet in small groups, discuss the Bible, communicate their intimate experiences to each other and regard themselves as the leaven of the Church. These little cells were animated by an intense moral ferment, a deep feeling and a sharp spirit of self-awareness; regional differences were especially marked in them.[21]

In his concluding statement above, R. Minder means by 'regional differences' the elements distinguishing Spener, the Alsatian Pietist who became a minister at Frankfurt and Leipzig and who was a moralist rather than a mystic, Francke, the North German from Lübeck who became the systematic organizer of the movement at Halle, and Zinzendorf, the great Silesian representative of mysticism in the Pietistic movement.

The words 'Pietist' and 'Pietism' refer to the book published in 1675 by Philipp Jakob Spener—*Pia Desideria*.[22] Spener had studied at Strasbourg and Basle. He had visited Geneva and had read the works of Luther, but, just as a mysticism based largely on feeling had asserted itself in a climate of dialectical Scholastic theology in the fourteenth and fifteenth centuries, so too did Spener want to go beyond a Lutheran orthodoxy that was too rigidly committed to pure formulae and give new life to the personal experience of faith. He accepted the teaching of the theologians of the conscience and especially that of Tauler (the *Theologia Deutsch*) and extended Luther's idea of justification by faith alone into an experience of rebirth in an active love of God and one's neighbour.[23] When he was in Frankfurt, from 1666 to 1686, he had groups of Christians meeting in his own home and then in other houses. These came to be known as *collegia pietatis* and at them members let themselves be permeated with the spiritual message of Scripture. He

143

refrained from being a reformer, but he did introduce at least one principle of renewal into the Church in his conviction that the minister had neither a monopoly nor a totality of charisms. The Spirit, he believed, was active in all Christians and in all groups of true Christians. All that was necessary was to let him be active. Without him, all that Scripture contained was a dead letter, a text like any other, not the word of God and his active presence, nourishing man's life and soul. What Spener repeated again and again to his 'basic communities'—for that was, after all, what his groups were—was the Pauline text: 'Let the word of Christ dwell in you richly, as you teach and admonish one another in all wisdom and as you sing psalms and hymns and spiritual songs (= songs inspired by the Spirit)' (Col 3:16).[24] The ecclesiological implications of this text are obvious.

Some of the strange manifestations that occurred in the Cévennes (see following section)—visions, sweating blood or tears of blood, and inner speaking—also occurred in Pietist circles, for example, in Halle at the beginning of the eighteenth century.

Nikolaus Ludwig, Graf von Zinzendorf (1700–1760), can certainly be described as a Pietist on the basis of his evident fervour for Jesus as saviour.[25] He went far beyond Pietism, however, in his unfailing affirmation of salvation by faith alone, as against a process of sanctification through experiences and spiritual progress, and his missionary zeal, which led the intimate pious groups to burst out into the world. His complex personality, his actions in the world and his ecumenical activity, however, do not come within the scope of this present study.

The word 'pietism' is often used today in a much wider sense, pointing to a sentimental kind of fervour and an indifference to exact teaching and demanding study.[26] In addition to this, the modern neo-Pentecostalism or Renewal in the Spirit has sometimes been described as pietistic.

THE 'PROPHETISM' OF THE CEVENNES[27]

I have put 'prophetism' between inverted commas, not because I want in any way to detract from the heroism of those Protestants who were defending their faith and their freedom of conscience, but because the spectacular manifestations of 'prophetism' which accompanied the revolt in the Cévennes were rather suspect.

The history of this movement cannot be understood without some knowledge of the dramatic circumstances of the period. Louis XIV was at that time pursuing a policy of bringing Protestants into the Catholic Church. The Edict of Nantes was revoked in 1685 and this was followed by the dragoons of Villars, the exodus of thousands of Huguenots, forced conversions to Catholicism, but in the Cévennes, the Church of the desert (see Rev 12:6) and armed resistance. From Holland, Pierre Jurieu encouraged the people of the Cévennes and even filled them with extravagant hopes, proclaiming the end of the papal empire in 1689 and the return of the exiles in 1710, and then in 1715. Literally released from his chains, he published in 1686 *L'Accomplissement des prophéties ou la délivrance de l'Eglise* and, in 1686–1689, *Lettres pastorales adressées aux fidèles de France qui gémissent sous la captivité de Babylone*. From 1689 to 1702, Jurieu went so far as to act as an employee of the Admiralty in England to stir up civil war in France. His fiery messages aroused a strong echo in the Cévennes and the Camisard uprising began in 1702. It was accompanied by a mixture of apocalyptic excitement—there were constant references to Joel 2:28–29—and military realism. The part played by a more or less unhealthy prophetism should not be exaggerated, but, in addition to demonstrations of biblical and prophetical exaltation on the part of those who conducted God's war, there were also scenes in which it is difficult to disentangle an intervention of the Spirit from a very unwholesome exaltation. The prophets, who were often very young, struck their heads, rolled on the ground, foamed at the mouth, fell to the ground as though in a cataleptic seizure, were shaken by convulsions and trembling and either uttered words in an unknown language[28] or 'prophesied' resistance, God's help and even a continuation of pitiless fighting and killing. After the Camisard uprising was over, Protestantism was restored under the leadership of Antoine Court, 'who was very severe with the prophets, whom he had seen at close quarters'.[29]

EDWARD IRVING[30]

A circle dedicated to apocalyptic and eschatological ideas existed in London during the first third of the nineteenth century. It had been founded and was led by the banker Henry Drummond. This 'school of prophets' was joined, in 1825, by the Scottish revivalist preacher Edward Irving, who was born in 1792 and had become a Presbyterian minister in 1815. The members of this circle lived in an atmosphere of charisms and in expectation of the imminent return of Christ. It was learnt in 1830 that certain ordinary people of Clydebank had received the gift of speaking in tongues. This was at once seen as a response to the prayers of the London revivalists, who without delay sent a delegation to Scotland. When its members returned, the London community also began to speak in tongues.

Because of Christ's expected return, the decision was taken to restore to the Church its Pentecostal purity and its early structure, including the functions of apostles, prophets, evangelists, pastors and teachers (see Eph 4:11). On 7 November 1832, Drummond appointed, by means of 'prophecy', the first apostle. This was not Irving, who died soon after, on 8 December 1834, in Glasgow, but John Bate Cardale. The Catholic Apostolic Church had come into existence. Its later history and the

'New Apostolic' secession do not come within the scope of our present research.

* * *

I am well aware of the fact that some of the data that I have provided concerning pneumatology in Reformed Christianity have been outrageously partial and oversimplified. I do not claim to have outlined the theology of the Spirit of those individuals and communities that have developed one—I have, for instance, not even mentioned Karl Barth or Emil Brunner—nor have I attempted to show what the activity of the Spirit was in those Protestant individuals and communities. It is, however very important to say something here, in conclusion, about what Emile G. Léonard regarded as a striking aspect of the Protestant believer—his individual expectation of divine intervention and his expectation of a revival of the Church.

The life of the Protestant communities has always been punctuated by 'revivals' going back to the activity of the Holy Spirit. Such revivals include, for example, the Methodist revival led by John Wesley in Great Britain from about 1729 onwards and in the United States from 1735 onwards,[31] the French revival movement of 1830,[32] the 1858 revival in the United States, the revival in Wales in 1905[33] and the activity of the Missionary Brigade in the Drôme region of France from 1922 onwards. This is, of course, no more than a bare list of names. It would be impossible for me to embark on a general study of the phenomenon known as 'revival' here.[34] I will therefore conclude by quoting a few lines written by a young Protestant preparing for the ministry, Yann Roullet, which were published in an article a year after he had been executed on 2 September 1944 in the concentration camp of the Struthof in Alsace:

> The Spirit of God goes before us. He acts or does not act ahead of us. May I call on that Spirit with all my strength and may he overwhelm my parish! Then I shall speak among the cypresses and beside the tombs and will receive a reply. It is probably needless for this revival or recall—who knows what to call it?—that believers should 'speak in tongues' or be shaken by convulsions. . . .[35]

NOTES

1. For Luther, see R. Prenter, *Spiritus Creator. Studien zu Luthers Theologie* (Munich, 1954); K. G. Steck, *Luther und die Schwärmer* (Zürich, 1955); P. Fraenkel, 'Le Saint-Esprit dans l'enseignement et la prédication de Luther, 1538–1546', *Le Saint-Esprit* (Geneva, 1963); M. Lienhard, 'La doctrine du Saint-Esprit chez Luther', *Verbum Caro*, 76 (1965), 11–38.
   For Calvin, see J. Pannier, *Le témoignage du Saint-Esprit. Essai sur l'histoire du dogme dans la théologie réformée* (Paris, 1893); A. Lecerf, *Introduction à la Dogmatique réfor-*

mée, II (Paris, 1938), pp. 173–240; M. Neeser, 'Raison, révélation et témoignage du Saint-Esprit dans la tradition protestante', *RTP* (1943), pp. 129–144; E. Grin, 'Expérience religieuse et témoignage du Saint-Esprit', *Et. Théol. et Rel.* (1946), 327–244; T. Preiss, *Le témoignage intérieur du Saint-Esprit (Cahiers théologiques*, 13) (Neuchâtel and Paris, 1946); W. Krusche, *Das Wirken des Heiligen Geistes nach Calvin* (Göttingen, 1957); G. W. Locher, *Testimonium internum. Calvins Lehre vom Heiligen Geist und das hermeneutische Problem* (Zürich, 1964); B. C. Milner, Jr, *Calvin's Doctrine of the Church* (Leiden, 1970); J. L. Klein, 'L'Esprit et l'Ecriture', *Et. Théol. et Rel.*, 51 (1976), 149–163.

2. For Karlstadt, apart from articles in dictionaries, see H. Barge, *Andreas Bodenstein*, 2 vols (1905); K. Müller, *Luther und Karlstadt* (1907); E. Hertzsch, *Karlstadt und seine Bedeutung für das Luthertum* (1932); R. J. Sider, *Andreas Bodenstein von Karlstadt. The Development of his Thought, 1517–1525* (Leiden, 1974).

3. M. M. Smirin, *Die Volksreformation des Thomas Müntzer und der grosse Bauernkrieg*, 2nd ed. (Berlin, 1952; tr. from Russ.); Norman Cohn, *The Pursuit of the Millennium. Revolutionary Millenarians and Mystical Anarchists of the Middle Ages*, 3rd ed. (London and New York, 1970), pp. 234–251; H. Fast, *Der linke Flügel der Reformation (Klassiker des Protestantismus*, IV) (Bremen, 1962), pp. vii-xxxiv; T. Nipperdey, 'Theologie und Revolution bei Münzer', *Archiv für Reformationsgeschichte*, 54 (1963), 145–181; E. Bloch, *Thomas Münzer, théologien de la révolution* (Paris, 1964; the original German book appeared in 1921, then in 1960); B. Töpfer, *Das kommende Reich des Friedens. Zur Entwicklung chiliastischer Zukunfthoffnungen im Hochmittelalter* (Berlin, 1964); W. Elliger, *Thomas Müntzer. Leben und Werk* (Göttingen, 1975); R. Schwarz, *Die apokalyptische Theologie Müntzer und die Taborlten* (Tübingen, 1977).

4. Thomas Müntzer, *Schriften und Briefe*, ed. G. Franz and P. Kirn (Gütersloh, 1968), p. 398, quoted by E. Bloch, *op. cit.*, p. 134.

5. P. Wappler, *Thomas Müntzer und die Zwickauer Propheten* (1908); N. Cohn, *op. cit.* (note 3), pp. 252–280; U. Gastaldi, *Storia dell'Anabattismo. I: Dalle origine a Münster (1525–1535)* (Turin, 1972). There is an immense bibliography: see H. J. Hillerbrand, *A Bibliography of Anabaptism, 1520–1630* (Elkhart, Ind., 1962).

6. Schmalkaldic Articles, III, 8: *Bekenntnisschriften* (Göttingen, 1952), pp. 453–454; *WA* 50, 245ff., Fr. tr. P. Jundt.

7. *Von den Konziliis und Kirchen*, 1539; *WA* 50, 646. In the Formula of Concord of 1577, the following definition of *Schwärmer* appears: 'Those who expect a heavenly illumination from the Spirit without any preaching of the Word of God are called enthusiasts'.

8. See the commentary on the third article of the Creed in the Little and the Great Catechism. According to the latter, 'Just as the Father is called creator and the Son is called saviour, so too must the Holy Spirit, because of his work, be called sanctifier. How does this sanctification take place? . . . In the first place, the Holy Spirit enables us to enter his holy community, the bosom of the Church, where he leads us to Christ by preaching. For neither you nor I would know anything of Christ, nor would we be able to believe in him or have him as Lord if the Holy Spirit did not place it in our hearts by the preaching of the gospel. The work is accomplished and Christ has gained a treasure for us by his passion, death and resurrection. If that work were to remain hidden, however, and if no one were to know anything about it, it would have been useless. So that this treasure should not remain buried, but so that we might benefit from it and enjoy it, God had the Word proclaimed and gave the Holy Spirit through it in order to bring and to communicate to us this treasure and this salvation. Sanctification is synonymous with leading to the Lord Christ to receive his benefits and what we would not have been able to obtain through our own efforts. . . . The Holy Spirit has a community of his own in this world. That community is the mother who gives birth to every Christian and feeds him by the Word of God which the Holy Spirit reveals and has proclaimed. He enlightens and inflames hearts so that they will grasp the Word, accept it, cling to it and remain faithful to it. Wherever he does not have the Word proclaimed and it does not penetrate into hearts so that it is understood, all is lost. . . .

Wherever Christ is not preached, the Holy Spirit is not at work—he who creates the Christian Church and who calls and brings together the members of that Church, outside of which no one can come to Christ.' Gerhard Sauter, *Kirche—Ort des Geistes* (Freiburg, 1976), pp. 59–106, has applied Luther's teachings to the present situation in the Church, but one is bound to ask whether this theology, which is dominated by its emphasis on Christ and the Word, can really be regarded as fully pneumatological. For this question, see M. Kwiram, 'Der Heilige Geist als Stiefkind? Bemerkungen zur Confessio Augustana', *TZ*, 31 (1975), 223–236, who has gathered together all the declarations. This, however, leaves me anxious for more.

9. *WA* 7, 538.

10. Paraphrase of the Magnificat; see *WA* 7, 546, 548; Letter to Spalatin in *WA, Briefwechsel* I, p. 57 ; *Traité du serf arbitre* (Fr. tr. in series *Je sers*) (1936), p. 110; Comm. on Galatians (1531) in *WA* 40, 574, 578.

11. The *Christianae Religionis Institutio* or 'Institutes' of 1536, final French edition of 1560 (*Institution chrétienne*), IV, c. 14, §8, end. See also J. Pannier, *op. cit.* (note 1), p. 75, and p. 125 for the First Catechism and the Confession of Faith of 1537. For Calvin's struggle against the Anabaptists, see 'Contre la secte phantastique et furieuse des libertins qui se nomment spirituels' of 1545, *Opera Calvini* in the *Corpus Reformatorum*, VIII.

12. In its Fr. tr. of 1541, reproduced in the Guillaume Budé collection, I, pp. 65ff. See also J. Pannier, *op. cit.*, pp. 82ff.

13. *Inst.* of 1541, *Opera Calvini* in *Corpus Reformatorum*, III, p. 368. See also Pannier, *op. cit.*, p. 106.

14. 'We know that these books are canonical and therefore a certain rule for our Faith, not so much because of the common consent and agreement of the Church as because of the inner persuasion and witness of the Holy Spirit, which enables us to discern them from other books of the Church. However useful the latter may be, it is not possible to base any article of Faith on them.'

15. See my *Vraie et fausse réforme dans l'Eglise* (1950), pp. 482–503, or in the later edition (1969), pp. 432–459; there are, at the end, references to liberal and rationalist interpretations. See also S. Castellion, quoted by Pannier, *op. cit.* (note 1), p. 116.

16. An immense number of books have been written about George Fox, the Quakers and the history of Quakerism. The following is a selection: George Fox's *Journal*, first pub. 1694 and frequently re-edited; see especially *The Journal of George Fox. A Revised Edition* by J. L. Nickalls, with an Epilogue by H. J. Cadbury and an Introduction by G. F. Nuttall (Cambridge, 1952); Robert Barclay, *An Apology of the True Christian Divinity, being on Explanation and Vindication of the Principles and Doctrines of the People called in Scorn, Quakers*, numerous editions, the Latin text dating back to 1676; (another) Robert Barclay, *The Inner Life of the Religious Societies of the Commonwealth* (new edition, 1876); J. R. Harris, ed., *New Appreciations of George Fox. A Tercentenary Collection of Studies* (1925); T. Sippell, *Werdendes Quäkertum. Eine historische Untersuchung zum Kirchenproblem* (Stuttgart, 1937); R. Knox, *Enthusiasm. A Chapter in the History of Religion* (Oxford, 1950), pp. 139–175, which consists mainly of anecdotes, stressing the eccentricities of the Quaker movement; P. Held, *Der Quäker George Fox, sein Leben, Werken, Kämpfen, Leiden, Siegen* (Basle, 1953); L. Eeg-Olafsson, *The Conception of the Inner Light in Robert Barclay's Theology. A Study in Quakerism* (*Studia Theol. Lundensia*, 5) (Lund, 1954); H. van Etten, *George Fox, fondateur de la Société chrétienne des Amis* (Paris, 1923); *idem*, *Le Quakerisme* (Paris, 1953).

17. See in note 16 especially R. Barclay (2); T. Sippell; R. Knox, *op. cit.*, pp. 139–142, 168–175.

18. See Norman Cohn, *op. cit.* (note 3), pp. 287–330, Appendix: 'The Free Spirit in Cromwell's England: The Ranters and their Literature'. There is evidence of the movement from 1646 onwards. It referred to three ages—those of the Father, the Son and the Spirit, which will be poured out over all flesh.

19. Lindsay Dewar, *The Holy Spirit and Modern Thought. An Inquiry into the Historical,*

Theological and Psychological Aspects of the Christian Doctrine of the Holy Spirit (London, 1959), pp. 154–157, 211–214.

20. There is an immense bibliography of Pietism. See, for example, the dictionaries. I would mention only A. Ritschl. *Geschichte des Pietismus*, 3 vols (Bonn, 1880); F. E. Stuffler, *The Rise of Evangelical Pietism* (*Numen*, Suppl. IX) (Leiden, 1965).

21. R. Minder, *Allemagnes et Allemands*, I (Paris, 1968), p. 113.

22. P. J. Spener, *Pia Desideria*, ed. Kurt Aland (Berlin, 1964). For Spener, see J. Wallmann, *aphilipp Jakob Spener und die Anfänge des Pietismus* (Tübingen, 1970); H. Bauch, *Die Lehre vom Wirken des Heiligen Geistes im Frühpietismus. Studien zur Pneumatologie und Eschatologie von Campegius Vitringa, Ph. J. Spener und Albrecht Bengel* (Hamburg, 1974): L. Hein, 'Ph. J. Spener, ein Theologe des Heiligen Geistes und Prophet der Kirche', *Die Einheit der Kirche. Festgabe Peter Meinhold* (Wiesbaden, 1977), pp. 103–126.

23. Spener was thus very close to Catholic piety: see J. Lortzing, 'Der Pietismus lutherischer Prägung als rückläufige Bewegung zum Mittelalter', *Theologie und Glaube* (1942), pp. 316–324. For Spener, it was thanks to Tauler that Luther became what he was: *Pia Desideria* (1964 ed.), p. 74. He wrote a preface to an edition of Tauler's sermons in 1681.

24. *Pia Desideria* (1964 ed.), p. 56.

25. There is a French *Vie* of Zinzendorf by F. Bovet in 2 vols (Paris, 1860). See also Erich Beyreuther, *Nicolas-Louis de Zinzendorf*, Fr. tr. E. Reichel (Geneva, 1967).

26. According to J. Baubérot, 'The adjective "pietist" is now used to describe a believer who is contaminated by moralism, an almost morbid distrust of theological criticism and intellectualism as a whole, and a total lack of political interest. The faults of Pietism seem to have been stressed much more than its positive qualities'. see his article 'Piétisme', *Encyclopaedia Universalis*, 13 (Paris, 1972), p. 57. G. Gusdorf has traced the influence of Pietism on eighteenth-century philosophical movements: *Dieu, la nature et l'homme au siècle des Lumières* (Paris, 1972), pp. 59–142; *idem, Naissance de la conscience romantique au siècle des Lumières* (Paris, 1976), pp. 244–275.

27. Original documents include Maximilien Misson, *Le théâtre sacré des Cévennes ou Récit des merveilles récemment opérées dans cette partie de la Province de Languedoc* (London, 1707); new ed. by Ami Bost, *Les prophètes protestants* (Paris, 1847); C. Bost, *Mémoires inédits d'Abraham Mazel et d'Elie Marion sur la guerre des Cévennes* (Paris, 1931); *Histoire des troubles des Cévennes ou de la Guerre des Camisards sous le règne de Louis le Grand*, new impression of the 3-vol. ed. of Villefranche, 1760 (published under the name of 'Patriote françois et Impartial'), 2 vols (Marseilles, 1975). Histories include H. Hennebois, *Pierre Laporte, dit Rolland, et le prophétisme cévenol* (Geneva, 1881); R. Knox, *Enthusiasm* (Oxford, 1950), pp. 356–371, who emphasizes above all the extravagant aspects of the movement and who accepts Brueys' fable, according to which a certain Du Serre trained children to imitate prophetic trances; A. Ducasse, *La guerre des Camisards. La résistance huguenote sous Louis XIV* (Paris, 1946), who is not objective; C. Almeras, *La révolte des Camisards* (Paris, 1959); E. Le Roy Ladurie, *Paysans de Languedoc*, 2 vols (Paris, 1966), pp. 330ff., for the apocalypse according to Jurieu. Finally, a work by a friend now dead, C. Cantaloube, *La Réforme en France vue d'un village cévenol* (Paris, 1951), chapter XII, pp. 205ff.; *idem*, article in the encyclopaedia *Catholicisme*, II (1950), cols 442–443. Historiography: P. Joutard, *La légende des Camisards* (Paris, 1977).

28. 'Speaking in tongues', which occurred sporadically among the mystics—I have already called attention to certain cases and I deal at some length with this phenomenon in Volume II in the section on the present-day Renewal—appeared among the 'prophets' of the Cévennes: Morton T. Kelsey, *Tongue Speaking* (London, 1973), pp. 52ff. J. V. Taylor, *The Go-Between God* (London, 1972), p. 219, notes that this phenomenon is not to be found either in Zinzendorf or in Wesley. One of Wesley's preachers, however, wrote in his diary on 8 March 1750: 'This morning the Lord gave me a language I knew not of, raising my soul to him in a wondrous manner'.

29. C. Cantaloube, article in *Catholicisme, op. cit.* (note 27), col. 443.

149

30. To the bibliography in my article 'Irvingiens' in the encylopaedia *Catholicisme*, VI (1967), cols 113–114, should be added R. Knox, *op. cit.* (note 16), pp. 550–558; C. Gordon Strachan, *The Pentecostal Theology of Edward Irving* (London, 1931).

31. The witness of the Holy Spirit, according to Wesley, enables light to be distinguished from darkness in order that we may know that we are children of God (cf. Rom 8:16), not, as in the case of Calvin, that we should know who is and who is not inspired: see Wesley's *Collected Works*, I, pp. 211ff. The Spirit is recognized by his fruits; see pp. 213ff.

32. Léon Maury, *Le réveil religieux* (Paris, 1892). For the problems raised in theology by a Wesleyan rather than a Calvinist influence, see J. Cadier, 'La tradition calviniste dans le Réveil du XIXe siècle', *Et. Théol. et Rel.*, 28 (1952/4), 9–28.

33. Once again, as during the time of the Camisards in the Cévennes, appeal was made to Joel 2:28–29. See H. Bois, *Le Réveil du pays de Galles* (Toulouse, n.d.; the preface is dated December 1905); J. Rogues de Farsac, *Un mouvement mystique contemporain. Le réveil religieux au pays de Galles (1904–1905)* (Paris, 1907). Compare J. Chevalier, *Essai sur la formation de la nationalité et les réveils religieux au pays de Galles, des origines à la fin du VIe siècle* (Lyons and Paris, 1924).

34. See C. G. Finney, *Lectures on Revivals of Religion* (new ed., London, 1910); H. Bois, *Quelques réflexions sur la psychologie des Réveils* (Paris, 1906); *Concilium*, 89 (1973; 'Religious Revival').

35. Yann Roullet, 'Découverte d'une paroisse', *Protestantisme français* (Collection *Présences*), by M. Boegner *et. al.* (Paris, 1945), pp. 107–135, especially p. 130.

9

THE PLACE OF THE
HOLY SPIRIT IN CATHOLICISM SINCE
THE COUNTER-REFORMATION

The close bond between the Holy Spirit and the life of the Church has always been not only experienced, but also affirmed throughout the centuries. Who could ever provide a balanced account of the holiness of so many of its members or describe the infinite variety of the forms assumed by that holiness? We know too that the Middle Ages saw the Holy Spirit as continuing to 'inspire' the Church's councils and teachers, the most important canonical decisions and even the election and activities of the ministers of the people of God.[1] The Church's life has always been seen as overshadowed by the Spirit *Dominum et vivificantem*. This is particularly true of the Church's faithfulness to the faith it has received from the apostles. The Fathers of the Church were especially convinced of this. Irenaeus expressed this conviction perhaps more clearly than the others. He showed faith dwelling in the Church as its proper place and supported by the testimony of the prophets, the apostles and the disciples. He described that faith as something that 'always makes us young again and, under the influence of the Spirit, like a costly drink contained in a precious vase, even renews the vase that holds it'. He goes on to say that 'in this gift the intimacy of the gift of Christ, that is to say, the Holy Spirit, is contained' and concludes by stressing that 'where the Church is, there is also the Spirit of God and where the Spirit of God is, there are also the Church and all grace. And the Spirit is truth.'[2]

I have already given this text from Irenaeus in the chapter on the early Church and another quotation, this time from Hippolytus, is also worth repeating here: 'The Holy Spirit conferring on those whose faith is correct the perfect grace to know how those who are at the head of the Church must teach and preserve everything'.[3] It is clear from this text that the charism of teaching was and is not automatically guaranteed to those in authority in the Church. The Spirit is guaranteed to pastors insofar as they are pastors of the *Church*, recognized by the Church as having the grace that dwells in it and as appointed or given by God himself.[4] This guarantee of faithfulness, of which the Spirit is the principle, is given to the *Church*. It is such a firm guarantee that to admit that the Church is capable of error is to impute a failure on the part of the Spirit.[5]

This was such a deep conviction that it was hardly thought necessary to express it. It is possible, however, to provide evidence of its existence.[6] The situation was different when the Church's faithfulness in its teaching and life was radically questioned, especially by the sixteenth-century Reformers. From that time onwards, in reaction to them, more and more statements were made about the unfailing faithfulness of the Church's Tradition because of the presence of the Holy Spirit who was promised to the Church by the Lord. The first apologists who were critical of Luther all reacted in this way. In 1523, for example, John Fisher insisted that the promise of the Spirit was not made simply to the apostles, but to the Church, until the end of the world.[7] The following statement was made at the 1528 Council of Sens:

> The universal Church cannot fall into error, being led by the Spirit of truth dwelling in it for ever. Christ will remain with the Church until the end of the world. . . . (The Church) is taught by the same one Spirit to determine what is required by the changing circumstances of the times.[8]

In Germany, Luther's opponents also concluded that the Church was guided by the Spirit: the Franciscan Conrad Schatzgeyer from 1522 onwards, Cochlaeus from 1524 onwards, the Dominican Mensing in February 1528, and Gropper in 1538. In 1533, John Driedo of Louvain published a treatise *De Ecclesiasticis Scripturis et Dogmatibus*, in which he demonstrated the inner mutual relationship between Scripture and the Church on the basis of the complementary activity in both of the same Spirit—'utrobique et unus et idem Spiritus loquens et docens'—and cited Jn 14:26 and 16:16, 13. Driedo's pupil Albert Pighi returned to the same argument in 1538 and 1544. Alphonse de Castro did the same in Paris in 1534. At the Council of Trent, the legate Cervini, the Fathers and the theologians justified, by appealing to the constant activity of the Spirit, the faithful handing down of the apostolic traditions and the trust that should be placed in those traditions as in the canonical Scriptures. The Council spoke only of apostolic traditions, but, in line with what had been taught by the Fathers, the other councils and the theologians of the Middle Ages, the activity of the Spirit was extended to doctrinal and ethical pronouncements made by the 'Church': 'In the general councils, the Holy Spirit has revealed to the Church, according to the needs of the times, many truths which are not explicitly contained in the canonical books' (Claude Le Jay; Girolamo Seripando; Pietro Bertano). Insofar as Christians were at that time aware of development in dogma, they tended to attribute this too to the help of the Holy Spirit.[9]

It is obvious that these statements, which are in themselves reasonable and traditional, concealed a tendency and even a temptation to give an absolute value to the Church as an institution by endowing its magisterium with an almost unconditional guarantee of guidance by the Holy Spirit. In opposition to the Reformation, there was an insistence on the fact that the letter of the Scriptures was not enough in itself and that there was a need for authentic interpretation. But whereas the Reformers attributed that interpretation to the Holy Spirit, the theologians of Trent ascribed it to 'the Church', since it was, they believed, in the Church that the Spirit was living, the Church itself that was the living gospel:

> There is no gospel if there is no Church. It is not that it is not possible to have Scripture outside the Church. . . . But the living gospel is the Church itself (*sed vivum Evangelium ipsa est Ecclesia*). Outside the Church, it is possible to have parchments or papers, ink, letters and characters, with which the gospel was written, but it is not possible to have the gospel itself. The apostles, who were filled with the Spirit, when they provided the creed, did not say: 'I believe in the Bible' or 'I believe in the gospel', but 'I believe in the holy Church'. It is in the Church that we have the Bible, that we have the gospel and that we have authentic understanding of the gospel, or rather, the Church itself is the gospel, written not with ink, but by the Spirit of the living God and not on tablets of stone, but on tablets of flesh of the heart.[10]

This was the beginning of a developing process that can be described as an affirmation of the part played by the Church and its authority and therefore, in the nineteenth century at least, a pervading sense of the primacy of the magisterium of the Church.[11] Thomas Stapleton (†1598), an Englishman who taught at Louvain, was undoubtedly most representative of this way of thinking. The reference to the help given by the Holy Spirit allowed him to attribute an almost unconditional value to authority as such and he insisted that, 'in questions of faith, believers should consider not *what* is said, but *who* says it'.[12]

Bossuet, whose teaching was followed in the French Imperial Catechism of 1806, defined the Catholic Church as the 'assembly or society of believers spread over the whole earth' and united by the Holy Spirit, who animates the Church, 'in which he has placed all his graces'. On the other hand, nineteenth-century catechisms, which followed and quite closely copied each other throughout the century until well into the twentieth, declared, for example: 'The Church is the society of believers established by our Lord Jesus Christ, spread over the earth and subject to the authority of its legitimate pastors' (Paris, 1852) and 'The Church is the society of Christians subject to the authority of its legitimate pastors, the leader of whom is the Pope, the successor of St Peter' (Paris, 1914).[13]

The magisterium itself refers to the Holy Spirit as the guarantee of its teachings and decisions,[14] including, for example, the definitions of the Mariological dogmas of 1854 and 1950. The only biblical references to which an appeal could be made in these teachings were quite remote; the basis for them was found in the faith of the Church, with the reservation that it was animated by the Spirit. This also accounts for the emergence of such doubtful formulae defining the magisterium as the *fons fidei*[15] and others such as 'Ecclesia sibi ipsi est fons'.[16] I have spoken elsewhere about the inflated emphasis that has been placed on the magisterium. The Reformers may have, if not exactly misunderstood, at least minimized the part played by the Church in the relationship between the believer and Scripture, but that is no reason for putting the magisterium in the place of the Holy Spirit to whose 'testimony' they appealed. Certain Catholic statements have fallen into this error. One one-sided emphasis should not be replaced by another. It is far better to integrate, recognize and make a place for all the gifts by which God communicates to us the truth of his Word.[17]

In his encyclical of 1897 on the Holy Spirit, *Divinum illud munus*, Leo XIII wrote: 'Hoc affirmare sufficiat, quod cum Christus Caput sit Ecclesiae, Spiritus Sanctus sit eius Anima', that is, 'if Christ is the Head of the Church, the Holy Spirit is its soul'.[18] This affirmation, which was quoted in the Encyclical *Mystici Corporis* of 1943, is far-reaching. Taken literally, it clearly points to an ecclesiological monophysitism. It is distasteful to Protestant Christians, because it seems to given an absolute value to the acts and structures of the Church. It also gave rise to a heated discussion among Catholic theologians about the uncreated soul and the created soul of the Church.[19] To go into this question would take us too far from the theme of this work, but it is worth noting here that the Augustinian text quoted by Leo XIII does not say exactly the same thing as the Pope aimed to say. The latter says: The Holy Spirit *is* the soul of the Church of which Christ is the Head. Augustine, however, said: What the soul does in our body, the Holy Spirit does in the Church; what the soul is for our body, the Holy Spirit is for the Body of Christ, which is the Church.[20] The statement, then, is functional and not ontological. This is an important difference, which was understood by Vatican II, which also took care to attribute the comparison to the Fathers.[21] I witnessed this prudent and precise way of speaking and know that it was intentional. I shall return later to the pneumatology of Vatican II.

The Holy Spirit has been very much alive in Catholicism since the Counter-Reformation and the restoration after the French Revolution. But what has been the situation with regard to ecclesiology in the past three or four hundred years? Bellarmine, who was the dominant theologian of this period, was above all a spiritual author and he was an Augustinian on the question of grace. Pneumatology is lacking in his teaching about the Church. Petavius (†1652) is famous for his theology of the personal relationship between the righteous soul and the Holy Spirit, but this theology lacks an ecclesiological extension. At the beginning of the nineteenth century, Möhler provided, in his book *Die Einheit* (1825), a radically pneumatological ecclesiology, but he later refused to prepare a new edition of this work, and what was preserved of his teaching is taken from his later book *Symbolik* (1832), with its resolutely Christological ecclesiology, in which the Church is seen as a 'continued incarnation'. This idea dominated the Roman school throughout the nineteenth century.[22]

M. J. Scheeben (†1888) combined Christological views with a pneumatological reflection, both of which he took to extreme conclusions or at least to extreme formulations. Examples of this can be found in his arguments concerning the character of baptism and ordination as giving the Church its structure, and his attribution of a special function to the Spirit in animating that Church. His analysis of the status of knowledge and Tradition in the Church is successful, but he is less successful when he calls the Church a 'kind of incarnation of the Holy Spirit'.[23]

The same formula is also found in Manning's writings, and I propose to deal at rather greater length with the Englishman's teachings about the Holy Spirit and the Church because he seems to me to be highly representative of the Catholic approach to the Spirit at the time that we are studying here. When he was still Archdeacon of Chichester, Manning (1808–1892) experienced a kind of conversion to the Holy Spirit. An ordinary believer who had read a volume of his sermons asked him why he spoke so little about the Holy Spirit.

> From that day I have never passed a day without acts of reparation to the Holy Ghost. I bought every book I could find on the work of the Holy Ghost and studied them. After five or six years I reached the last step to which reason alone could lead me, namely that the unanimous witness of the universal Church is the maximum of historical evidence for the revelation of Christianity. But the historical evidence is only human and human evidence is fallible after all. Then, and not before, I saw that the perpetual presence and office of the Holy Ghost, etc., raises the witness of the Church from a human to a Divine certainty. And to Him I submitted in the unity of the one Faith and Fold. Since then the Holy Ghost has been the chief thought and devotion of my whole soul.[24]

To confine ourselves to external order and the public sphere, Manning's intention was expressed above all in two books. In 1865, he published *The Temporal Mission of the Holy Ghost, or Reason and Revelation*,[25] the sub-title reflecting the author's concern, as confided to us in the above statement. Then, in 1875, the seventh edition of *The Internal Mission of the Holy Ghost* appeared.[26] In this book, Manning sets out a highly structured doctrine of the Spirit in the following order: grace, the theologal virtues, the gifts of the Holy Spirit (Manning's main source here was the treatise by Dionysius the Carthusian), the fruits of the Spirit, the beatitudes, and a final chapter on devotion to the Holy Spirit. The Mystical Body is mentioned frequently, but the author does not speak about the charisms in the sense of a 'pneumatology'. At the beginning of the book, he summarizes the contents of his previous book in the following way:

> I have pointed out how the Church or the mystical Body of Christ is in its structure imperishable and in its life indefectible, because it is indissolubly united to the

155

Holy Ghost, the Lord and Life-giver; I have shown also how, because it is indissolubly united to the Spirit of Truth, it can never fail in the knowledge of the perfect revelation of God; and how, because its knowledge can never fail, its voice is also always guided by the continual light and assistance of the Spirit of Truth. It can therefore never err in enunciating or declaring the revealed knowledge which it possesses.

Manning was looking for an absolute rock of truth and because of that he became a Roman Catholic. He at once committed himself to the cause of papal infallibility and wanted the definition of this teaching to be almost excessively extensive.[27] He was convinced that the Holy Spirit was connected in an indefectible manner to the Mystical Body and that the union between the two was similar to the hypostatic union. After quoting Eph 2:22 in chapter I of his earlier book, *The Temporal Mission,* Manning had this to say about this union:

> The union therefore of the Spirit with the body can never be dissolved. It is a Divine act, analogous to the hypostatic union, whereby the two natures of God and man are eternally united in one Person. So the mystical body, the head and the members, constitute one mystical person.

Clearly this is passing rather quickly over the historicity of the life of the Church.[28] I do not want to stress too much this excessive and, as such, untenable position. I feel justified in having given rather a lengthy analysis because Manning's very forceful approach is characteristic of the situation in which the Holy Spirit was placed in Catholicism of the period we are considering here. At that time, the Spirit was seen, on the one hand, as the principle of holy living in the souls of individuals—this was the 'internal mission'—and, on the other, as guaranteeing acts of the institution, especially its infallible teaching.[29] This certainly does not constitute a pneumatology.

By pneumatology, I mean something other than a simple dogmatic theology of the third Person. I also mean something more than, and in this sense different from, a profound analysis of the indwelling of the Holy Spirit in individual souls and his sanctifying activity there. Pneumatology should, I believe, describe the impact, in the context of a vision of the Church, of the fact that the Spirit distributes his gifts as he wills and in this way builds up the Church. A study of this kind involves not simply a consideration of those gifts or charisms, but a theology of the Church. If, by the Church, we meant, even without saying so explicitly—although many have affirmed it!—the institution, the clergy, the hierarchy or the magisterium, then Manning's earlier work would suit our purpose admirably. He speaks of the Mystical Body, of the whole body, but what he has principally in mind is the infallibility of the magisterium and above all the infallibility of the Sovereign Pontiff as the 'organ of the Spirit in the Church and in the world'. The Spirit, according to Manning, only makes the structures that have resulted from the incarnation present and active, and this is probably why he and even Scheeben spoke about the activity of the Spirit in incarnational terms.[30] There is also very little about the Holy Spirit in the otherwise remarkable and very useful study of the Mystical Body of Christ by E. Mersch. The encyclical *Mystici Corporis* of 1943 contains a profound theology of the Holy Spirit, but it never reaches the point where it becomes a full pneumatology because it is restricted by its concentration on the institution.

There is no separation of the activity of the Spirit from the work of Christ in a full pneumatology. Everything that I have said so far points to the impossibility of making such a division. A pneumatology of this kind, however, goes beyond simply making present the structures set up by Christ; it is the actuality of what the glorified Lord and his Spirit do in the life of the Church, in all the variety of forms that this activity has assumed in time and space. This is, I think, the meaning of the rather hermetic statement by Nikos Nissiotis, who has criticized the Catholic Church on more than one occasion for what he calls its 'Christomonism': 'A true pneumatology describes and comments on life in the freedom of the Spirit and in the concrete communion of the historical Church, the essence of which is neither in itself nor in its institutions'.[31]

In the final chapter of this volume we shall examine how the Second Vatican Council initiated precisely this kind of pneumatology, the truthfulness of which will emerge gradually throughout the work.

NOTES

1. References to various studies and an abundance of texts will be found in my *Tradition and Traditions* (Eng. tr.; London and New York, 1966), Part One, Excursus B, pp. 119–137.
2. Irenaeus, *Adv. haer*. III, 24, 1 (Fr. tr. F. Sagnard, *SC* 34, pp. 399ff.). See also above, pp. 71–72, note 30.
3. Hippolytus, Prologue to the *Apostolic Tradition* (Fr. tr. B. Botte, *SC* 11, p. 26).
4. This is the meaning of the famous statement by Irenaeus: 'charisma veritatis certum secundum beneplacitum Patris', *Adv. haer*. IV, 26, 2 (ed. W. W. Harvey, p. 40). See R. P. C. Hanson, *Tradition in the Early Church* (London, 1969), pp. 159ff.
5. This was formally stated by Tertullian, *De praescr*. 28, 1–3 (*SC* 47, pp. 124–125), c. 200 A.D.
6. See, for example, Cyril of Jerusalem, *Cat. Myst*. XVI, 14 (*PG* 33, 937); John Chrysostom, *De S. Pent. Hom*. 1, 4 (*PG* 50, 458; Fr. tr. under the direction of M. Jeannin by M. C. Portelette, *Œuvres complètes de S. Jean Chrysostome*, III (Bar-le-Duc, 1869), pp. 263–264). See also Augustine and many of the texts in my book, *op. cit*. (note 1). It is useful in this context to cite the terms in which the Seventh Ecumenical Council (787; Nicaea) begins and justifies its definition of the cult of images: 'Following the royal way and pursuing the divinely inspired teaching of our holy Fathers and the tradition of the Catholic Church—for we know that it is of the Holy Spirit, who dwells in the Church. . . .': Actio VII: Mansi, 13, col. 370; *DS* 600.
7. *Assertionis Lutheranae confutatio* (1523)—there is no modern edition. For the history summarized in this chapter, see my book, *op. cit*. (note 1), pp. 156–176; J. Ermel, *Les*

sources de la Foi. Concile de Trente et Œcuménisme contemporain (Tournai, 1963); G. H. Tavard, *Holy Writ or Holy Church: The Crisis of the Protestant Reformation* (London and New York, 1959).

8. Mansi, 32, col. 1158D-E.

9. M. Hofmann, *Theologie, Dogmen und Dogmenentwicklung im theologischen Werk Denis Petau's* (Frankfurt and Munich, 1976), pp. 177 and 533.

10. Cardinal Hosius (†1579), *Opera omnia* (Cologne, 1584), I, p. 321, cf. p. 551; II, pp. 169, 244, 246, 398, 399, on the article 'Credo sanctam Ecclesiam catholicam' as containing the whole of faith. It was quite common to make a contrast between the 'vivum cor Ecclesiae' and the 'mortuae chartaceae membranae Scripturarum': see Staphylus, *In causis Religionis sparsim editi libri* (Ingolstadt, 1613), p. 24.

11. I have retraced this history in my book, *op. cit.* (note 1), chapter 6, pp. 177–221. E. Dublanchy's article 'Eglise' in *DTC*, IV, Part Publication XXXII (1910), cols 2108–2224, is characteristic of this tendency to confine ecclesiology to the magisterium.

12. This is the title that Stapleton gave to chapter V of Book X of his *De Principiis fidei doctrinalibus* (1572). See also H. Schützeichel, *Wesen und Gegenstand der kirchlichen Lehrautorität nach Thomas Stapleton* (Trier, 1966).

13. See E. Germain, 'A travers les catéchismes des 150 dernières années', *Recherches et Débats*, 71 (1971), 108–131.

14. See Clement XIV, Breve *Dominus ac Redemptor*, suppressing the Society of Jesus (21 July 1773): 'Divini Spiritus . . . adiuti praesentia et afflatu'. A more serious case was Pius IX's Bull *Ineffabilis Deus*, on the dogma of the Immaculate Conception (8 December 1854): 'Catholica Ecclesia, quae a Sancto semper edocta Spiritu columna est ac firmamentum veritatis' (*Collectio Lacensis*, VI, col. 836); see also Leo XIII, Encyclical *Divinum illud munus*, on the Holy Spirit (9 May 1897) (*DS* 3328); Pius XII, Constitution *Munificentissimus*, defining the dogma of the Assumption (1 November 1950): 'Universa Ecclesia in qua viget Veritatis Spiritus, qui quidem eam ad revelatarum perficiendam veritatum cognitionem infallibiliter diriget' (*AAS*, 42 [1950], 768; *Denz.* 3032; not in *DS*).

15. This term is found, for example, in C. Pesch, *Compendium Theologiae dogmaticae*, I, No. 301, and in J. V. Bainvel, *De Magisterio vivo et Traditione* (Paris, 1905), p. 56.

16. See H. Dieckmann, *De Ecclesia* (Freiburg, 1925), II, note 670; J. Deneffe, *Der Traditionsbegriff* (Münster, 1931), pp. 147–148. It was also unfortunately used by Pius XII, in his allocution on the centenary of the Gregoriana (7 October 1953; *AAS*, 45 (1953), 685); 'Sub tutela ductuque Spiritus Sancti sibi fons est veritatis'.

17. I appreciate the truth of the following statements, but I would have liked the Holy Spirit to have been given his rightful place: Pius XII, Encyclical *Humani generis* (*AAS*, 42 [1950], 569; *DS* 3886): 'Una enim cum sacris eiusmodi fontibus Deus Ecclesiae suae Magisterium vivum dedit'; Vatican II, Constitution on Revelation, *Dei Verbum*, 10: 'Munus autem *authentice* interpretandi verbum Dei scriptum vel traditum soli vivo Ecclesiae Magisterio concreditum est'; the word italicized by me is very important.

18. *AAS*, 29 (1896–97), 650; *DS* 3328.

19. References in U. Valeske, *Votum Ecclesiae*, I (Munich, 1962), p. 161, note 17; my book *Sainte Eglise* (Paris, 1963), pp. 503, 643.

20. Augustine, *Sermo* 267, 4 (*PL* 38, 1231), cited by Leo XIII and Pius XII; *Sermo* 268, 2 (*PL* 38, 1232–1233).

21. Constitution on the Church, *Lumen Gentium*, 7, 7: 'Dedit nobis de Spiritu suo, qui unus et idem in Capite et in membris existens, totum corpus ita vivificat, unificat et movet, ut Eius officium a sanctis Patribus comparari potuerit cum munere, quod principium vitae seu anima in corpore humano adimplet', with reference to Leo XIII, Pius XII, Augustine, John Chrysostom, Didymus and Thomas Aquinas. See also *Ad Gentes divinitus*, 4.

22. See my *L'Eglise de S. Augustin à l'époque moderne* (Paris, 1970), pp. 417–423, 428–433. For Scheeben, see pp. 429, 433–435.

23. This formula will be found in Scheeben's *Dogmatik*, III, §276, no. 1612.

24. Taken from autobiographical notes edited in 1890 and published in E. S. Purcell's *Life of Cardinal Manning, Archbishop of Westminster* (London, 1895), II, pp. 795–796.

25. *The Temporal Mission of the Holy Ghost or Reason and Revelation* (London, 1866). My quotation (above, p. 156) will be found on p. 61.

26. H. E. Manning, *The Internal Mission of the Holy Ghost* (London, 7th ed., 1875). My quotation (above, pp. 155–156) will be found on p. 3.

27. 'The definitions and Decrees of Pontiffs, speaking ex cathedra, or as the head of the Church and to the whole Church, whether by Bull, or Apostolic Letters, or Encyclicals, or Brief, to many or to one person, undoubtedly emanate from a divine assistance, and are infallible' (*The Temporal Mission*, pp. 81–82). In 1865, Manning had, in view of the proposed Vatican Council, suggested the following text: 'Vivae vocis oraculum a Summo Pontifice prolatum circa fidem, mores vel facta ut aiunt dogmatica seu circa veritates fidei morumque questionibus circumstantes infallibile esse' (Mansi, 49, col. 171). He excluded, however, the idea of infallibility inherent in the Pope's person.

28. According to Quirinus (that is, Döllinger), Manning said that the definition of papal infallibility would be a 'victory of dogma over history': see *Römische Briefe vom Konzil* (Munich, 1870), p. 61.

29. The following recent studies are interesting in that they reveal this tendency: P. Nau, 'Le magistère pontifical ordinaire au premier concile du Vatican', *RThom*, 62 (1962), 341–397; J. J. King, 'The Holy Spirit and the Magisterium Ecclesiae', *American Ecclesiastical Review*, 148 (1963), 1–26; C. Larnicol, 'A la lumière de Vatican II. Infaillibilité de l'Eglise, du corps épiscopal, du Pape', *Ami du Clergé*, 76 (1966), 246–255, 257–259, especially 254b.

30. Despite his thesis on the distinctive and personal gift and indwelling of the Holy Spirit, Scheeben attributed the anointing of Christ's humanity to the Logos and believed that the Spirit was only the means. See his *Dogmatik*, V, §222; *Mysterien des Christentums*, §51, 5.

31. See the symposium *Le Saint-Esprit* (Geneva, 1963), p. 91.

ADDITIONAL NOTE

FORGETTING THE HOLY SPIRIT

The Holy Spirit has sometimes been forgotten. It is not difficult to find examples of this. Karl Adam's *Das Wesen des Katholizismus* (1924) was rightly held in high esteem during the first half of this century. Yet we find in it: 'The structure of Catholic faith may be summarized in a single sentence: I come to a living faith in the Triune God through Christ in His Church. I experience the action of the living God through Christ realizing himself in His Church. So we see the certitude of the Catholic faith rests on the sacred triad: God, Christ, Church.'[1]

There is at present a desire and even a need for a short formula of Christian faith. Several have already been suggested, and some of these have been collected and discussed by J. Schulte in his *Glaube elementar. Versuche einer Kurzformel des Christlichen* (Essen, 1971). Regrettably, in the formulae suggested by G. Scherer, by groups of students and of mothers there is an insistence on man and on Christ as a 'man for others', but a rather disturbing absence of any reference to the Holy Spirit and the Church. On the other hand, however, the brief formulae suggested by readers of the French journal *Informations Catholiques Internationales*, 471 (1 January 1975), p. 12 were remarkably Trinitarian.

In an article in *L'Aurore*, published on 2 March 1978 and entitled 'Attention! Hiéroglyphes!', Fr Bruckberger, a passionate critic of the French bishops and modern religious teaching, attempted to 'define briefly (for my readers) what is essential in Catholic faith'. He spoke firstly of 'God' and then of Christ, who has 'risen into heaven, where he reigns with his body, soul and divinity, at the right hand of his Father'. He then continues: 'Is that all? Not at all! How would we be able to console ourselves for such a physical absence? He has, of course, left us with the account of his life, and the Scriptures bear witness to him. He has also left us with the Church which, through its sacraments, embodies us in the Christian life and enables us to share in the divine life.' Fr Bruckberger concludes by enlarging on the gift of the Eucharist. Of course, too much stress should not be laid on the content of a newspaper article. Nevertheless, the total omission of the Holy Spirit, the Paraclete, and the immediate passage from Christ to the Church and the sacraments are significant.

SUBSTITUTES FOR THE HOLY SPIRIT

In a suggestive but very short article, without any references, P. Pare noted that there has always been a teaching about the Holy Spirit in the Western Church, but little of it has entered its living faith or its liturgy.[2] (This would need to be checked; in the meantime the criticism is welcome.) The liturgy of the Western Church, Pare points out, is centred on the eucharistic presence and therefore on the incarnation and the redemption, and the relationship between the second and the first Person. Rome, Pare suggests, appears to have replaced the Holy Spirit and let him be overshadowed by the Pope, the Virgin Mary and the cult of the Blessed Sacrament. This criticism is certainly exaggerated, as this present book shows in its own way. Nonetheless, Pare is criticizing something not entirely fanciful: here is some evidence for it. I shall confine myself to references to the three realities mentioned by Pare himself: the Eucharist, the Pope and the Virgin Mary.

M. J. Scheeben, whose work we have already mentioned, attempted to explain in depth the doctrine of the infallibility of the pontifical magisterium as defined by the First Vatican Council in 1870.[3] He compared this dogma with the one defined in 1854 on the Immaculate Conception of Mary, saying that Mary and the Pope were two closely related 'seats of wisdom'. He connected the meaning of this with the mystery of the Eucharist and believed that 'the Eucharist, Mary and the Holy See are the most important links (*die vorzüglichsten Bindeglieder*) by which the Church is established, maintained and shown to be true, total, firm and living communion with Christ'.[4]

One of the most fervent advocates of the dogma of infallibility at the Council was Mgr Mermillod. In a sermon that he gave in Rome in January 1870, he declared: 'There are three sanctuaries: the crib, the tabernacle and the Vatican. There are three (a word is missing here): God, Jesus Christ and the Pope. What do we want? We want to give you Jesus Christ on earth. We have seen him at Bethlehem in the form of a child. We see him today in the form of an old man.'[5] Despite the great and genuine respect that I have for Mgr Mermillod, I regard these words as perfectly ridiculous, which excuses them from being blasphemous. Mermillod, who was made a cardinal by Pius IX, preached a sermon on the theme of the three incarnations of our Lord—in Mary's womb, in the Eucharist and in the Pope.[6]

Fr R. Plus, whose books on spirituality were so widely read in the first half of this century, devoted three consecutive chapters in one section of one of his books to this theme: Mary, the Pope, the Mass.[7] Possibly under the influence of Fr Plus, the directors of the Apostolate of Prayer and the Eucharistic Crusade chose for their congress in June 1945 the general theme: 'The Apostolate of Prayer in the service of Christ by devotions to the Sacred Heart, the Eucharist, the Blessed Virgin and the Pope'.[8]

Mgr Lépicier, who also became a cardinal, spoke of Abyssinia, where he had been working as a missionary, as a country 'in which the great Catholic devotion to those "three white things" ' (as he called them in preaching to the natives)—'the Host, the Virgin Mary and the Pope—flourished magnificently'.[9] The same rather imaginative theme of the 'three white things' was taken up by the Canadian Association Mariale in Paris at their church of Saint-Michel.[10]

For Mgr Marcel Lefebvre, the 'three white things' are 'The three main gifts that God has given us: the Pope, the most holy Virgin and the eucharistic sacrifice'.[11]

I now propose to consider each of these three realities in turn. It will become apparent that there is an element of truth and depth in an assimilation of the function of each of them to the Holy Spirit, but certainly not in any way that might encroach on the place occupied by and the part played by the Spirit.

1. *The Eucharist*

P. Pare undoubtedly had the spirituality of the (Real) Presence in the Eucharist in mind when he wrote his article. I do not wish to suggest any particular reference in this context, but I am bound to point out that the part played by the Holy Spirit in the Eucharist—not only in the change of the bread and wine into the body and blood of the Lord, but also in our communion—has hardly been developed. The Eucharist is seen and experienced in an essentially Christological perspective: the intimate presence in the Eucharist is the presence of Christ. This does not meant that it is not authentic or that it does not produce the fruits of grace! I shall be dealing with the pneumatological aspect of the Eucharist in Volume III of this book.

2. *The Pope*

The following remarks on the papacy do not detract in any way from what I have already said in the preceding chapter and what I shall say in Volume II, namely that there is a close link, based on God's faithfulness, between the Holy Spirit and the apostolic ministry. The Popes themselves have explicitly taught that the Holy Spirit is present and active in our personal lives and in the Church: it is sufficient to cite the encyclicals *Divinum illud munus* of Leo XIII (9 May 1897) and *Mystici Corporis Christi* of Pius XII (29 June 1943). Many of the Church's most official statements, however, have insisted forcibly on the external, visible and jurisdictional principles of unity, such as the magisterium and, above all, the papal authority. Here are four relatively recent examples:

> The Catholic Church is one with a unity that is visible and perfect throughout the whole world and among all peoples, with a unity, the beginning, the root and the indefectible source of which is the supreme authority and the 'excellent principality' of blessed Peter, the prince of the apostles and of his successors in the Roman throne.[12]

> So that the episcopate should be one and undivided and so that, through the close mutual relationship of the pontiffs, the universal multitude of believers might be preserved in the unity of faith and communion, setting blessed Peter above the other apostles, he established in his person the lasting principle and the visible foundation of each unity. The eternal temple was built on its strength and the loftiness of the Church reaching up to heaven rose on the firmness of that faith.[13]

> The one who made (the Church) unique also made it one . . . 'one body and one spirit' (Eph 4:4) . . . with a concord so great and so absolute among men that it is the agreement and the harmony of minds that form the necessary foundation. . . . For this reason, Jesus Christ established in the Church a living authentic and permanent magisterium that he provided with his own power and instructed with the spirit of truth.[14]

> Together with those sacred sources (Scripture and tradition), God has given to his Church a living magisterium to throw light on and explain those matters that are contained in the deposit of faith only in an obscure and so to speak implicit manner.[15]

The Popes who were responsible for the above texts have also spoken of the Holy Spirit.[16] Although I fully appreciate the part played by the Church's magisterium, I do not think that it can be denied that the Popes have for a very long time insisted on it as the principle of unity in the Church. In this matter, Vatican II was much more explicit in giving the Holy Spirit his rightful place.[17]

In this section I refrain from discussing the many expressions of excessive devotion to the Pope, some of which border on idolatry, like those which speak of a presence of Christ under the pontifical species, in a way analogous to that presence under the eucharistic species. A great deal could be written about this question, but it has no place in our present discussion, since it is an unedifying aspect of past history in the Church.

3. The Virgin Mary

This is a very large subject. On the one hand, it is necessary to acknowledge the criticisms that have been made of Catholic teaching about Mary and recognize their possible correctness. On the other, however, it is very important to remain conscious of the deep bond that exists between the Virgin Mary and the Spirit, and consequently of a certain common function despite the absolute disparity of the conditions.

The criticism is very serious. It is made mainly by Protestants and can be summarized as follows:[18] Catholics attribute to Mary what really belongs to the Holy Spirit and, in extreme cases, they give her a place that should be occupied by the Paraclete. We Catholics do indeed attribute to her the titles and the function of comforter, advocate and defender of believers in the presence of Christ, thought of as a fearsome judge. Mary's maternity is such that, thanks to her, we are not left as orphans. She reveals Jesus, who in turn reveals the Father. She forms Jesus in us[19] and thus performs a rôle which should properly be attributed to the Spirit.

Mary has also been called the 'soul of the Church'—this title has also been applied to the Holy Spirit. Many spiritual men and women have, of course, spoken of Mary's presence in their souls and have claimed that she has guided their lives and that they have experience of this that is similar to an experience of the presence and inspiration of the Spirit.[20] Elsie Gibson has said: 'When I began the study of Catholic theology, every place I expected to find an exposition of the doctrine of the Holy Spirit, I found Mary. What Protestants universally attribute to the action of the Holy Spirit was attributed to Mary.'[21] It is, in fact, hardly possible not to react as Elsie Gibson did when we read this text by Bernardino of Siena, quoted in an encyclical letter by Leo XIII, who was, a few years later, to write a fine encyclical on the Holy Spirit, *Divinum illud munus*: 'All grace that is communicated to this world comes to us by a threefold movement. It is dispensed according to a very perfect order from God in Christ, from Christ in the Virgin and from the

Virgin in us.'[22] Bernardino adds to this that Mary has at her disposal 'a certain jurisdiction or authority over the temporal procession of the Holy Spirit, to such an extent that no creature has ever received the grace of any virtue from God except through a dispensation of the Virgin herself'. This is clearly unacceptable.

Even if we reject this unacceptable statement, however, the matter is not closed. There is a deep relationship between Mary, the mother of God, and the Holy Spirit. That relationship derives from the mystery of salvation, the Christian mystery as such.[23] This is surely why, in the Latin liturgy, a prayer to the Holy Spirit was included with each commemoration of the Virgin Mary, just as Paul was always commemorated with Peter. It is, of course, true to say that certain Catholic spiritual writers expose themselves to criticism by attributing to Mary an immediate effectiveness in grace and the spiritual life and, in extreme cases, by ascribing to Mary what is inalienably the work of God and the Holy Spirit.

The part played by Mary is situated within that played by the Holy Spirit, who made her the mother of the incarnate Word and who is the principle of all holiness and of the communion of the saints. Mary has a pre-eminent place in the Christian mystery as the model of the Church and of universal intercession. This is the work of the Spirit in her. That is why Christians try to model their lives according to the image of Mary, who welcomed Christ and gave him to the world, and they pray to her so that this may be accomplished in them. They expect this from Christ himself, acting through his Spirit, but they are convinced that Mary co-operates in their activity by virtue of being a model of intercession. This accounts for their experience of Mary embracing in a warm and concrete realism their experience of the grace of Christ and his Spirit. The communication of Christ is, after all, accompanied by a memory of Mary, and the Christian mystery would lack an important dimension if it excluded or passed over the part played by Mary. Mary is the first recipient of grace and the first to have been associated with the sovereign action of the Spirit in Christ. Protestants are right to reject an attribution to Mary of what belongs only to God, but they are wrong if they remain closed to the witness borne by Catholic and Orthodox Christians to the benefit in their lives in Christ of a discreet Marian influence.

I am, of course, aware how inadequately I have dealt with this question in these few pages. I would like to quote in its entirety the extremely dense section devoted to the rôle of the Holy Spirit in the Virgin Mary in Paul VI's Apostolic Exhortation *Marialis cultus* of 22 March 1974. Here at least is the prayer of Ildefonsus of Toledo (†667) quoted therein: 'I pray to you, I pray to you, holy Virgin: that I may receive Jesus myself from that Spirit who enabled you to conceive Jesus. May my soul receive Jesus through that Spirit who enabled your flesh to conceive that same Jesus. . . . May I love Jesus in that Spirit in whom you adore him yourself as your Lord and in whom you contemplate him as your Son.'[24]

NOTES

1. Karl Adam, *The Spirit of Catholicism* (Eng. tr.; new ed., London, 1932), p. 51.
2. P. Pare, 'The Doctrine of the Holy Spirit in the Western Church', *Theology* (August 1948), 293–300.
3. M. J. Scheeben, 'Die theologische und praktische Bedeutung des Dogmas von der Unfehlbarkeit des Papstes, besonders in seiner Beziehung auf die heutige Zeit', series of articles in *Das ökumenische Concil vom Jahre 1869*, II, pp. 503–547; III, pp. 81–133, 212–263, 400–418.
4. M. J. Scheeben, *op. cit.*, III, p. 102.
5. J. Friedrich, *Geschichte des Vatikanischen Konzils*, III (Nördlingen, 1887), p. 587; quoted by Lord Acton, *Briefwechsel Döllinger-Acton*, ed. V. Conzemius, II (Munich, 1965), p. 77.
6. A. Dansette, *Histoire religieuse de la France contemporaine*, I (Paris, 1946), p. 414.
7. R. Plus, *Face à la vie*, 2nd series (Toulouse, 1926), pp. 93–94; section VII: 'Fêtes et dévotions', chapters CXII, CXIII, CXIV.
8. *Doc. cath.* 942 (8 July 1945), col. 481.
9. Alverne, 'La visite apostolique de Mgr Lépicier en Erythrée et Abyssinie', *L'union des Eglises*, 10 (January/February 1928), 415.
10. A. Richard, 'Faut-il incarner l'Eglise? Les trois blancheurs', *L'Homme nouveau* (7 March 1976).
11. Mgr Lefebvre, homily at Ecône 18 September 1977, on the occasion of the thirtieth anniversary of his episcopal consecration: pub. in *Le coup de maître de Satan. Ecône face à la persécution* (Martigny, Switzerland, 1977), pp. 30–41.
12. Pius IX (the Holy Office), in a letter dated 16 September 1864, rejecting the aims of the Association for the Promotion of the Reunion of Christendom: *AAS*, II (1919), 372; *DS* 2888.
13. Vatican I, Constitution *Pastor aeternus* (18 July 1870), Prologue: *DS* 3051. At the council itself, Mgr Dupanloup and Mgr Ginoulhiac remarked that the Pope was not the principle of unity in faith; Christ was. (Is this Christomonism?) See Mansi 51, 955B and 957C respectively.
14. Leo XIII, Encyclical *Satis cognitum* (29 June 1896): *DS* 3305.
15. Pius XII, Encyclical *Humani generis* (12 August 1950): *DS* 3886;
16. Leo XIII mentions the Spirit explicitly in *Satis cognitum: AAS*, 28 (1895–96), 715.
17. See the Constitution on the Church, *Lumen Gentium*, 7, 3: 'The same Spirit, giving the body unity through himself and through his power and through the internal cohesion of its members . . .'; 12, 1; 27, 3: 'The Holy Spirit unfailingly preserves the form of government established by Christ the Lord in his Church'; Constitution on the Church in the Modern World, *Gaudium et spes*, 40, 2; Decree on the Church's Missionary Activity, *Ad Gentes*, 4; 15, 1: 'The Holy Spirit, who calls all men to Christ by the seeds of the word and by the preaching of the gospel, stirs up in their hearts the obedience of faith . . . gathers them into one people of God'.
18. The most detailed and most fully documented expression of this criticism will be found in Lucien Marchand, 'Le contenu évangélique de la dévotion mariale', *Foi et Vie*, 49/6 (September/October 1951), 509–521.
19. A. C. Placi, quoted by R. Laurentin, *RSPT*, 50 (1966), 542, note 139.
20. As in the cenacle of Montmartre (10 January 1953).
21. Elsie Gibson, 'Mary and the Protestant Mind', *Review for Religious*, 24 (Mary 1965), 396–397, quoted by L. J. Suenens, *A New Pentecost* (London, 1977), pp. 197–198.
22. Leo XIII, Encyclical *Iucunda semper* (1894): *AAS*, 27 (1894–95), 179. Complete texts and a criticism of them will be found in H. Mühlen, *L'Esprit dans l'Eglise* (Paris, 1969), II, pp. 149ff. I can add other texts and data to these, including the following which, despite its anecdotal nature, is still significant. I have in front of me a calendar for 1955 from the Libreria Editrice Vaticana. On one page, there are two pictures: on one side, Pius XII, on

the other, the Assumption of the Blessed Virgin. Thursday 19 May, 'Ascensione N.S.'; six days later, Sunday 29 May, there is no sign of Pentecost and all that I can see is 'S. Maria M[ediatrice]'.

23. Apart from Mühlen, *op. cit.* (note 22), who is critical, see R. Laurentin, 'Esprit Saint et théologie mariale', *NRT*, 89 (1967), 26–42; L.-J. Suenens, *op. cit.* (note 21), pp. 196–197. See also the *Société française d'Etudes Mariales*, 25 (1968): 'Le Saint-Esprit et Marie, I: L'Evangile et les Pères'; 26 (1969): 'II: Bible et Spiritualité' (mainly documentary studies); Mariological Congress at Rome (1975). R. Laurentin has written about almost every aspect of this question in his very informative bulletins in *RSPT*, 50 (1966), 542; 54 (1970), 287–290; 56 (1972), 438, 478–479; 58 (1974), 296, note 110; 60 (1976), 321, note 37, 322, note 44, 452–456; 62 (1978), 277ff. Laurentin has also touched on the same question in his *Catholic Pentecostalism* (London, 1977), pp. 195–200: 'Mary, Model of the Charismatic'.

24. Ildefonsus, *De Virginitate perpetua Sanctae Mariae*, 12 (*PL* 96, 106).

10

THE PNEUMATOLOGY OF VATICAN II[1]

[*Note:* I have used the following initials in this chapter when referring to the documents of Vatican II: *AA* = *Apostolicam actuositatem*, Decree on the Apostolate of the Laity; *AG* = *Ad Gentes*, Decree on the Missions; *CD* = *Christus Dominus*, Decree on the Bishops' Office; *DV* = *Dei Verbum*, Constitution on Revelation; *GS* = *Gaudium et spes*, Constitution on the Church in the Modern World; *LG* = *Lumen Gentium*, Constitution on the Church; *PO* = *Presbyterorum ordinis*, Decree on the Ministry and Life of Priests; *SC* = *Sacrosanctum Concilium*, Constitution on the Liturgy; *UR* = *Unitatis redintegratio*, Decree on Ecumenism.]

During the Second Vatican Council (11 October 1962–8 December 1965), the Orthodox, Protestant and Anglican 'observers' frequently criticized the texts that were discussed for their lack of pneumatology. Many of these 'observers' have continued to criticize the Catholic Church for this lack since the Council, but it is debatable whether this criticism is still justified. It was certainly justified at the time. This is clear from a study of the way in which the text of *Lumen Gentium*, developed—see (note 1 below) the article by Mgr Charue and the comments by C. Moeller—or a reading of the excellent Constitution on the Liturgy, the only document that remained almost unchanged after the work of the preparatory commissions. It would be tedious to go through every document and every conciliar discussion in search of references to the Holy Spirit. There are at least 258 of them in the conciliar texts! An enumeration of them would not, however, be sufficient as a basis for a pneumatology. They might only be used, as a commentator—unjustly, in my opinion—observed, to 'give a sprinkling of the Holy Spirit' to a text that was basically not pneumatological. I propose therefore to try to draw attention to the elements of true pneumatology that were present at the Second Vatican Council and have since then been active in the Catholic Church.

1. The Council preserved the Christological reference which is fundamentally biblical and the essential condition for the soundness of any pneumatology. The pneumatology of the Council is not pneumatocentric. It stresses that the Spirit is the Spirit of Christ;[2] he carries out the work of Christ and builds up the Body of Christ. Again and again, the Holy Spirit is

called the principle of the life of that Body, which is the Church.[3] The Council also preserved—and did well to preserve, since it contained an important truth—the idea that the Holy Spirit guarantees the faithfulness of Tradition and the truth of the solemn pronouncements of the magisterium.[4]

2. The idea of the Mystical Body was not, however, put forward by the Council as the only definition of the Church, as a resolution at Vatican I, Cardinal Franzelin and Pius XII had all proposed, nor was the theme of a 'continuous incarnation', which dominated the nineteenth and the first half of the twentieth centuries, followed at the Council. Mühlen is quite right in noticing this. In *Lumen Gentium*, there is a comparison between the visible and the spiritual, and the human and the divine, aspects of the Church and the union of the two natures in Christ. This comparison is made for the purpose of attributing to the Holy Spirit the task of animating the Church as an event here and now: 'Just as the assumed nature inseparably united to the divine Word serves him as a living instrument of salvation, so, in a similar way, does the communal structure of the Church serve Christ's Spirit who vivifies it by way of building up the body' (*LG* 8, 1). The Spirit, then, is not an impersonal force—the creed, after all, describes him as 'Lord'. He remains the Spirit of Christ. The Council took up the New Testament idea that we have already encountered in Irenaeus, of the ecclesial function of sanctification as a participation in Christ's anointing by the Spirit:

When the fullness of time had come, God sent his Son, the Word made flesh, anointed by the Holy Spirit. . . . (*SC* 5).

In order that we might be unceasingly renewed in him (cf. Eph 4:23), he has shared with us his Spirit who, existing as one and the same being in the head and in the members, vivifies, unifies and moves the whole body (*LG* 7, 7). Christ has . . . filled it (the Church) with his Spirit (*LG* 9, 3).

The Lord Jesus, 'whom the Father has made holy and sent into the world' (Jn 10:36), has made his whole Mystical Body share in the anointing of the Spirit with which he himself has been anointed (*PO* 2; reference in a footnote to Mt 3:16; Lk 4:18; Acts 4:27; 10:38).

God consecrates priests so that they can share by a special title in the priesthood of Christ. Thus, by performing sacred functions they can act as the ministers of him who in the liturgy continually exercises his priestly office on our behalf by the action of his Spirit (*PO* 5, 1).

3. The Council went beyond what Mühlen called a 'pre-Trinitarian monotheism'. Whereas the idea of God that predominated in Vatican I was not explicitly Trinitarian, the teaching contained in several of the documents of the Second Vatican Council is based on a Trinitarian view of the 'economy' of creation and grace. This applies firstly to the principle that the Father's initiative led to the mission of the Word, the Son, and that of the

Spirit (see *LG* 2–4; *AG* 2–4; *GS* 40, 2) and secondly to the consequence that the Church is called the people of God, the Body of Christ and the Temple of the Spirit (see *PO* 1; *AG* 7, 3 and 9, end). What is more, in accordance with the admirable formula of Cyprian that inspired me in *Chrétiens désunis*, the Church is also shown by Vatican II to be the 'people made one with the unity of the Father, the Son and the Holy Spirit'.[5] Even better, the Council also called the Church one, 'the highest exemplar and source of this mystery' being 'the unity in the Trinity of Persons, of one God, the Father and the Son in the Holy Spirit' (*UR* 2, 6).

Because of this Trinitarian view, the Church is seen to be a community of worship in spirit and in truth, in accordance with the logic of *ab*, *per*, *in* and *ad*—from the Father, through the Son, in the Spirit, to the Father—so well outlined by C. Vagaggini.[6] The intention of the conciliar document on the liturgy is essentially practical, with the result that this theology is developed very little in it. It is, moreover, more Christological than pneumatological. The Spirit, however, has a place in the other conciliar documents which refer to the doxological function of the Church (see, for example, *PO* 2 and 5) and especially in the review of the sacramental rites that the Council required and that has been carried out since the Council ended. This return of the Spirit to our liturgical celebrations calls for a detailed study.[7]

There has, of course, never been any serious problem with regard to baptism. What is more, I have already spoken about baptism from the point of view of Scripture and I shall return to this question when I discuss 'baptism in the Spirit'. The new ritual of confirmation includes the fourth- and fifth-century Eastern formula, 'The seal of the gift of the Spirit', combining the two ideas of the seal and the gift, both of them pneumatological.

A contrast has sometimes been made between the Latin Church's theme of the priest playing, at the level of the sense, the part of Christ and acting *in persona Christi*, and the Eastern practice of the priest invoking the Spirit, who is the Person who is acting. It cannot be denied that there are two theological traditions and two liturgical styles, but it would be superficial to separate them or place them in opposition to each other. The two quotations above from *Presbyterorum ordinis* show that they are closely associated. The renewed ritual of the ordination of priests includes the prayer: 'Make your servants here present priests of Jesus Christ through renewing them by your Holy Spirit' and, for bishops, restores the consecratory prayer from Hippolytus' *Apostolic Tradition*.

The part played by the three Persons is developed in a very remarkable way in the renewed rite of the sacrament of penance or reconciliation. This is particularly clear in the unfortunately little-known long text of the formula of absolution:

> Jesus Christ . . . poured out his Holy Spirit on the apostles so that they would receive the power to remit sins. Through our ministry, may Jesus Christ himself deliver you from evil and fill you with the Holy Spirit.

The Holy Spirit, our helper and defender, has been given to us for the remission of sins and in him we can approach the Father. May the Spirit illuminate and purify your hearts, so that you will be able to proclaim the wonders of him who has called you from darkness into his wonderful light.

The most important achievement of the Council in this sphere was undoubtedly the introduction of epicleses into the new eucharistic prayers, the second of which is taken almost word for word from the prayer of Hippolytus, which is the earliest liturgical text in existence. There was no epiclesis in the pre-conciliar Roman canon. It would have been easy to introduce one; a reference to the Holy Spirit could have replaced the reference to blessing in the two prayers of consecration of the gifts and of sanctification of the faithful: 'Bless and approve our offering. . . . Let it become for us the body and blood of Jesus Christ . . .' and 'Then, as we receive . . . the sacred body and blood of your Son, let us be filled with every grace and blessing'. It would be sufficient to see uncreated Grace as the principle of created grace. The other eucharistic prayers, however, each include two epicleses, one with the consecration or sanctification of the gifts in mind, and the other so that the Spirit will sanctify, fill and unite believers in Christ, within a framework of absolute praise in the communion of saints. The Spirit, then, is given as the place, the climate and the active agent of the sacrament of the body and blood of the Lord. I shall deal at greater length in Volume III with the pneumatology of the Eucharist, a subject of the greatest concern to me.

4. One of the most important ways in which the Holy Spirit has been restored to the pneumatological ecclesiology of the Council was in the sphere of charisms.[8] This meant that the Church is built up not only by institutional means but also by the infinite variety of the gifts that each person 'has the right and duty to use in the Church and in the world for the good of mankind and for the upbuilding of the Church . . . in the freedom of the Holy Spirit who "breathes where he wills" (Jn 3:8): at the same time, they must act in communion with their brothers in Christ and especially with their pastors' (AA 3). A new theology, or rather a new programme of 'ministries', giving the Church a new face that is quite different from the one that the earlier pyramidal and clerical ecclesiology presented, has developed since the Second Vatican Council on the basis of these charisms used for the common good and the building up of the Church. I have discussed this question elsewhere and shall not repeat here what I have already said. I will show in Volume II why it is important and under what conditions it is possible to call the Spirit, who makes the Church by these means, 'co-institutive' of the Church. Going beyond all legal provisions, the Holy Spirit is entrusted with the task of making sure that 'the form of government established by Christ the Lord in his Church' is unfailingly observed (LG 27, 3).

170

The Spirit 'blows where he wills'. He is an 'event'. The Council recognized this aspect of the Holy Spirit and placed it within its proper context. The social structures are, for example, at the service of the Spirit (*LG* 8, 1). He makes the gospel a contemporary reality and enables men today to understand the Word of God (*DV* 8, 3; 23). He prompts developments in the religious life (*LG* 44 and 45) and, in the case of apostolic or missionary initiatives, 'often anticipates the action of those whose task it is to rule the life of the Church' (*AG* 29, 3). It is also to the Spirit that the Council attributed the perpetual renewal that the Church has to undergo if it is to be faithful to its Lord—as we might well expect from the Council of the *aggiornamento* (*LG* 9, end; cf. 8, 3; *GS* 21, 5; 43, 6; *PO* 22, 2). The Council was also anxious that ccumenical endeavour should continue, 'without prejudging the future inspiration of the Holy Spirit' (*UR* 24, 2). The whole ecumenical movement, the Council believed, came in the first place from the Holy Spirit (*UR* 1, 2; 4, 1), who is also at work in the other Christian communities.[9]

5. At the same time as giving a higher value to the charisms and in conjunction with this renewed emphasis, the Council also reassessed the importance of the local churches. Karl Rahner was of the opinion that the most valuable new element introduced by the Council was the idea of the local church as the realization of the one, holy, Catholic and apostolic Church.[10] It was defined as such by the Council (*LG* 26, 1; *CD* 11, 1) and both these definitions include an affirmation that the people of God called and gathered together in this way is in fact called 'in the Holy Spirit'. The Church as a whole is presented as a communion of churches, with the Holy Spirit as the principle of that communion. This is very clear from the conciliar texts (see, for example, *LG* 13; 25; 49; *AG* 19, 3; *UR* 2, 2 and 6; *Orientalium Ecclesiarum* 2). A theology of the catholicity of the Church that seeks to express some of the aspects of the Orthodox *sobornost'* is outlined in *Lumen Gentium* 13: 'In virtue of this catholicity each individual part of the Church contributes through its special gifts to the good of the other parts and of the whole Church. Thus through the common sharing of gifts and through the common effort to attain fullness in unity, the whole and each of the parts receive increase.' The 'sacred Tradition' is preserved by the 'entire holy people united with their shepherds' (*DV* 10, 1), who share in the prophetic functions of Christ. The Council even went so far as to state: 'The body of the faithful as a whole, anointed as they are by the Holy One (cf. Jn 2:20, 27), cannot err in matters of belief. Thanks to a supernatural sense of the faith which characterizes the people as a whole, it manifests this unerring quality. . .' (*LG* 12, 1). As Ignace Ziadé, the Maronite Archbishop of Beirut, said: 'The Church is the mystery of the pouring out of the Spirit in the last times'.[11]

6. If the fullness that must be recapitulated in Christ is preceded by a material preparation in the history of this world, then the Spirit must already be active in history. Several times in different documents, the conciliar Fathers speak of the Spirit of the Lord 'who fills the whole earth' (*PO* 22, 3; *GS* 11, 1), 'who . . . directs the unfolding of time and renews the face of the earth (and) is not absent from this development' (*GS* 26, 4) and who works on man and turns him towards God (*GS* 41, 1). The same constitution on the Church in the Modern World also insists that the Spirit makes a new creature of the Christian (*GS* 22, 4; 37, 4), but neither this affirmation nor the others referring to the Spirit are developed in the document.

It is therefore possible to say that there are signs of a true pneumatology in the teachings of the Second Vatican Council. The Council provided the texts, but the truth of that pneumatology has to be confirmed in the life of the Church. The whole people of God knows that it has the task of building up the Church and that lay people have to contribute their gifts or charisms to this task. The local churches are still looking for ways of life that are peculiar to them. The chapter on conciliarity that was opened by Vatican II has not yet been brought to an end. There have been many crises, but there have also been generous initiatives. The Catholic Renewal which began in Pittsburgh in the U.S.A. in 1967 and which has spread throughout the world is clearly part of this living pneumatology, since the Spirit is undoubtedly experienced in that movement, at least according to the testimony of those who follow it. Is it perhaps the response to the expectation of a new Pentecost that Pope John XXIII expressed more than once in connection with the Council?[12] It is at least part of that response, but the total response is much greater and much more mysterious. The entire life of the Church is unfolding in the breath of the Spirit of Pentecost.

Pneumatology, like ecclesiology and theology as a whole, can only develop fully on the basis of what is experienced and realized in the life of the Church. In this sphere, theory is to a great extent dependent on praxis. Paul VI brought to a close the Council inaugurated by John XXIII and repeated his predecessor's desire for a new Pentecost. Some years after the close of the Council, he was able to say: 'The Christology and especially the ecclesiology of the Second Vatican Council should be followed by a new study and a new cult of the Holy Spirit, as an indispensable complement of the conciliar teaching'.[13] With these words, then, I will close this volume, since they to a very great extent justify the attempt that I make in the rest of this work to provide such a pneumatology.

NOTES

1. See especially G. Barauna, ed., *Vatican II. L'Eglise de Vatican II* (*Unam Sanctam*, 51b) (Paris, 1966), especially the contributions by O. Rousseau, pp. 39–45, C. Moeller, pp. 102–104, M. Philippon, P. Smulders, B. van Leeuwen, and H. Schürmann, pp. 541–557, on the spiritual charisms; C. Moeller, article in *Theological Issues of Vatican II* (Notre Dame, Indiana, 1967), pp. 125–126; H. Cazelles, 'Le Saint-Esprit dans les textes de Vatican II' in H. Cazelles, P. Evdokimov and A. Greiner, *Le mystère de l'Esprit-Saint* (Paris, 1968), pp. 161–186; H. Mühlen, *L'Esprit dans l'Eglise*, II (*Bibl. Œcum.*, 7) (Paris, 1969), pp. 9–114; A. Charue, 'Le Saint-Esprit dans "Lumen Gentium"' and J. G. Geenen, 'Ecclesia a S. Spiritu edocta. Heilige Geest en Heilige Kerk in de transmissie der Openbaring volgens de dogmatische Constitutie "De divina Revelatione" van Vaticaan II', *Ecclesia a Spiritu Sancto edocta. Mélanges théologiques. Hommage à Mgr Gérard Philips* (Gembloux, 1970), pp. 16–39 and 169–199 respectively.

2. 'Communicando Spiritum suum'. *LG* 7, 1; 'Spiritus Christi': *LG* 8, 1; 'Spiritum Christi habentes': *LG* 14, 2, etc.

3. Some twenty texts can be quoted here: see *AA* 3, 2; 29, 3; *CD* 11, 1; *LG* 21, 2, etc.

4. See, for example, *LG* 25, 3; 43, 1; *DV* 8, 9 and 10. The 'help of the Holy Spirit', however, extends even further: see *GS* 44, 2.

5. *LG* 4; in a note, there is reference to Cyprian, *De orat. Dom.* 23, Augustine and John Damascene.

6. C. Vagaggini, *Theological Dimensions of the Liturgy* (Eng. tr.; Collegeville, Minn., 1976), chapter 7.

7. There is an outline in *Notes de Pastorale liturgique*, 133 (April 1978), 19ff.

8. Simple, but important references will be found in *LG* 4; 7, 3; *AG* 4; 23, 1; 28, 1. More formal and dense texts: *LG* 12; *AA* 3, 4. See also H. Schürmann, *op. cit.* (note 1).

9. *LG* 15; *UR* 3, 2 and 4; 4, 9. H. Mühlen, *op. cit.* (note 1), pp. 175–242, has used these texts as the basis for a very positive assessment of the value of the non-Catholic communions as Churches. The theological problem is to know whether the Spirit makes use of all his ecclesial effects when the ecclesial sacrament is imperfect. It is, however, quite true that the pneumatic ecclesiology of the local Churches enables us to assess the other Churches more positively: see P. J. Rosato, 'Called to God in the Holy Spirit. Pneumatological Insights into Ecumenism', *Ecumenical Review*, 30 (1978), 110–126.

10. K. Rahner, 'The New Image of the Church' (Eng. tr.), *Theological Investigations*, X (London, 1973), pp. 3–29, especially pp. 7ff.

11. I published Mgr Ziadé's intervention of 1963 in *Discours au Concile Vatican II* (Paris, 1964), pp. 37–42; see also pp. 31–36, where Cardinal Suenens' intervention on the charismatic dimension of the Church appears. Suenens also said: 'The time of the Church, which passes through the centuries to the parousia, is the time of the Holy Spirit'. Both these texts are very significant and had a deep influence on the Council.

12. See the official collection *Acta et Documenta Concilio œcumenico Vaticano II apparando*, Series I (*Antepreparatoria*), Vol. I: *Acta S. Pontificis Ioannis XXIII* (Vatican City, 1960), p. 24, the discourse at Pentecost, 17 May 1959; the Council was convoked as to a new Pentecost. In the summer of 1959, there was the following prayer for the Council, addressed to the Holy Spirit: 'Renova aetate hac nostra veluti Pentecostem mirabilia tua' (p. 48). See also the letter of 28 May 1960 to Cardinal Alfrink with a broadcast of the celebration of Pentecost in mind (p. 87); and John XXIII's discourse on the day of Pentecost, 5 June 1960: 'È infatti nella dottrina e nello spirito della Pentecoste che il grande avvenimento del Concilio Ecumenico prende sostanza e vita' (p. 105).

13. General audience on 6 June 1973: see *Doc. cath.*, 1635 (1 July 1973), p. 601. In the Apostolic Exhortation *Marialis cultus* (22 March 1974), there is also, after a pneumatological discussion of the mystery of Mary (26), an invitation to 'think more deeply about the activity of the Spirit in the history of salvation' (27).

SOME UNUSUAL TERMS

AGE (Gr. AEON) A period regarded not only as a certain length of time, but also as a certain rule or a certain state at the spiritual level. It is variously translated: as 'this world' or 'this age' (2 Cor 4:4) or as 'the world to come' or 'the age to come' (Heb 6:5).

CIRCUMINCESSION (CIRCUMINSESSION) This is a translation of the Greek *perichōrēsis* and points to the divine Persons' being one within the other, their interpenetration, their mutual interiority; see Jn 10:38; 14:10; 17:21.

DOXOLOGY (DOXOLOGICAL) Act or a formula of praise, as, for example, at the end of the eucharistic prayer or of a psalm recited chorally.

ECONOMY (ECONOMIC) The unfolding of what God does in the history of the world to make his plan of salvation known and to have it realized.

EPICLESIS (EPICLETIC) Invocation of the Holy Spirit or a celebration including such an invocation.

EPITIMIA(I) Practice or practices suggested or imposed by a spiritual father in the Eastern Church, corresponding to some extent to what we would know as the 'penance' indicated by a confessor.

HEGUMENOS The head or superior of a monastery in the Eastern Church.

HESYCHASM (HESYCHAST) The school of spirituality, originating in Sinai in the fourth century, which can be summarized as silence, solitude and recollectedness (returning to within).

KENOSIS Emptying oneself: see Phil 2:7. A renunciation of the manifestation of oneself in glory or in obvious splendour.

MODALISM Error in the dogma of the Trinity according to which the Word or the Spirit are seen as simple modes by which divinity is manifested.

PROCESSION In the theology of the Trinity, the way in which one Person is derived from the other consubstantially within the unity of the same divinity.